# DOING BUSINESS IN
# RUSSIA

# CBI

## *Initiative Eastern Europe*

# DOING BUSINESS IN
# RUSSIA

**ALM CONSULTING • BRITISH GAS
FRERE CHOLMELEY BISCHOFF
KPMG PEAT MARWICK**

**KOGAN
PAGE**

**Note:** This book has been written on the basis of information and law current as at January 1993.

First published in 1993

Kogan Page Limited
120 Pentonville Road
London N1 9JN

**British Library Cataloguing in Publication Data**

A CIP record for this book is available from the British Library.

ISBN 0 7494 0695 X

Typeset by DP Photosetting, Aylesbury, Bucks
Printed in England by Clays Ltd, St Ives plc

# Contents

# The Contributors

***Frere Cholmeley Bischoff*** is a leading London law firm with offices throughout Europe specialising in international business transactions. Frere Cholmeley Bischoff lawyers have considerable experience of advising on Russian affairs. The firm's offices in London and Berlin and the Moscow representative office have been acting on behalf of a number of Eastern European enterprises and institutions.

***KPMG Peat Marwick*** is the UK member firm of KPMG, one of the largest international firms of accountants, tax advisors and management consultants. KPMG Moscow provides assistance to Russian and multinational companies doing business in Russia. KPMG's Moscow office is authorised to undertake accounting, auditing, consulting, and advisory business. In addition it is helping Russia privatise and restructure its state-owned organisations.

***British Gas*** (Global Gas) is responsible for the downstream development of British Gas' worldwide activities, principally in the gas business, gas related investment and project development work, including gas-fired power generation.

British Gas successfully undertook a demonstration of their polyethylene pipe laying capabilities in St Petersburg last autumn as a first stage in their gas distribution activities in Russia.

***Moscow Narodny Bank Limited*** has been incorporated in the City of London since 1919 and provides a comprehensive range of international and merchant banking products and services to corporate, government and private customers with particular emphasis on business related to the economies of the former Soviet Union and of Central Europe.

**ALM Consulting** is a Moscow-based financial and legal consulting firm assisting Russian and Western companies in their trading and investment transactions in Russia.

**CIT Research Ltd** specialises in international communications research. Founded in 1981, CIT covers the main global telecoms fields, including an annual report on communications in Eastern Europe. With 750 clients world-wide, 75 per cent of CIT's turnover comes from outside the UK.

**ExcelInform Ltd** is a Moscow-based business consulting company primarily providing advice on marketing in Russia.

**Brown & Root** is a world leader in project management, engineering, construction, operations and maintenance. It operates in the oil and gas, petroleum and chemical, civil, industrial, environmental, power and pulp and paper sectors, employing over 40,000 people worldwide.

   The company manages its Europe, Africa and CIS operations out of London but has an office in Moscow and representation in Baku, Azerbaijan. Brown & Root is a subsidiary of Halliburton Company of Dallas.

**Nicholas Louis** is a consultant with many years' experience in advising international companies on their Russia activities.

**Dr Michael Bradshaw** is a lecturer in the School of Geography and Associate Member of the Centre for Russian and East European Studies at the University of Birmingham. His research interests include regional problems in Russia and foreign investment in the former Soviet Union. He is editor of *The Soviet Union: a New Regional Geography* (Belhaven Press, 1991), and author of *Siberia in a Time of Change* (EIU, 1992) and *The Economic Effects of Soviet Dissolution* (RIIA, 1993).

# Preface

Russia is undergoing a difficult and painful process of transforming itself into a free market and a stable democracy. The constitutional and economic crises now facing the country are preoccupying foreign ministries throughout the world. That could be a signal for companies to write off the market, but it would be unwise to dismiss too lightly the commercial scope resulting from the wholescale reorientation of one of the world's superpowers.

Russia has many strengths which will become more apparent in the medium term. It occupies one seventh of the world's land surface and, with a wealth of mineral resources, it has a population of 148 million and an impressive record of scientific achievement.

The economic 'shock therapy' undertaken by the Yeltsin government at the beginning of 1992 has established the free enterprise ethic and has set in train the liberalisation of the market. As Russia is reintegrated into the world economy and as the programme of rapid privatisation is developed, opportunities for western traders and investors are progressively opening up.

Many of the first entrants have become involved in the development of natural resources, above all oil and gas. As multilateral aid contracts come on flow, there are going to be increasing opportunities to supply Russian organisations as they re-equip. Nor should consumer goods be overlooked, as the experience of Littlewoods in St Petersburg testifies. Examples of other commercial developments include Amersham International's two hi-tech joint ventures, the proposal by British Airways to set up a new airline, Air Russia, and Cable & Wireless's commitments in telecommunications.

Any western company active in Russia would admit to the difficulties of operating in a market unsupported by a normal legal, financial and commercial infrastructure. Finding ways to set up profitable ventures is a prolonged and complex process. This book is designed to give practical guidance to western companies getting involved in the market. It draws principally on the expertise of Frere Cholmeley Bischoff, KPMG Peat Marwick, Moscow Narodny Bank, British Gas, ALM Consulting, Brown & Root, CIT Research Ltd, ExcelInform Ltd, Nicholas Louis and Dr Michael Bradshaw at the University of Birmingham. The CBI thanks them all for the very substantial efforts they have made in putting this book together. The CBI would also like to thank Littlewoods, Amersham International and KBC Process Technology for sharing their experience of the Russian market in the case studies. Other significant contributions were received from Alexander Mamut, James Kitcatt, Elena Agranovskaya, Sergey Punzhin, Nadezhda Kuklina, Dmitri Bogdanovich, Marina Ievleva, Jackie Carpenter and Calum Chace.

As the potential of Russia unfolds I hope this book proves useful to western companies in developing profitable business in this challenging and exciting market.

Alan Lewis, CBE
Chairman, CBI Initiative Eastern Europe
April 1993

*Part I*

# A Business Revolution?

# 1

# Russia and its Potential

## ALM Consulting

The Russia of today is in the throes of revolutionary change. After more than 70 years of communist rule, the country is fast becoming a modern, market-oriented democracy. This chapter looks at Russia's historical development and some of the factors crucial to its resurgence.

## THE DEVELOPMENT OF RUSSIA

From 1721, in the reign of Tsar Peter the Great, until the 1990s, the Russian state was the centre of a huge empire. At the end of the 18th century it included the Baltic Republics, the Ukraine, Byelorussia, part of Poland, Bessarabia and the Northern Caucasus. In the 19th century it encompassed Finland, Transcaucasia, Kazakhstan and Central Asia. The whole area was governed by the Emperor, an hereditary monarch who held supreme autocratic power – a position confirmed by the 'Basic State Laws'.

The February Revolution of 1917 disposed of autocracy in Russia, and on 1 September 1917 the provisional government declared the country a republic. Later, as a result of the October Revolution led by the Bolsheviks, a 'dictatorship of the proletariat' was established and the Russian Soviet Federal Socialist Republic (RSFSR), to be part of the Union of Soviet Socialist Republics (USSR), was created. The fundamental characteristic of this new Union was the concentration of all levers of power in the hands of the Communist Party.

The communist system existed for 74 years. The foundations for its collapse were laid by Mikhail Gorbachev, General Secretary of the Communist Party and later President of the Soviet Union. Gorbachev's policies of *glasnost* (openness) and *perestroika* (restructuring), initiated in April 1985, which were intended to

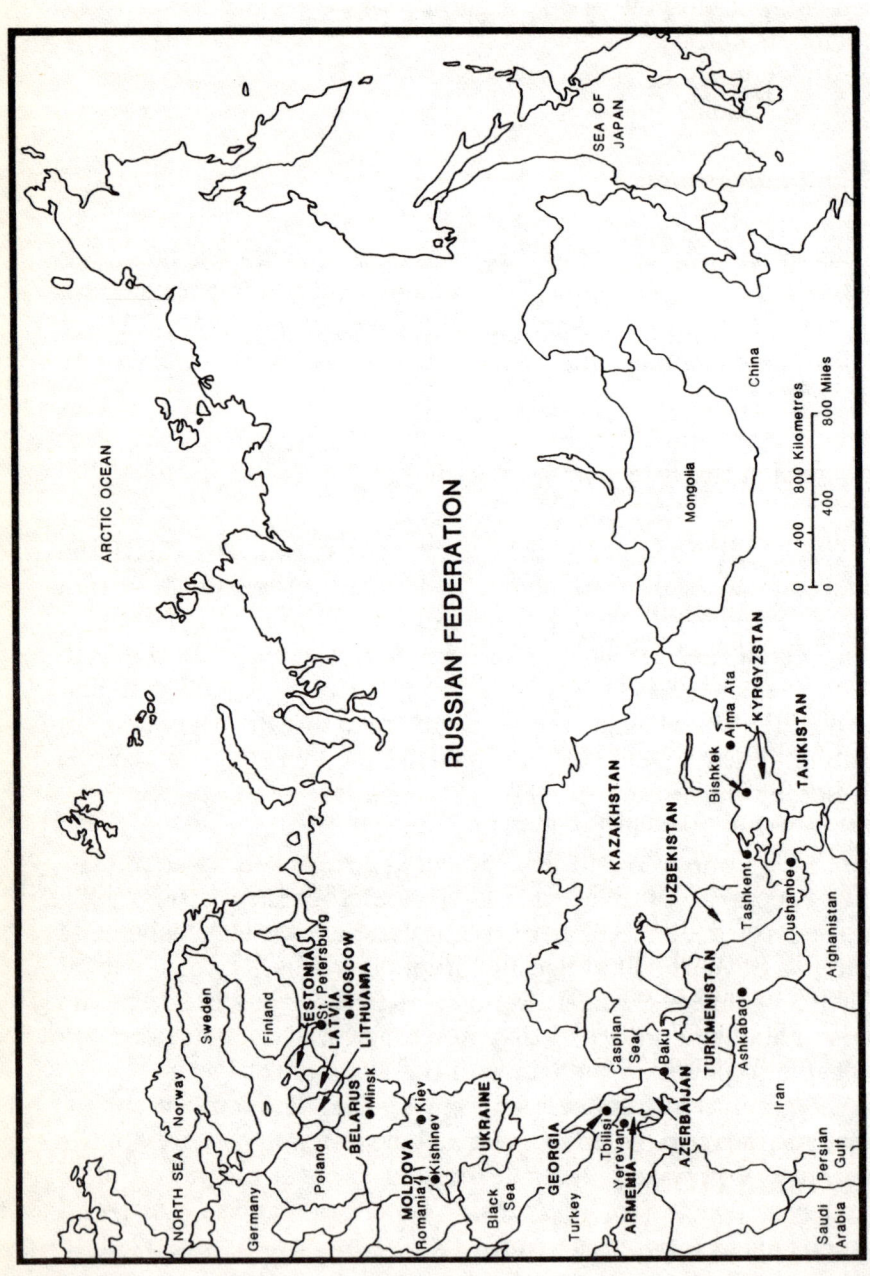

**Map 1.1** *The former Soviet Union*

Source:  School of Geography, University of Birmingham

modernise and invigorate the socialist system, in fact unleashed forces that could not be contained. Most importantly, the process of democratisation led to direct elections for the office of President of Russia. Backed by democratic legitimacy, the emphatic winner, Boris Yeltsin, was able to establish a power base strong enough to abort the attempted coup in Moscow on 21 August 1991 – a *putsch* initiated by several members of the government and Party hierarchy with the aim of reversing the course of democracy and returning to a totalitarian administrative system.

### The CIS and independence

The failure of the August coup provided the catalyst for a complete regeneration of Russia's political and social system. The existing order had been clearly rejected by its subjects and in the ensuing months a new framework emerged, based on national sovereignty and independence. In Minsk on 8 December 1991, the leaders of Russia, Byelorussia and the Ukraine signed an Agreement on the Creation of a Commonwealth of Independent States (CIS). This event signalled the final demise and disintegration of the economic and political superpower – the Soviet Union – into a number of independent states.

A fortnight later the new Commonwealth was enlarged by the Alma Ata Declaration, signed by 11 states – Azerbaijan, Armenia, Belarus, Kazakhstan, Kirghyzstan, Moldova, the Russian Federation, Tadzhikistan, Turkmenistan, Uzbekistan and the Ukraine. The Alma Ata Declaration proclaims the Commonwealth neither a state nor a union of states. Co-operation between the members is to be conducted on the basis of equality through co-ordinating institutions created on a uniform basis.

On 24 December 1991 the Soviet Union resigned as a member of the United Nations. Its place was taken by the Russian Federation, which also took over the seat of the USSR as a permanent member of the Security Council. On 25 December the Soviet President Mikhail Gorbachev, by now effectively redundant, resigned and on 1 January 1992, by agreement between Gorbachev and Yeltsin, the Soviet Union formally ceased to exist.

## PROSPECTS FOR POLITICAL AND ECONOMIC TRANSFORMATION

The central figure in Russia's immediate future is almost certain to be

Boris Yeltsin. Elected President in June 1991 on an anti-totalitarian and anti-communist platform, Yeltsin continues to enjoy considerable support from almost all sectors of Russian society, and in particular among people without strong political convictions. Boris Yeltsin came from the highest echelons of the Communist Party of the Soviet Union and, as the city Party leader in Moscow in the mid-1980s, gained a reputation as a radical reformer and opponent of corruption and party privilege.

Despite the emergence of a number of diverse factions in the final years of Soviet rule, the fall of the one-party state left something of a vacuum within Russian politics which is only now being filled by organised groupings. The 'left' was split following the August coup and the 'right' only started attaining a structure in the spring of 1992. Meanwhile, the loosely defined 'centre' comprises a number of political parties and movements, most of which differ only very little from each other.

Perhaps the only genuine force so far to emerge in Russian politics as an alternative to Boris Yeltsin and the radical market reform strategy is the 'Civic Union' – an alliance of small parties based around Mr Arkady Volsky and the Russian Vice-President, General Alexander Rutskoi. Mr Volsky, a former executive in the Central Committee of the Soviet Communist Party, is the head of the Union of Industrialists and Entrepreneurs, an organisation representing enterprise managers and bureaucrats. During the course of 1992 several of Volsky's allies were appointed to senior posts within the government and Volsky himself is believed to have been a major influence behind the relaxation of credit controls in the summer of 1992.

Between them, Mr Volsky and General Rutskoi attract considerable support from assorted opponents of current policies, including some die-hard communists and nationalists. Indeed, the Civic Union's calls for the abandonment of the economic shock therapy programme and the restoration of a protective customs regime may find favour among any sector of society with some nostalgia for the old order. However, the policies actually espoused by the Civic Union contain few throwbacks to the old system, and many observers believe that the grouping has attracted support from the old guard simply because it has formed a focal point for opposition to the government.

The appointment of Viktor Chernomyrdin, a more conservative figure, to replace Yegor Gaidar as Prime Minister at the end of 1992 is likely to lead to a policy shift towards the Civic Union's line. Chernomyrdin is himself an industrialist and, although several of the key members of the former government's economic team retained their portfolios after the December 1992 Congress of People's Deputies, it is widely thought that the pace of change in Russia will slow in 1993 and 1994.

Probably the fundamental factor in Russia's political and economic transformation is the privatisation process. The emergence of a property-owning middle class is seen as crucial to the development of a modern, stable democracy. Following its decriminalisation in the late-1980s, private enterprise accounted by the end of 1992 for 10–12 per cent of Russia's GNP. Now the task is to transfer the country's vast infrastructure of state-owned enterprises into private hands. Although slow starting (as elsewhere in Eastern Europe) this process is probably now largely irreversible.

## GEOGRAPHY AND CLIMATE

The Russian Federation covers most of Eastern Europe and Northern Asia, stretching 2500–4000 kilometres from north to south and 9000 kilometres (11 time zones) from west to east – in total 17,054,400 square kilometres (over 15 per cent of the land on Earth). It contains 20 autonomous republics, 1045 cities and about 2200 townships. The east and parts of the south are largely mountainous and the rest, about 70 per cent of the surface area, is made up of vast plains.

About 120,000 rivers are over 10 kilometres long, with navigation or floating of timber possible on 400,000 kilometres of water. These rivers are the main sources of water for cities and industrial enterprises, and the larger rivers of Siberia are used for deriving hydro-electric power.

The country also has about two million fresh water and salt water lakes. The largest of these are the Caspian and Lake Baikal. More than 40 per cent of the territory of Russia (over 700 million hectares) is covered in forests, with total reserves calculated at 79 billion cubic metres. Especially large areas of forestation are to be found in the Taiga regions of Siberia, the far east and the north-eastern parts of Russia. These regions are also the main provinces for hunting and the fur industry.

The greater part of Russia has a temperate climate. The severest and most strongly continental climate is in Siberia and the Northern part of the far east. Here there is permanently frozen soil (permafrost) and average winter temperatures of around –50C. In the north the permafrost can reach a depth of 500 metres. The south

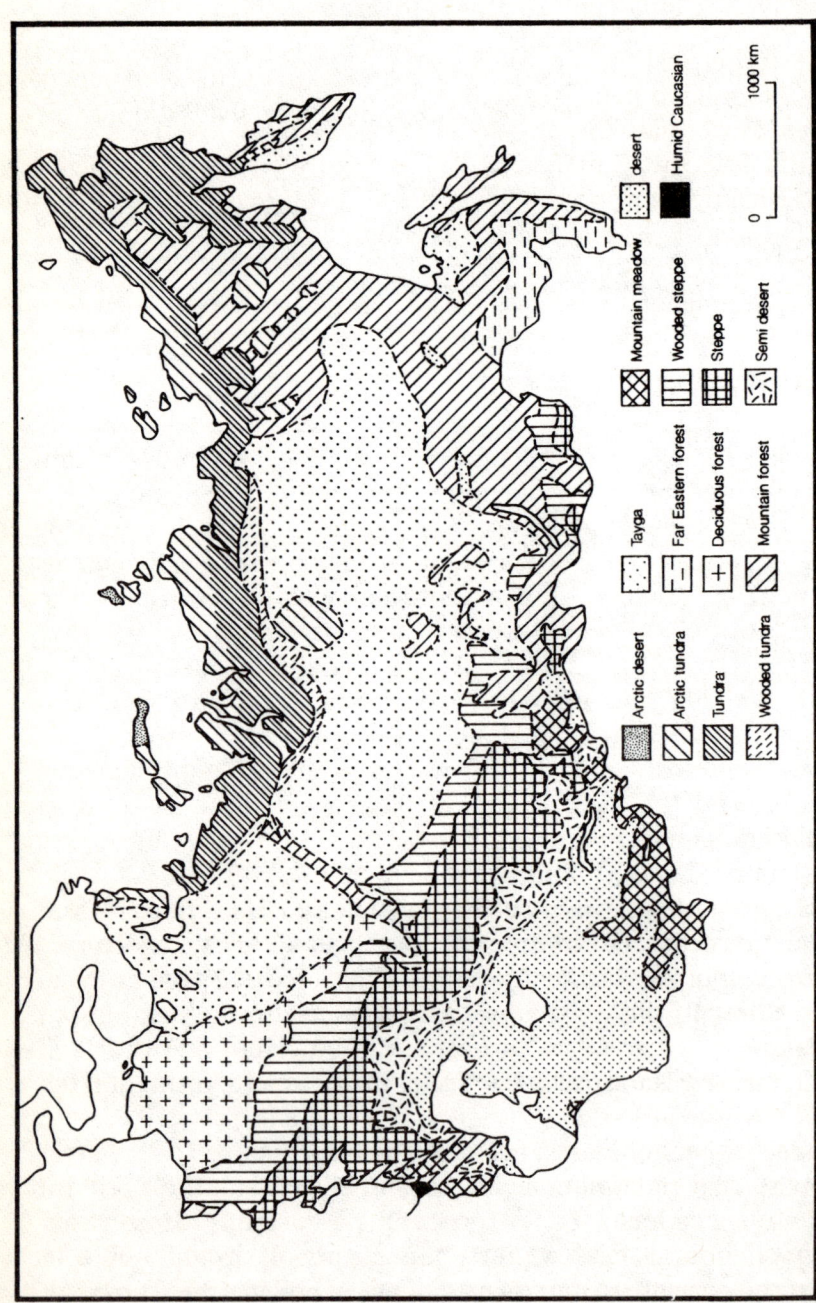

**Map 1.2** *Major landscape regions*

Source: Based on Mellor, REH (1982) *The Soviet Union and its Geographical Problems*, Macmillan, London, p9.

of the far east has a monsoon climate with cool, largely snowless winters and a cool, wet summer.

## HUMAN RESOURCES

The Russian Federation is a multi-national country. On its territory live over 148 million people of more than 100 different nationalities and tribes. More than 72 per cent of the population live in cities – 9 million in Moscow, 5 million in St Petersburg and over 1 million each in Nizhniy Novgorod, Novosibirsk, Sverdlovsk, Kuibyshev, Omsk, Chelyabinsk, Kazan, Perm, Ufa, Rostov and Volgograd.

In 1990, 75 million Russians were in active employment, the vast majority (68.2 million) working for state-owned enterprises. Of the rest, 5 million worked in agriculture (4.1 million on state and 0.9 million on private farms) and 1.7 million worked in co-operatives. Heavy unemployment is expected during 1993 (forecasts range from 4 million to 13 million). The worst hit areas are expected to be those based around heavy industry and defence factories and those with an underdeveloped infrastructure, such as the Kurganskaya and Amurskaya *Oblasts* (administrative regions) and the Tuva autonomous republic.

The overall standard of education is high. The country boasts a 99 per cent literacy rate and the teaching (especially of scientific and quantitative subjects) is of a very high quality. Education is free and compulsory to the age of 16. Many go on to higher education and competition at university level is intense.

## AGRICULTURE

In Russia, agriculture accounts for over 20 per cent of the country's GNP and, directly or indirectly, a third of the work-force. Traditionally, output has consisted mainly of grain and animal products, though the tiny private sector has concentrated on vegetables.

Russian farming is currently undergoing a complete overhaul. The country's traditional peasant agriculture, nationalised and collectivised under the communists, is in effect being restored as farmers are to obtain the right to own the land they work and the size of holdings will be reduced. Until the beginning of 1992, almost all of Russia's agricultural land was in the hands of around 26,000 enormous state farms. Most of these organisations are now breaking up and restructuring according to the wishes of their workers. While some small family farms have already emerged, much of the land is now managed either by associations – where individual plots are controlled by individual farmers, but machinery and so forth is shared – or co-operatives. Only 10 per cent remain in state ownership and these will no longer receive subsidies.

As elsewhere in Eastern Europe, the agricultural sector plays a major role in Russia's political situation. Social stability, so necessary for the implementation of radical reform, is to a great extent dependent upon the food market. However, the success of the current farm reforms is itself simultaneously dependent on the fundamental reformulation of the country's infrastructure, and in particular the general reorientation of industry. Domestic factories have been producing machinery unsuitable for smaller farms and in insufficient quantities. Huge amounts of agricultural output are lost during transportation, storage and processing. It is hoped that the solution to these problems lies in privatisation (of manufacturing and the retail industry) and the creation of exchanges for agricultural produce.

## RAW MATERIALS

The Russian Federation is extremely rich in natural resources. It has the world's largest reserves of gas, coal, iron ore, other metallic ores, asbestos and various other chemicals, and is also estimated to possess 6 per cent of the world's known oil deposits. But the country's performance as regards the exploitation of this indigenous wealth presents a gloomy picture. Many of the mining industries are experiencing serious difficulties as a result of years of under-investment.

Russia has over 300 reserves (deposits) of iron ore, most of which are high grade, containing over 55 per cent iron. The largest reserves are on the Kola Peninsula, the Urals, Western Siberia, the Krasnoyarsk region, Southern Yakutsk and in the far east. On the Kola Peninsula and the in Krasnoyarsk area are also to be found the main reserves of sulphate ores.

On top of this Russia has considerable reserves of various other metals including copper, lead, zinc, tin and aluminium-based deposits. There are large mines of platinum (mostly in the Urals), silver (in Siberia) and gold (also in both Siberia and the Urals).

Substantial reserves of diamonds are now being mined in the western parts of Yakutsk. The quality of the ores and the quantity of diamonds is comparable to those produced in South Africa and Zaïre. Reserves of high quality jewellery-grade diamonds have been found in the Urals area.

## COMMUNICATIONS

Russia has an extensive network of connections between its major cities and developed centres for communication with other countries. In general the transport sector has been in decline for some years, but the new political and commercial climate has produced several major initiatives to update the industry.

Russia's ports are generally divided into four categories according to their technical and volume capacity – though some, such as St Petersburg, Novorossiysk and Nakhodka are unclassified. The principal ports are shown in Table 1.1.

Russia has an extensive rail network connecting all the major cities. The lines are mostly five-foot gauge and capable of carrying large volumes of freight. However, to send goods by rail currently involves some risks. The system is generally inefficient (though it is the subject of a major electrification programme) and cargo has been known to vanish completely.

Also the road system is generally underdeveloped. The condition of the roads is very poor, even within cities, and some of the furthest-flung areas can be barely accessible at all. Given the relatively low level of private car ownership among Russian citizens, this sector may be one of the last to benefit from investment and modernisation.

For some years, most Russians have preferred to travel between cities by plane. The country also has a wide network of airports up to

**Table 1.1** Principal Russian sea ports

| | |
|---|---|
| Black Sea Basin | Novorossiysk |
| Baltic Basin | Leningrad |
| | Vyborg |
| | Kaliningrad |
| Far-Eastern Basin | Nakhodka |
| | Vladivostock |
| Northern Basin | Archangel |
| | Murmansk |
| | Onyega |
| Caspian Basin | Astrakhan |

international standards. Sheremetyevo 2 airport in Moscow, Russia's main international airport, has a capacity of 2100 passengers per hour. Also airport complexes in Rostov-on-Don and Vladivostock, Samara, Murmansk and Kaliningrad are now in operation, while St Petersburg's Pulkovo airport has recently undergone substantial modernisation.

It is planned eventually to take the country's airports out of the control of the airlines and turn them into individual joint stock companies. These would be partly privately owned and responsible for their own financing and regulation. This should open the way to increased competition and, in the longer term, the emergence of small private airlines in Russia.

## TRADE POTENTIAL

Partly as a reflection of the priorities developed through the Comecon organisation, the Russian economy is to an extent geared towards exporting primary goods and importing manufactured produce. Much of the country's industry is, or was, in the military sector, and the consumer goods which are produced tend to be unreliable and, surprisingly for a country that is in the forefront in space technology, outdated. Russia's principal imports are shown in Table 1.2.

**Table 1.2** *Principal imports*

|  | *Jan–Aug 1991* | *Jan–Aug 1992* | *Change* |
|---|---|---|---|
| Grain (metric tonnes, million) | 11.4 | 16.7 | +46% |
| Frozen meat (metric tonnes) | 312,000 | 256,000 | –18% |
| Coffee beans (metric tonnes) | 27,500 | 13,000 | –53% |
| Tea (metric tonnes) | 86,500 | 32,000 | –63% |
| Sugar (metric tonnes, million) | 2.5 | 2.1 | –16% |
| Medicines (US$, million) | 595 | 762 | +28% |
| Machinery and equipment (US$, billion) | 8.9 | 8.0 | –10% |
| Steel and cast iron (US$, million) | 612 | 208 | –66% |
| Pesticides (US$, million) | 388 | 314 | –19% |
| Knitwear (US$, million) | 475 | 350 | –26% |
| Textile clothing (US$, million) | 510 | 459 | –10% |
| Cotton textile (metres, million) | 41.5 | 13.7 | –67% |
| Silk textile (metres, million) | 2 | 1.6 | –20% |
| **Total imports (US$, billion)** | **26.8bn** | **21.7bn** | **–19%** |

Accordingly, considerable opportunities exist for Western firms prepared to seek markets on Russian territory. A Presidential Decree in November 1991 substantially liberalised Russia's foreign trade regime and signalled a move towards free trade principles and reliable customs procedures. The negotiating parties on the Uruguay Round have agreed that Russia's accession to the GATT is desirable and Russia is currently seeking to develop favourable trading links with the EC.

## 2

# Economic Transformation

## *ALM Consulting*

On 28 October 1991, President Boris Yeltsin, in an address to the Russian parliament, announced that Russia was to transform its economy to a market-based system. Whereas previous reforms introduced under Soviet rule had been afflicted by inertia or, if effected, had only dabbled with market principles, the new Russian administration was prepared to embark on a programme of radical and fundamental economic restructuring.

Although a number of itemised and finely scheduled plans were formulated in the late-1980s for moving the Soviet economy towards the market, the present Russian government is not committed to a pre-defined agenda. Such a policy would be unlikely to succeed in the volatile political and social situation prevailing in the aftermath of the Soviet Union's collapse. However, the current leadership does have a coherent strategy. Known in the Russian press as 'Gaidaronomics', after Yegor Gaidar, the former acting Prime Minister regarded as its principal architect, it consists of a series of reforms designed to open up the Russian economy and instil market disciplines. This chapter will examine the main elements of the programme and to begin with, it outlines the background against which they are introduced.

## THE SOVIET LEGACY: COMMAND ECONOMICS

From the 1920s to the 1980s Russia, as part of the USSR, operated a centrally planned economy tilted towards broad and rapid industrialisation. The key features of this system were:

- Agriculture was collectivised and the country's capital base nationalised – private ownership of the means of production was illegal.

- The allocation of resources and output levels for all sectors were dictated by the 'plan', promulgated by the central authorities and enforced by the State Planning Committee (Gosplan).

- Producer and retail prices were fixed and maintained for long periods, with low prices on basic goods a fundamental principle of social policy. All types of goods – from screwdrivers to milk – would leave the factory with their retail price already indelibly marked on them.

- Foreign trade was undertaken only by state-owned Foreign Trade Organisations (FTOs) – one for each sector of the economy. Most trade was with other members of the socialist bloc.

This system supported brisk economic growth both before and in the immediate aftermath of World War II, but by the late-1960s inherent inflexibilities in its structure were being exposed. The response of the Brezhnev administration was merely to tinker with existing mechanisms, a policy which failed to arrest a decline in the rate of economic growth. The effects of this were mitigated by the oil price shocks of 1973 and 1979, from which the USSR benefited considerably. None the less, the period from the mid-1960s to the mid-1980s came to be regarded as one of stagnation.

### Perestroika

Although trumpeted at the time as 'radical', the economic reforms initiated by Mikhail Gorbachev under the banner of *perestroika* in fact amounted to little more than familiar Soviet regenerative tactics – patriotic calls for more effort and attempts to impose stricter discipline. Only in the late-1980s were positive adjustments made to the economic system, in the form of increased autonomy for enterprises and the demonopolisation of foreign trade. The role of the plan was reduced and enterprises shifted to 'self-financing'. However, in reality these reforms were similar to those already attempted elsewhere in Eastern Europe with, at best, only limited degrees of success.

It was not until 1990 that genuine efforts were made to introduce market dynamics to the Soviet economy. The development of a private sector, first envisaged in 1988 with the passing of the Law on Co-operatives, was given a concrete basis with the amending of the Soviet Constitution to accommodate 'collective' and 'personal' ownership and the enactment of a Law on Enterprises designed to place all enterprises, whether under private, collective or state ownership, on an equal footing.

Another principal element of *perestroika* was decentralisation. More and more decisions were taken at the local level, and by 1991 almost 50 per cent of state enterprises were under republican control. The governments of the republics also assumed considerable legislative competence, and the Russian Republic had already passed numerous laws aimed at providing the foundations for a market economy before the events of summer and autumn 1991. At the time, though, these had limited effect as the real levers of power remained ultimately in Union hands.

## STABILISATION AND LIBERALISATION

The first phase of the transition programme involved the removal of various controls and restrictions operating in the economy, and simultaneously the imposition of strict financial discipline through austere fiscal and monetary policies.

### The freeing of prices

On 2 January 1992 fixed prices were lifted on machinery and equipment, consumer goods, services and labour. The straightforward and immediate aim of this measure was to enable supply and demand mechanisms to determine price levels, thus eliminating the chronic shortages, long queues and distortions in relative prices which were so characteristic of the command economy. With a reliable price structure in place, the production of sought-after goods would be encouraged and the production of unwanted goods deterred.

Price controls were retained on a dozen basic foodstuffs, some municipal services, electricity and fuels. Limits have been fixed on the profits of sellers for the time being. Rates of permissible profit rises were fixed, with the long-term aim of removing all restrictions of this kind. However, the continued monopolisation of many sectors of the economy means that these restrictions on the prices of staple items will be retained for the foreseeable future. Furthermore, the appointment of Viktor Chernomyrdin as Prime Minister at the end of 1992 is likely to lead to a slowdown in the price liberalisation.

### Credit and monetary policy

Also at the beginning of 1992, the government introduced strict controls on credit and the money supply designed to prevent the 'corrective' inflation which followed price deregulation from spiralling into hyperinflation. In fact a number of political compromises in the middle of 1992 led to a relaxation of this policy, with the central bank printing billions of roubles to bail out severely indebted enterprises. However, in the final quarter of 1992 spending was reined in once more, and month-on-month inflation fell from 33 per cent in November to 25 per cent in December.

### Welfare provision

In order to soften the blow of the austerity programme and to facilitate the movement of workers from loss-making to profitable production, the budget provides for resources to be allocated towards providing a 'safety net' for the unemployed. Those who lose their jobs following the closure or restructuring of an enterprise are entitled to unemployment benefit up to 90 per cent of their previous average wage. After six months this drops to 75 per cent of the minimum wage.

## INSTITUTIONAL CHANGE

At the heart of Russia's economic reform programme is the removal of the main economic structures from state control. This means shifting ownership of enterprises from the state to the private sector and reorganising infrastructural sectors such as banking. It is recognised that these changes should be achieved in the shortest possible time, otherwise the financial discipline which is slowly developing will not take hold beyond the short term.

### Privatisation

The government hopes to have completed the privatisation of most state-owned enterprises within three or four years. The programme introduced provides for a combination of compulsory and voluntary privatisation, with an emphasis placed on encouraging employees to obtain an interest in the ownership of the firm they work for.

There are several possible methods of privatisation, depending on the size and type of enterprise concerned, and the government is keen to ensure that the process is flexible – the important thing is that the transfer takes place as speedily and as fairly as possible. Already a number of small concerns have been sold off, and larger enterprises have transformed themselves into joint stock companies ready for the sale of shares during 1993 and 1994.

In order to enable all individuals (many of whose savings have been eroded completely by inflation) to participate fully in the privatisation process, 'vouchers' with a face value of R10,000 are being issued free to every Russian citizen, regardless of their age, income, social status and so forth. These can be used to purchase an interest in a privatising enterprise, or are freely tradable for cash.

### Independent banking structures

The reconfiguration of the Russian banking sector is a crucial element in the overall reform programme, as it will be a factor determining whether small private enterprises can get off the ground. The Soviet banking system since 1988 had consisted of the state bank (Gosbank) and a number of subordinate institutions operating as monopolies in particular sectors of the economy (practically all foreign currency transactions, for example, were carried out through the Vneshekonombank.) It bore very little resemblance to Western models, being essentially a vehicle for conveying funds to production units to enable the fulfilment of the plan. The banks did hold deposits for enterprises and individuals, but most people preferred to stash any savings they accumulated under their mattresses. Reflecting the modest economic importance of the rouble, the banking system as a whole performed generally only a limited function.

As a natural corollary of the liberalisation of prices, the strict fiscal policies and the moves to make the rouble convertible, Russia's entire banking system is in the process of being restructured. The aim is to create a Western-style two-tier banking system, with an independent central bank regulating the money supply, stabilising the currency and so forth, and private commercial banks accepting deposits and making loans to individuals and businesses.

Already around 2000 new commercial banks have sprung up in Russia, but as yet few operate purely on market considerations. Most were set up by state enterprises, either individually or in association with others in the same sector. Since deposits continue to be hard to come by, these banks are heavily reliant on their shareholders and, as a result, are unable to offer long-term credit to new borrowers.

The transformation of the banking sector is also becoming bogged down by the perpetuation of old practices, including the system whereby all payments between enterprises pass through the central bank. In this respect the introduction of Western technology and know-how is very important. Several aid programmes provide for this, and the opening of branches in Russia by a number of Western banks should stimulate the process.

# 3

# A New Legal Framework

*Frere Cholmeley Bischoff*

For nearly three-quarters of a century Russia was a republic of the USSR, operating an economy based on state ownership of assets and the central planning of economic activity. The first concrete moves away from this model were taken at the Union level during 1988, but the process picked up little momentum until the USSR was dissolved and its republics gained independence at the end of 1991. This is a result of the fact that, although the republican economies traditionally formed only a part of an enormous whole, a noticeable consequence of the separatist forces which arose following political liberalisation in the late-1980s was that more effective economic laws tended to be passed at republican level. Inevitably, these laws attained a new significance when the nation's assets and resources came firmly into republican ownership.

Russia has now established almost all of the basic foundations of a market system, and is rapidly developing a comprehensive legal framework capable of regulating all types of economic activity. This chapter examines the principal legal aspects of Russia's new commercial environment, and focuses in particular on legal guarantees relating to property ownership, foreign investment and foreign trade.

## THE NEW COMMERCIAL ENVIRONMENT

### Private enterprise

The legal basis for conducting commercial activities in Russia is to be found in the 1990 Law on Enterprises and Entrepreneurship (the Enterprise Law). This enactment is one of several passed during 1990 which, though apparently part of an evolutionary process of derestricting private enterprise that included the USSR Laws on Individual Labour Activity (1986) and Co-operatives (1988), in fact marked a decisive break with the country's socialist past. In effect, the state's long-established right to be involved in any business being done on Russian territory was removed. Instead the Enterprise Law provides that the state and administrative bodies are generally precluded from interfering in the activities of enterprises except in cases specifically envisaged by law and within the limits of their authority.

As well as this, the Enterprise Law outlines the basic conditions for doing business ('conducting entrepreneurial activity') in Russia generally. The following are the main principles:

- Any firm or individual, whatever their national origin, can conduct entrepreneurial activity once duly registered for such purposes by the state.

- Financial resources, intellectual and other property rights can be obtained and used on a contractual basis.

- Enterprises operate on an equal footing irrespective of their ownership, legal and organisational status.

- Enterprises have the right to operate in any sector or branch of the economy, and to carry out any type of lawful activity envisaged by their founding documents and Russian legislation.

### Limits to state intervention

Mindful of how practices developed under central planning can perpetuate, legislation has also been passed actively preventing administrative organs from meddling in the affairs of independent economic agents. The 1991 Law on Competition and the Restriction of Monopolistic Activities on Goods Markets targets several forms of government intervention as incompatible with the proper functioning of a competitive market. Specifically prohibited are various forms of control by state bodies over enterprises' commercial or trading operations and the involvement of government officials in decision making or the ownership of individual concerns.

More generally, the law prevents state organs from adopting acts which create favourable conditions for individual enterprises at the expense of others, thereby impeding competition. In principle a legal means therefore exists for challenging government subsidies and other state forms of aid (including tax breaks and cheap loans). However, this notion is unlikely to develop to any great extent for some time yet.

### Contracts

During 1991 new Fundamental Principles of Civil Legislation of the USSR were enacted, with a view to the adoption of modern civil codes by the constituent republics. Although intended as an outline statute, the Fundamental Principles are considerably more market-orientated than Russia's 1964 Civil Code, and, until an updated civil code is actually passed, they will be applied. Central to the Fundamental Principles are the provisions relating to contracts, which move towards establishing an assumption of contractual supremacy under Russian law. Whereas previously many aspects of an accord between two parties were pre-defined by the plan or fixed norms, contractors are now generally free – as in developed market economies – to agree on the conditions which suit themselves.

### Labour relations

Several pieces of legislation concerning labour relations were enacted during 1991 and 1992, including most importantly a USSR Law on the Resolution of Individual Labour Disputes, a Russian Federation Law on Collective Contracts and Agreements, and an Act amending the Russian Labour Code. Generally, the role of the trade unions has been reduced and, while certain procedures developed under the old system are retained, Russian labour law is being brought into line with West European norms.

### Bankruptcy and liquidation

A Law on Bankruptcy was finally adopted by the Russian parliament at the end of 1992, and should come into force in spring 1993. In the meantime, the main legislation in this area is a Presidential Decree allowing companies to be declared bankrupt, which was not ratified and is considered to be unenforceable. Also, some provisions relating to the liquidation of companies are to be found in the Enterprise Act, but comprehensive rules on this subject are long overdue.

## OWNERSHIP

The Russian Federation Law on Ownership and Property, passed in

December 1990, recognises that assets may be under private, state or municipal ownership. The following basic principles of ownership are established:

- Unless the law specifically provides otherwise, any type of assets can be the subject of property rights, including land, buildings and enterprises.

- The owner of the property has the right to own, use and dispose of that property at his or her discretion.

- Any expropriation must be lawful and any damage must be compensated in full.

## PRIVATISATION

With the basic notions of property ownership in place, the process of dividing up assets owned by the State and transferring them to private hands – pivotal to the creation of a market system – could be undertaken. By the end of 1992, Russia had enacted a set of far-reaching laws forming the basis for the privatisation of state-owned enterprises.

The main points of the privatisation programme are:

- Small firms are sold off through auctions or competitive tendering.

- Larger firms are transformed into joint stock companies, with their shares then transferred to private owners.

- Employees qualify for various benefits and incentives, according to the privatisation plan adopted.

- Vouchers, distributed free to every Russian citizen, can be used to purchase shares or other interests in privatising enterprises.

By the end of 1992, the privatisation process was beginning to gather momentum. The Russian government hopes to privatise most of the country's largest state-owned enterprises during 1993 and 1994.

## LAND

Two enactments in 1991 – a Law on Land Reform and a Russian Land Code – have paved the way towards full rights in land for any firm or individual. Currently Russian citizens can own land but, until recently, substantial constitutional restrictions existed on their ability to sell or otherwise transfer it. Amendments to the Constitution passed at the December 1992 Congress of People's Deputies should allow a new, more liberal Land Code to be passed in 1993. This is expected to establish the right of full title to land for Russian individuals and enterprises and, provided some commercial investment is undertaken, also for foreigners.

Although many Russians, particularly in Moscow, are now becoming the owners of their residences, for the moment the most common types of interest in land are a lease or a right of use. However, the privatisation process enables citizens to purchase plots of land, so real estate ownership is set to become more widespread.

## FOREIGN INVESTMENT

Crucial to the success of Russia's economic transformation is the attraction of foreign capital into the economy. Already several thousand enterprises with foreign capital from over 60 countries have been registered in Russia. Between them they employ about 130,000 people and, in 1991, produced goods and services then valued at R11 billion.

The Foreign Investment Law, together with a number of bilateral treaties concluded with individual countries (including the UK), affords strong protection for investments made by foreigners. In particular, full and immediate compensation must be paid in the event of any expropriation. Thus Russian foreign investment legislation is generally in line with that of most developed countries.

Other legislation is planned to reinforce this broad framework over the next few years. According to a programme adopted in the summer of 1992, laws are to be passed in several stages relating to the activities of foreign investors in all areas of the Russian economy.

## FOREIGN TRADE

A Presidential Decree 'On the Liberalisation of Foreign Economic Activity on the Territory of the Russian Federation', issued in November 1991, formed the basis for a substantial liberalisation of the foreign trade regime in Russia. Subsequent legislation has established a relatively straightforward system for the payment of import and export duties and completion of other customs formalities. A notable development is the abolition of the requirement for formal registration of Russian exporters and importers except where 'strategically important' raw materials are concerned.

### Currency regulations

A number of laws on banking and monetary matters have been enacted with a view to establishing a market-based financial system in Russia. The legal foundations for achieving 'internal convertibility' have been laid, and the remaining restrictions on currency operations are set to be removed in the course of the transition programme.

**4**

# Sources of Law

## *Frere Cholmeley Bischoff*

The importance of the rule of law during the transition from a centrally planned to a market economy cannot be overestimated. It is no use enacting laws designed to foster market dynamics and, more importantly, allowing individual enterprises and not government bodies to set their own agendas, if such rules cannot be enforced between subjects and the state itself.

A modern, democratic Russia is now being built on the principle of the division of powers, with legislative power exercised by the Supreme Soviet, executive functions performed by the President and judicial control effected by the Constitutional Court, the Supreme Court and the Supreme Arbitrazh. Also the exact and proper observation of laws on Russian territory is enforced by the Procurator's office, headed by the Procurator General.

This chapter outlines the procedure for enacting laws and the basic structure of state administration currently operating. It then examines the system likely to emerge under a planned new Constitution and highlights some of the legal consequences of the handover of power from the Union to the republic level which occurred at the end of 1991.

## LEGAL SOURCES

The principle legislative organ in Russia is the Supreme Soviet. Draft laws, together with the grounds for their creation, are initially scrutinised by the Presidium and various other permanent commissions, chambers and committees of the Supreme Soviet, including the Legislative Committee and, if approved, are sent for discussion by the Supreme Soviet in full session. Each bill is subjected to two readings unless passed without amendment at the first reading. Otherwise the law is voted on article by article, part by part and as a whole during its second reading. If approved, the law is then adopted by a resolution, which commonly also includes provisions relating to the amendment or replacement of any existing laws and appropriate transitional arrangements. The law then comes into force upon its signature by the President – in many cases this has occurred some time after the Supreme Soviet has passed the law.

Currently a number of laws are being passed by decree of the Russian President. Such decrees can only be set aside by the Supreme Soviet – or its parent body, the Congress of People's Deputies – if they contradict the Constitution.

Generally, adherence to the Constitution is enforced by the Constitutional Court of the Russian Federation. This forum resolves questions relating to the consistency with the Constitution of all legislation, international treaties, political parties and other civil groupings, as well as settling jurisdictional arguments.

### Central government

The government consists of the President and the Council of Ministers. All ministers are nominated by the President, and the Prime Minister is put forward by the President for adoption by the Supreme Soviet. Laws issued by the Council of Ministers take the form of instructions or resolutions. Individual ministers or the entire Council can be removed on a vote of no confidence by the Congress of People's Deputies.

### Regional and local government

Russia has a number of autonomous republics, regions, *oblasts*, cities and districts. The apportionment of powers between central and local government is currently a highly contested issue, and new arrangements are in the process of being drawn up. In general, local councils have jurisdiction over valuable resources situated on or under their territory, can enact laws on certain limited matters and have the right to initiate legislation to be passed centrally. Further powers are often granted by individual laws.

## A NEW CONSTITUTION

Russia has a written Constitution establishing the country's fundamental laws. At present the old Soviet Constitution, now amended hundreds of times, is still being used. This document is generally regarded as a major obstacle to continued reform, and a modern Russian Constitution has been drafted to take its place. However certain quarters, most notably the Congress of People's Deputies (a body partly democratically elected under Soviet rule and consisting mostly of conservative forces) are opposed to the drafts, which would replace many existing structures and necessitate new elections. None the less, one of the outcomes of the Congress held at the end of 1992 was an agreement with the President that a referendum on the basic principles of a new Constitution would be called, and this is to be held in April 1993.

Under the most recent draft Constitution:

- The President is the head of state of the Russian Federation and represents the country in domestic and international affairs. Direct elections to the office will be held every five years, and the same person may be re-elected only once. The President is the leader of the government and can issue decrees and instructions carrying the force of law throughout the territory of Russia.

- The Supreme Soviet is the federal parliament and sole legislative organ of the Russian Federation. It is in permanent session, with elections held every four years, and consists of two chambers: the State Duma and the Federal Assembly. Among its main competences are the power to amend the Constitution, call referendums, adopt the federal budget and dismiss the President, the Vice-President and judges of the Supreme Courts.

- Legislation can be initiated by deputies, various parliamentary committees, the President, the Federal Assembly, republican, regional and district assemblies, the courts and any electoral group numbering not less than one million people.

- Draft laws and bills are considered first by the State Duma and secondly, if approved, by the Federal Assembly. On approval by the Federal Assembly, they are sent for signature by the President and are then officially published. A law comes into force either as laid down in the law itself, or if there is no such provision, seven days after publication.

## LEGAL CONSEQUENCES OF RUSSIAN INDEPENDENCE

The process of building up a body of law capable of addressing any aspect of societal relations which may occur is, of necessity, an evolutionary one. Just as conditions in society change, so must the law. In a sense this occurs automatically in common law countries through the precedental force of decisions handed down by the courts. In civil law systems, such as Russia, this updating is effected formally through periodic revision of the basic legislative acts, usually in a manner which reflects developments in the courts and other judicial fora. However, on a day-to day basis lawyers can be guided, if not bound, by interpretations of the law made by the courts in individual cases. Thus civil law systems are generally no less responsive than common law ones to changes in attitudes, practices and custom.

The USSR, a federal state built on socialist principles, developed in this way a comprehensive, if unique, set of laws governing every sphere of activity relevant to its political and economic structure. Consequently upon the dissolution of the USSR, Russia, having rejected socialism and instead started moving towards a market system, was confronted with laws mostly passed to augment and reinforce structures which were to be replaced, and which were as a result to a great extent irrelevant to its newly defined priorities. But if it declared ineffective any enactment passed in the name of the USSR it would leave itself to a large extent lawless – although several laws, including the Civil Code, were passed at the republican level (on the basis of federal 'fundamental principles') these did not amount to a full legal system. Even the most prolific of legislatures could not hope to develop almost instantly a set of laws to parallel those of the countries whose example it was now seeking to follow. Instead the approach favoured was to announce that Russian law was to have priority, but USSR laws were still valid to the extent they were not inconsistent with them. Thus the USSR law would 'fill in the gaps' of Russian law until Russia was able to perform this function with new laws of its own.

Had the Russian authorities actually followed this policy strictly, therefore, there would be lacunas in the law only to the extent that matters were incapable of being addressed by the lengthily developed USSR laws. However, in practice the Russians have done something slightly different – operating a policy of regarding USSR laws as effective only in *areas* in which no Russian law exists. So if the Russians have passed a law, however brief or general, in a given sphere it is the *only* applicable law on the matter in question.

While this approach indeed ensures that the applicable laws on a certain matter do not contain any provisions which may be anachronistic in the conditions now prevailing, it also means that the legislative layer is unusually 'thin'. It is, therefore, perhaps not by accident that recently passed Russian laws tend to be somewhat declaratory by nature (many contain a number of broad principles but few mechanisms for actually putting them into effect). Accordingly, any analysis of recent Russian laws is likely to contain at least some predictive component.

# 5

# Russia and its Trading Partners

## ALM Consulting

Russia's trading links are altering drastically as its political and economic priorities are reassessed. Until recently it was part of a huge economic apparatus covering the whole of the Soviet Union. Industry was oriented towards producing for this and the wider socialist zone through internal mechanisms and the Comecon network. But since the late-1980s traditional ties have been disappearing as, first, *perestroika* diminished the importance of the 'plan' and then the individual countries of the Soviet bloc turned their backs on international communism.

As a result, in 1992 Russia became a net importer. Between January and August exports were worth US$21.5 billion (34 per cent down on the same period in 1991) and imports US$21.7 billion (19 per cent down), whereas in 1991 the same months had produced a trade surplus of US$6 billion. Overall turnover has fallen by over a quarter, reflecting the breakdown of old arrangements and industry's struggle to adapt to new markets. This chapter outlines the emerging framework for relations between Russia and the West, the former members of Comecon, the previously Soviet states and its own autonomous republics.

**Table 5.1** *Trade turnover (US dollars, billion)*

|  | Jan–Aug 1991 | Jan–Aug 1992 | Change |
|---|---|---|---|
| Industrialised nations | 33 | 26.1 | –21% |
| Less developed countries | 7 | 5.6 | –20% |
| Former Comecon | 15 | 7.8 | –48% |

| Table 5.2  *Trading partners* | |
|---|---|
| European countries | 68% |
| Asia | 21% |
| Africa | 2% |
| America | 9% |
| Australia | 0.1% |

# RUSSIA'S LINKS WITH THE WEST

### *The European Community*

A whole new basis for relations between Russia and the EC is currently in the process of being developed. The Russian government clearly regards the EC as its principal trading partner of the future, and businesses in the EC are expressing a growing interest in selling their products on the Russian market.

The accord signed by the EC and the USSR in December 1989 (basically a model 'first generation' agreement) has therefore been thoroughly overtaken by events. At the same time it is recognised that Russia is not yet ready to enter an Association Agreement along the lines of those the EC concluded with Poland, Hungary and Czechoslovakia in 1991. Accordingly a Partnership and Co-operation Agreement falling somewhere between the two is being negotiated. Such an Agreement provides for improved trade access as well as close co-operation in a number of key sectors.

### *The United Kingdom*

Close and friendly relations between the peoples of Russia and the United Kingdom have existed for hundreds of years and remain

| Table 5.3  *Principal EC trading partners* | |
|---|---|
| | *Turnover (US dollars, billion)* |
| Germany | 7.6 |
| Italy | 3.1 |
| France | 2.1 |
| UK | 1.5 |
| Netherlands | 1.4 |

strong today. This fact was recognised in a treaty signed by the two parties during a visit by the Russian President Boris Yeltsin to London in November 1992. This document envisages wide co-operation between the two countries in a number of areas. In particular, an agreement on economic co-operation provides for the creation of an inter-governmental committee on trade and invest-ment, with direct involvement for interested businesses.

### The United States

Trade between Russia and the United States increased during the perestroika years and, despite a recent drop, can be expected to pick up further in the years ahead. This should be facilitated by a new trade agreement based on that signed by the US and the Soviet Union and ratified by the US Congress in November 1991. Most importantly, this agreement will grant Russia 'most favoured nation' status.

### CoCoM

An important factor in trade relations between many Western countries and Russia is the Co-ordinating Committee for Multilateral Export Controls (CoCoM). This organisation was established during the days of East–West confrontation to restrict exports of high technology by its members (the NATO countries except Iceland, plus Japan) to communist administrations in Eastern Europe.

Perhaps surprisingly, some CoCoM restrictions still exist. However the contemporary emphasis is on preventing the re-export of equipment by Russia and other members of the CIS to regimes which CoCoM regards as dangerous and unstable. To this end a new coactive body, likely to number the ex-Soviet republics among its participants, is being created. Already several controls have been lifted, including those on communications technology (except fibre optics, which will probably be removed soon). The curbs most likely to remain in force are on munitions, high-speed computers and advanced machine tools.

## RELATIONS WITH FORMER COMECON COUNTRIES

Until recently, Russia's foreign economic relations were pursued largely through the Council for Mutual Economic Assistance (Comecon). Set up in 1949, the goal of this organisation was to establish the international division of socialist labour. In broad terms, the Soviet Union supplied raw materials to the other member countries (Poland, Czechoslovakia, Hungary, Romania, Bulgaria, Cuba, Vietnam, Mongolia and, until reunification, the GDR) and received machinery, manufactured products and processed food in return. Trading was carried out through a central accounting body, with suppliers and customers having no direct contact. All transactions were conducted using the 'transferable rouble', a means by which a somewhat arbitrary value was assigned to products traded.

However, the functioning of the Comecon system was contingent upon its member countries operating command economies and, as most of the states have moved away from this model, so trading between them has been placed on a different footing. Since January 1991 transactions between Comecon states have been carried out at world market prices using convertible currencies. This change removed the fundamental components from the Comecon mechanism and the organisation was formally liquidated in 1992.

The collapse of Comecon has led to a dramatic downturn in the volume of goods moving between its former member states. The total share of former Comecon countries in Russian trade has fallen from over 60 per cent in 1989 to 25 per cent in 1991 and 19 per cent in the first eight months of 1992. The general breakdown of long-standing arrangements has left some East European factories without the inputs to which their production lines are tailored, and Russian plants without parts and servicing for their machines.

During 1992, Russia and its ex-Comecon partners began the process of formulating new trading and other commercial ties on a country-by-country basis. Year-long agreements have been concluded with several states, incorporating the following features:

- Fixed prices in hard currency are designated to 'priority products' (such as food and raw materials).

- Special account-settling mechanisms are set up, allowing for various clearing methods including barter payment calculated in convertible currency.

- Government payment guarantees are provided to be channelled through banks.

The various elements of these agreements are indicative of a broader market-oriented foundation to ties between the countries which is likely to be developed in future accords.

New links are also being forged at the enterprise level. Joint chambers of commerce and industry have been formed and industrial managers' representative bodies have signed co-operation agreements aimed at providing mutual assurances of supplies. A novel development is the establishment of a 'Trans-National Stock Exchange', an organisation aimed at co-ordinating trade between small and medium-sized businesses within the former Comecon's geographical boundaries.

## RELATIONS WITH FORMER SOVIET REPUBLICS

Until the end of 1991 Russia was a republic of the Union of Soviet Socialist Republics. This was a 'federal, multi-national state formed on the basis of socialist federalism' (Article 70 of the USSR Constitution) which issued legislation for, and concluded international treaties on behalf of, its constituent republics. All-Union legislation consisted of laws, decrees and other enactments adopted by various state organs which ensured a uniformity of legal regulation throughout the territory of the USSR.

The end of the Soviet Union was formally brought about when Russia, Ukraine and Byelorussia, and shortly after the other Soviet republics (except Georgia and the Baltics) signed the Agreement on the Creation of a Commonwealth of Independent States (Azerbaijan has since pulled out). This stated in its preamble that 'the USSR no longer exists as a subject of international law and geopolitical reality'. Its former republics are now independent sovereign states, each having sole jurisdiction over, and responsibility for, its own internal affairs. All are now internationally recognised as such and have become individual members of the United Nations.

### Nature of the CIS

The CIS is a unique supranational organisation born more of necessity than a spirit of comity. It possesses none of the characteristics of a state or federal structure and has no legislative power to bind its members. In essence, it simply provides a platform on which the strong interdependence of its constituent states can be managed.

Indeed it is felt in many circles that the CIS provides no more than a transitional mechanism for peacefully dismantling many of the ties developed under centralised communist rule. Certainly the direction of public opinion throughout the former USSR remains in favour of increased regionalisation. However, it is these centrifugal forces and an attendant rise of nationalism which have created a potentially explosive situation and which make the existence of a negotiating forum especially vital. Thus a crucial element in the original CIS agreements is the recognition of the inviolability of existing borders between the signatory countries.

### Extent of Commonwealth co-operation

The fields in which the member states of the CIS are due to co-operate are determined by the economic, military and other links forged during the decades of Soviet governance. The principal vehicles created to effect this co-ordination are the Council of Heads of State, convened at least twice yearly, and the Council of Heads of Government, which meets at least every three months. Council meetings have a rotating presidency, and each state has one vote with decisions reached by consensus. Councils have also been set up in other spheres (for example defence and the railways) to co-ordinate activities at the ministerial or managerial level.

### Economic co-operation

The new foundations for economic co-operation between Russia and the other members of the CIS are currently in the process of being laid. The rigid framework of economic interdependence developed during the years of Soviet rule was based largely on the system of central planning, and has to an extent eroded in congruence with the switch to market relations between enterprises. In particular, world prices are now generally charged for goods traded between enterprises in different CIS member countries. None the less, a number of ties are *de facto* still in place, not least because they require more effort to dismantle than to maintain.

Underscoring economic relations within the CIS is the continued use of the rouble for financing all transactions within and between the member states. At the centre of this 'rouble zone' is undoubtedly Russia, which both mints all units of the currency and runs a large trade surplus with most of the CIS – a reflection of its mineral wealth and comparatively well-developed industrial base. In fact it is partly these attributes of the rouble zone which threaten eventually to pull it apart. Despite controlling all the printing presses for the rouble, Russia does not determine economic policy within the other states in which it is used. During the first half of 1992 other republics pursued less stringent credit policies than Russia, thereby creating inflationary pressures on Russian territory resented by monetarist influences in its government. In response Russia announced that it would only accept payments for its products from other CIS countries in roubles granted by its own central bank. Thus a distinction arose between roubles issued by Russia and roubles credited by other CIS states' central banks. This is the first step on a road towards the introduction of separate national currencies, which is anyway the long-term aim of most of the CIS countries. (Ukraine introduced its own 'coupons' – a move towards its proposed new currency the *grivna* – at the end of 1992, and several other states, most notably Azerbaijan and Moldova, have already made concrete moves in this direction.) In the long run it may well be that the only countries to remain in the rouble zone will be Russia, Kazakhstan, Uzbekistan, Belarus, Kirghyzstan and Armenia. These republics agreed to set up an Interstate Bank for Mutual Settlements at the CIS Bishkek summit in October 1992.

However, there remains a perception within the CIS that many of the economic links formulated under Soviet rule are mutually advantageous and should be renewed. This seems likely to be effected initially in a piecemeal fashion through bilateral and multilateral agreements, rather than strictly through the channels of the CIS. A number of treaties have already been concluded between republics of the former Soviet Union, including those not members of the CIS. It is envisaged that these might build into a coherent system of co-ordinated economic relations and even constitute a legal basis for a new 'Economic Commonwealth'.

### Customs policy

Also anticipated in the original CIS agreement was the creation of a 'common economic space.' In fact this proved impossible from the outset as different states pursued different pricing and customs policies in the immediate aftermath of the Soviet Union's collapse. In Russia, a Presidential Decree of 27 December 1991 introduced a system of fines for unlicensed exporting of various products to other member states and shortly afterwards mounted border controls at major crossing points to prevent such activities.

However, during the course of 1992 new arrangements were drawn up by several republics setting up an embryonic customs union, which may eventually be extended to cover most of the CIS. The original members – Russia, Kazakhstan, Kirghyzstan, Tajikistan and Uzbekistan – agreed to create a common customs territory with common rules and no internal barriers. Belarus, Moldova and

Armenia also agreed to the idea in principle and in September 1992 Russia announced that it was setting up new controls on its borders with non-signatories – Azerbaijan, Georgia, Ukraine and the Baltics.

To complement the new customs arrangements an Agreement on Freight Transit was adopted by ten CIS member countries (all except the Ukraine) in February 1991. This laid down fixed procedures for dealing with products exported from and imported to one CIS state via another CIS state to or from a third country outside the Commonwealth. The basic provisions of the Agreement are:

■ Customs formalities must be completed in the receiving or despatching state, and are recognised by all the other contracting republics.

■ Goods in transit are exempt from customs duties and inspection.

■ Re-export is generally prohibited of goods exported from one contracting state for sale in another.

At the time of writing, therefore, certain aspects of the CIS's internal market are in place while others remain to be determined. Given the unstable economic and political conditions which persist in the member states, though, there is some uncertainty whether the agreements which have been signed will be implemented. The exact nature and orientation of the new system will thus become clearer during 1993, but a stable regime is unlikely to emerge for some years yet.

## RUSSIA AND ITS REPUBLICS

As its alternative formal name suggests, the Russian Federation is itself a federal state. Under Soviet rule it included 16 'Autonomous Republics' and 5 'autonomous regions'. This was changed in April 1992 when a new Federation Treaty upgraded the status of the main regions to full republics. These republics have their own parliaments and considerable powers of self-government, including certain rights to pass local laws. The new Treaty – to be part of the long-awaited new Constitution – essentially grants jurisdiction over most military, foreign and economic issues to the centre and devolves control over mineral resources and tax-collecting rights to the republics and 55 smaller regions.

However, the separatist forces prevalent throughout the region have led to a number of complications in establishing a workable federal structure. The over-centralisation of the Soviet system is perhaps now in some danger of being replaced by over-regionalisation. Two republics, Tatarstan and Checheno-Ingushetia, refused to sign the Treaty altogether, while others imposed strict conditions for their acquiescence. In general, decisions of the central authorities are often ignored at the local level and several republics have imposed restrictions on import and export operations. Accordingly, since trade may be appreciably affected, the situation in some of these areas is examined in more detail.

### Tatarstan

Recent calls for Tatar independence go back at least to the summer of 1990, when the republic's Supreme Soviet drafted plans for economic sovereignty and local laws on ownership, trading and so forth. This position was reinforced in March 1992, when 61.4 per cent supported a referendum on sovereignty in spite of a ruling by Russia's Constitutional Court that the wording of the question put to voters was unconstitutional.

At the time of writing it is unclear exactly what form future relations with Russia will take. Surrounded geographically by other parts of the Russian Federation, the outright secession of Tatarstan would be physically very complicated. Indeed the Tatar government claims that this is not in any event its aim, and it wishes instead to conclude a bilateral treaty granting Tatarstan some form of 'associated' status with the Russian authorities. A step in this direction was taken in December 1991 when an agreement signed by the two governments granted the Tatars full jurisdiction over oil deposits situated on their territory. A new Tatarstan Constitution, likely to be a key factor in this matter, looks set to be delayed until a full agreement has been signed.

### Checheno-Ingushetia

Another republic which failed to sign the Federation Treaty was Checheno-Ingushetia. The position with this republic is very complex as the Chechen constituency unilaterally seceded from the Russian Federation in 1991 (its leader, General Dudaev, announced the creation of an independent Chechen Islamic Republic) while the Ingush part, it seems, is willing to stay. The stated aim of the Chechen government is to attract its neighbouring republics into a fundamentalist North-Caucasian Federation. Future developments

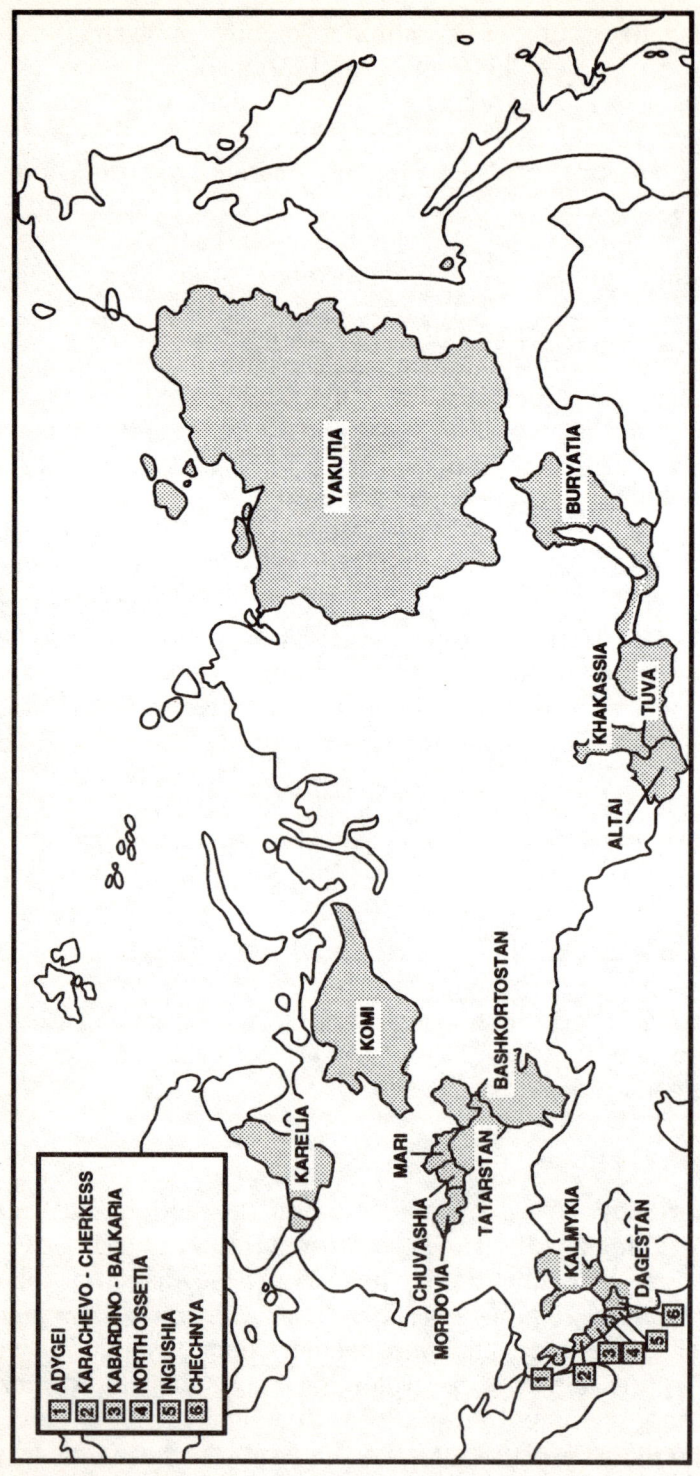

**Map 5.1** *Russia's autonomous republics*

Source:  School of Geography, University of Birmingham

are thus uncertain but trading links are, at best, likely to be disrupted.

### Bashkiria

The largest autonomous republic of the Russian Federation, in terms of population, is Bashkiria. In spite of conflict with the Russian authorities over various aspects of economic policy, the Bashkirian government is committed to remaining within the Federation and signed the Treaty in April. However, the Bashkirians wish to complement this with bilateral accords on property, taxation, budgetary and other matters. One such agreement has already been reached allowing the republic to retain up to 75 per cent of foreign exchange earnings.

### The Crimea

A converse situation has arisen in the Crimea. Currently part of the Ukraine, the area seems to be gearing itself for reunification with Russia, from which it was transferred in 1954. Following the grant of wide self-governing powers in April 1992, including jurisdiction over land and natural resources and control over the pace of economic reform, migration and education policy and military movements on its territory, the Crimean parliament within two weeks declared the peninsula an independent republic. Under pressure from the Ukrainian parliament this declaration was subsequently rescinded, but it seems likely that further moves towards separation will be made in the future.

# 6
# Market Intelligence
*KPMG Peat Marwick*

Marketing and market research used to be irrelevant under the conditions prevailing in the Soviet Union. In the past only one or two contacts needed to be cultivated and the market absorbed everything. Now it is necessary to find out who the end-users are, who will buy and who has the money. It must be stressed that finding a market is not likely to be as difficult as identifying a secure source of payment. The potential market for a particular product may appear vast, but exploiting it may prove problematic at this stage because of the lack of foreign exchange reserves.

## STATISTICS

The enormous state bureaucracy of the command economy thrived on collecting statistics and regurgitating them in a way that would support its goals. Available statistics are frequently outdated and incomplete and, beyond what was officially published, difficult to obtain. Measures of national wealth are based on the so-called Net Material Product, which excludes the service sector and represents about 85 per cent of GDP. Economic data are distorted by the use of artificial indicators. Statistics based on the private sector are often not collated.

The State Statistical Committee publishes statistics on foreign trade. Commodity and other exchanges regularly publish statistics on trading conditions, volumes, prices and deals relating to their area of activity. These are often quoted in Russia's financial press.

There are a number of companies offering statistical information on Russia and the former Soviet Union. More and more studies are becoming available on various sectors – in particular, commodity production, oil and gas. There have been studies of consumer tastes which attempt to bridge the information gap. They show that established brands achieve high rates of recognition, but they give very little information on who has money to spend.

Market sizes for particular products and future consumption patterns – in particular for new services with which people or enterprises are unfamiliar (eg, insurance and pension plans) – are difficult to judge. Existing results tend to be misleading since they often concentrate on cities such as Moscow and St Petersburg.

## SOURCES OF INFORMATION

The DTI's Russian desk keeps information on the Russian economy, on the various regions and autonomous republics and some market sector information. It provides general market advice on various aspects of doing business in Russia and has published a brief profile of business in Russia. The DTI's World Aid Section gives advice on hard currency projects funded by the World Bank, the European Community and the European Investment Bank. It may also be worth approaching the TACIS representative in Russia to see what sort of projects are likely to be approved.

The Eastern Europe Trade Council is an advisory group, appointed by the British Overseas Trade Board, which promotes trade opportunities and disseminates market information. It has a reference library containing information on legislation, trade directories, trade journals and market sector specific information. It produces a bi-monthly bulletin containing market pointers and new sources of information.

Banks that have representative offices in Russia may be able to provide information on trading conditions, payment difficulties and acceptable or recommended payment terms. Some of them publish economic reports and bulletins.

The British Embassy's Commercial Section is a first point of contact for many newcomers in Russia. It collects market information, information on trade conditions and investments, and provides a good background on how to start and where to go. The Commercial Section tries to keep up to date with contacts in the various ministries and circles of businessmen, and undertakes some research on potential partners if requested. The new consulate in St Petersburg also provides some commercial services.

BSCC, formerly the British Soviet Chamber of Commerce,

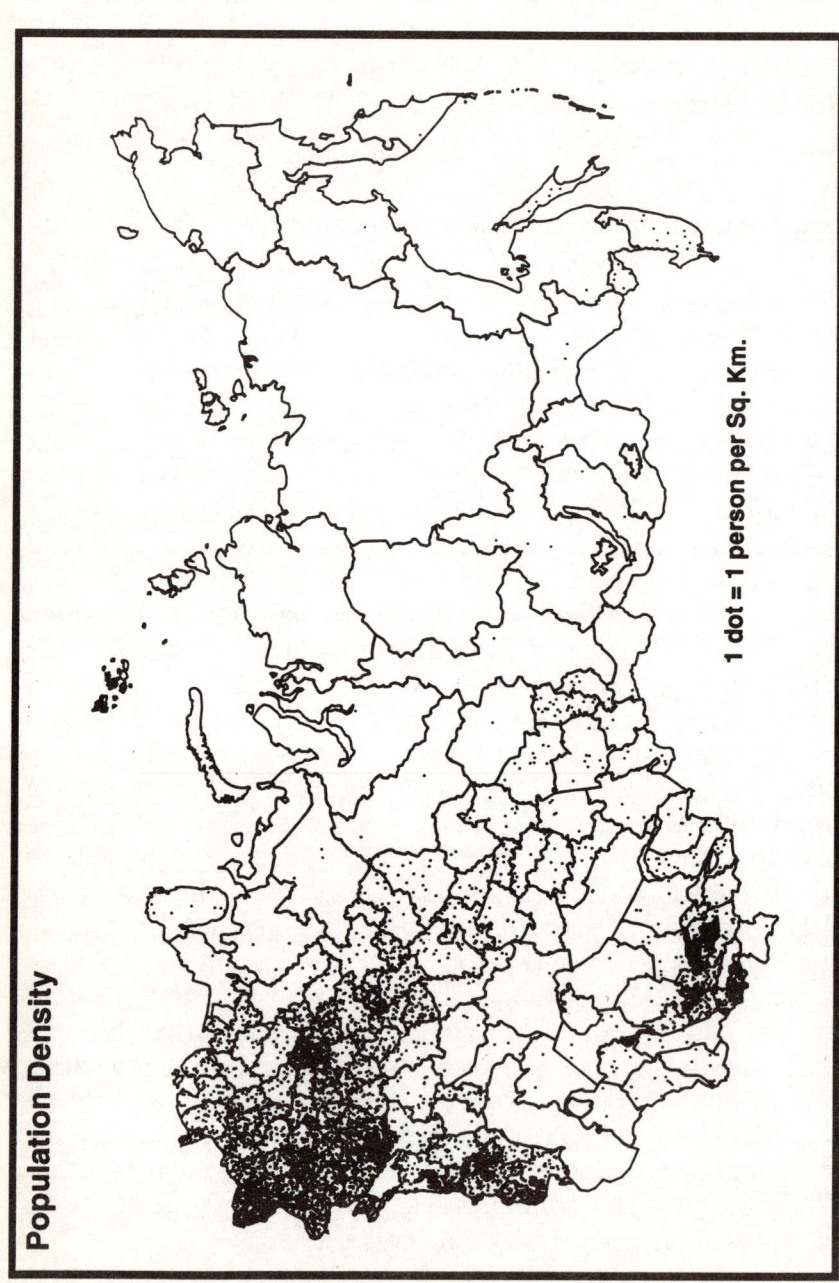

**Population Density**

1 dot = 1 person per Sq. Km.

**Map 6.1** *Population density*

Source:  School of Geography, University of Birmingham

organises regular trade missions. It offers a membership scheme to interested companies and provides regular meetings for members. The BSCC is geared towards smaller companies which account for 90 per cent of its membership. It works in conjunction with a number of regional chambers of commerce which have experience of organising trade missions and fairs.

### Ministries and governmental bodies

The ministries continue to cast their shadows on most economic activity. It is often simpler and quicker to address queries about particular companies under their jurisdiction directly to them. The Russian government created the Russian Agency for International Co-operation and Development (RAICI) in January 1993. The Agency takes over from the Committee on Foreign Investment and has been given very broad powers including 'to form and realise state policy in attracting foreign investment including loans and credits for the economy'. It is also supposed to register foreign investments and monitor technical assistance. It will have regional branches as well as branches abroad. However, it is a new body and it is difficult to know at this stage how functions will be shared with other bodies involved at present with foreign investment. City authorities and regions now also want to manage their own industries and privatisation programmes, control their own natural resources and collect their own taxes and these are a good source of information on local conditions. Investors should develop good relations and sometimes negotiate directly with them.

### Business circles

It is now possible to influence end-users and enterprises. Therefore a much wider range of contacts is necessary than just the ministries or the Foreign Trade Organisations. It may also be necessary to promote contacts with peripheral organisations such as trade associations and new business circles. Local entrepreneurs are often overlooked because they have not developed much influence yet: however they may provide interesting insights and potential for business. There are many opportunities beyond Moscow and St Petersburg.

### Professional advisers

Useful information on investments is much harder to obtain than information on trade. There are numerous publications but often the information is contradictory and of little value on its own. Investment opportunities must be analysed and compared with actual practice. Professional advisers who have set up offices in Russia are a valuable source of information and are well aware of conditions facing their clients and of pitfalls facing investors. They will help you understand the difficulties in valuing businesses and profit forecasting in relation to a fledgling market.

## TRADE FAIRS AND TRADE MISSIONS

Specialised and general trade fairs are organised all over Russia. Trade fairs provide a useful way of making contact in Russia with technical specialists, engineers, enterprises and other end-users. The structure of the fairs has mirrored changes in the economy: for example, there are fairs exhibiting small-scale farming machinery to the new private farmer. Fairs and exhibitions help you to test the market, attract customers, meet wholesalers and carry out some initial research. They may also help identify potential business representatives.

As a first step, trade missions can help exporters gain an insight into market potential and get into contact with end-users and companies in complementary lines of business. Missions are organised by BSCC in conjunction with local chambers of commerce and industry.

Seminars and other educational campaigns, lectures and demonstrations are also useful ways of getting your product known about by end-users. Emphasis should be placed on sharing technical points rather than a hard sell.

## PUBLICATIONS

In addition to a wealth of publications devoted to business in Eastern Europe in general, there are a number of English language journals and publications specifically on Russia. General business publications in English include *Delovie Lyudi* (formerly *Business in the USSR*), *Commersant, Russia Express*, the *BSCC Bulletin* and *Moscow Business Week*. There are also some sectoral publications in English such as *Moscow Computer News* and *Oil and Gas Bulletin*. These can all be obtained in the UK.

Russian language publications cover a wide spectrum. There are some financial and legal papers: for example, *Ekonomycheskaya*

*Gazeta* (Economic Gazette), *Finansovaya Gazeta* (Financial Gazette), *Finansy* (Finances) and *Pravitelstvenny Vestnik* (Legal Journal). Find out which trade publications cover your industry: in this way you will learn about the state of technology, possible investment projects and import needs.

There are a few English language directories of companies. For example, an oil and gas directory, a directory of health care users and buyers and of other industrial endusers (see Appendix 2). Lists of companies seeking partners or co-operation agreements are circulated by a number of organisations: however these do not give information on creditworthiness or a company's standing.

# 7

# Business Culture

*Nicholas Louis*

## ARRANGING A VISIT

To travel to Russia one still needs a visa. The hosting company should send a formal telex or fax invitation to the local Russian embassy, stating the exact dates and purposes of the intended visit and listing the full particulars of those invited. It is best to rely on an experienced travel agent, since the visas are often issued at the last moment and may be cause for last-minute panic. Should the visit need to be prolonged, a visa extension can be obtained locally without too many problems.

It is best to arrange an agenda well in advance of the meetings, so as not to waste precious time on general overviews upon arrival. Business cards are a must and some people have bilingual cards prepared, although this requires some knowledge of Russian. In any case, several simple phrases of greeting may come in extremely useful and will be much appreciated.

It is appropriate to ask the receiving party to book a hotel; alternatively the travel agent may advise on a convenient place to stay. Some Russian companies have guest houses which, though saving on the accommodation costs, should be looked at before taking up the offer. In rural centres they are often much better and safer than the local hotel. International direct-dial phones are still an uncommon luxury outside Moscow, so it may be worthwhile agreeing a fixed time for your office to call a particular number. Hotels do not normally have switchboards with direct numbers to the room, and the reception rarely passes on messages.

Transportation for getting from the international airport to the hotel should be pre-arranged, as there have been several cases of travellers being mugged and left in the road with no luggage.

Domestic flights are frequently delayed in winter time due to the weather, and year round due to lack of fuel. To be sure of arriving on time, journeys can be made by train. There are usually four-berth compartments: if the journey is overnight, drinking sessions into the small hours of the morning with your travelling companions are not uncommon.

## GETTING DOWN TO BUSINESS

Once contacts are established and common ground for doing business is laid, you may be invited to the home of your host, which is considered a great honour. Often Russians are shy of inviting foreigners for fear of embarrassing them with the spartan surroundings. The invitation is usually for dinner to meet the family and it is common to bring some flowers for your hostess and perhaps a small gift. Outdoor sports and family outings are popular, so if you end up staying the weekend you may be invited out to the 'dacha' (country house). As in the West, with all the big decisions being made on the golf course, in Russia they are reached during hunting or fishing trips.

Any advice on how to manage a business should be provided with the utmost courtesy. Needless to say, engineers in the oil and gas industry would be offended if a Westerner came along and started telling them how to drill a well properly. Most of the shortcomings that do exist are due to isolation from colleagues abroad and lack of hard-currency funds to purchase equipment and spares. Any creative offers, such as barter of such items against a supply contract will go a long way towards cementing a relationship.

Rarely is a deal struck during the first visit and travel expenses should be budgeted for. One should be patient, but firm. Foreigners have always been treated like VIPs, but it is only recently that the myth that all foreigners, Americans in particular, are millionaires has been shattered.

Russians often being gullible, are on the whole friendly and open-hearted, but beware the new breed of 'beeznesman'. Though foreigners have also been given a bad name by some of the shadier characters making their way to Russia, there are the same sort of 'sharks' on the receiving end awaiting the next victim. Promises are made, deals are struck and time, if nothing else, is lost. References are very important for both sides and care should be taken to make sure that meetings are taking place with the company in question and not a private spin-off company of the individual welcoming you.

The greatest shortage in Russia is in information. One of the best gifts is a reference manual or a subscription to a periodical publication on the area of business under discussion. Some companies have become popular by offering their clients English language courses.

When travelling within the country it would be wise to ask for a guide or have somebody in the party speaking Russian. Many promising business deals have fallen through due to simple language communication problems. It is still not unusual for Russian companies to send correspondence in Russian, expecting the receiving company to have it translated. Should a deal be struck, its successful execution often depends on the motivation of the English-speaking person at the hosting company. He would also be the person nominated to oversee and report on the progress of the contract.

Much attention should be paid to the preparation of presentation documents. If goods or equipment are being offered for sale, national safety or health approval certificates will need to be obtained, so it may be useful to have a copy of the relevant EC or other certificates on hand. Experience of sales to other former Eastern bloc countries is usually a good reference point and many industry standards within ex-Comecon countries are still quite similar.

Dress for meetings is formal. When meeting or parting with somebody it is common to shake hands – not just when one is first introduced. According to unwritten protocol the meeting parties always sit opposite each other during negotiations. When seeing people at ministries or Foreign Trade Organisations, it is expected that meetings start punctually and usually on the hour. Due to the shortage of meeting rooms one may find another anxious group peering through the door at the end of the allocated hour.

At the end of a visit it is usually expected that an invitation for a reciprocal visit be extended. Russians travelling abroad pay their return air fare, but expect to be put up and entertained by the hosting party. This is an opportunity to get to know the people you are dealing with and to extend the same courtesies as were offered when visiting them. Some of their fondest memories carried back may be not of the tour of the plant, but of the visit to the bowling alley or the local pub. A good sense of humour is highly valued, but beware of the endless glasses of vodka!

*Part II*

# The Business Infrastructure

# 8

# Convertibility

## *KPMG Peat Marwick*

A market is not conceivable without economic interaction both within Russia and with the rest of the world. A convertible rouble would encourage the return of flight capital, stimulate foreign direct investment and eliminate the need to protect the domestic market with export controls. It would also expose Russian businesses to competition from abroad and thus throw the country into the deep end of the world economy.

Under the Soviet regime, the rouble measured output and represented the value central planners assigned to goods and particular transactions. It could not be converted into foreign currency nor readily exchanged for goods. Fixed prices and shortages of goods meant that the amount of printed money was largely irrelevant. Money could simply be confiscated with scant regard for the people who had to use it: in January 1991, R100 and R50 bank notes were simply taken out of circulation.

## REFORMS

At this stage of Russia's transformation, a fully convertible rouble is a somewhat academic proposition. Politicians and economists have still to grasp its practical implications. Some ministers regularly insist that the rouble will soon be convertible while introducing measures to try and hold foreign currency in the country. However, these measures have contributed to the uncertainty which hampers government action and foreign investments.

Full convertibility involves a number of major steps: freeing prices; disentangling the monetary legacy of the Soviet Union; unifying the maze of different exchange rates; developing a foreign exchange market; and floating and pegging the rouble to a sustainable rate of exchange.

### Freeing prices

The possibility to convert money into domestic consumer goods is a central expectation that people have of money. Freeing prices is one of the first stages in achieving convertibility because it enables a proper value to be placed on goods and, despite the nominal decrease in purchasing power, makes the rouble worth possessing because it is backed by goods. Most prices were freed in January 1992 except for basic commodities such as bread and energy which are subsidised through a super-profit tax. However, without a proper market, prices are still for the most part fixed by monopoly producers.

### Disentangling the rouble zone

Some of the ex-Soviet republics are still using the rouble as their currency, conducting internal trade in roubles and running enormous trade deficits with Russia. Russia is trying to improve its control over credits in roubles granted to banks and enterprises outside Russia by distinguishing roubles which it has issued from roubles resulting from credit extensions. Other CIS members are quitting the rouble zone altogether and introducing their own currencies, or have introduced rouble substitute coupons to protect themselves from Russian inflation. The whole process has suffered from the inability of CIS members to co-ordinate their macroeconomic stabilisation and exchange reform plans.

### Developing a foreign exchange market

One of the major stumbling blocks on the road to convertibility is the lack of a proper foreign exchange market, without which it is difficult to find a correct parity for the rouble. Trading sessions on the Moscow Interbank Currency Exchange (MICE) take place twice a week, but turnover there is very small because of the lack of currency on offer. It also takes days to transfer money to banks with access to the exchange. Voluntary sales of currency represent barely nine per cent of weekly market turnover. Volumes of foreign currency trade in the whole of Russia are estimated by the central bank to be between $100 and $200 million a week, and that figure includes the street market. The existing exchange arrangements and official channels seem to have no impact on the supply of hard currency to the economy. The amount of foreign currency which has to be mandatorily exchanged has not increased since July 1992.

### Unifying various rates of exchange

The Soviet Union left behind it a complex maze of different exchange rates that were applied to different types of transactions and valuations. In January 1992, the official Union rate of R1.7 to the dollar was effectively devalued by the introduction of a new central bank rate of R110 to the dollar. However, a special rate was also introduced at R55 which was used to calculate the mandatory surrender of foreign currency by exporters. Also authorised were the weekly (later bi-weekly) sessions at MICE which set the market rate. As of 1 July 1992, a limited internal convertibility was introduced and a unified rouble exchange rate is now set twice a week by the Bank of Russia, based on the MICE rate. This rate must now be used for calculating payments and settlements between economic entities, for accounting purposes, for computing tax liabilities and calculating the mandatory surrender of foreign currency.

### Pegging the rouble

Once Russia achieves fiscal and monetary stability, the goal will be to peg the rouble at a sustainable exchange rate and defend it with the help of the G-10 stabilisation fund. However, the stabilising fund will only appear once conditions that will allow stabilisation are in place. The rouble will remain unattractive until policies are seen to be working.

## CONVERTIBILITY ISSUES

### Trading activities

The government, out of dire necessity, has imposed a heavy burden on exporters. Fifty per cent of foreign currency earnings must be disposed of no later than fourteen days after having been received. Joint ventures with over 30 per cent foreign participation are allowed to convert the entire 50 per cent amount at an exchange rate agreed upon with authorised banks, while other enterprises are required to sell 30 per cent of the required 50 per cent of export proceeds directly to the central bank at the central bank market rate. The 20 per cent portion which is not sold directly to the central bank was intended to allow for a more liquid hard currency market and an adequate supply of foreign currency for importers and foreign investors who wish to repatriate their profits.

These measures have been taken without adequate preparation and have driven the rouble down. The partial surrender requirement of foreign exchange encourages under-invoicing and the bypassing of official and interbank channels. The Central Bank alleges that Russian companies maintain illegal accounts outside Russia. A number of joint ventures and foreign-owned companies have agreements with their banks to swap the roubles resulting from the surrender requirements back into hard currency on the day they exchange, thereby incurring a set fee rather than face the risk of seeing their earnings dwindle.

### Hard currency trade within Russia

Only those goods produced in foreign countries and bought by trade organisations in hard currency via bank transfer may be sold for hard currency in Russia. Goods purchased in Russia or produced in Russia must be sold for roubles. Although no measures have so far been taken, the Prime Minister, Mr Chernomyrdin clearly intends to clamp down on hard currency trade within Russia in an attempt to make the rouble more attractive.

### Foreign currency accounts

Companies incorporated in Russia, including those with foreign capital, may hold accounts in foreign currency but can only keep accounts abroad with permission. They may obtain foreign currency through commercial banks or through exchanges.

Resident individuals have the right to buy foreign currency at domestic exchanges through authorised banks, or licensed exchanges. They may open foreign currency accounts, are allowed to deposit currency without justifying its origin and draw from it as they choose. In reality it is difficult for Russian citizens to withdraw more than US$500 unless they have plans to travel abroad.

### Repatriation of profits

In theory, there are no restrictions on the transfer of net profits, provided they are covered by hard currency profits. The 50 per cent of hard currency proceeds remaining after the mandatory conversion may be legally repatriated as dividends to the foreign shareholder.

However, potential investors are still wary because they do not have confidence that they will be able to bring their money out once profits have been generated. Not all banks are able to handle large volumes of hard currency.

The government's attempts to establish confidence in the rouble are hampered by the persistence of cash bank note shortages and the lack of demand for the rouble. More importantly, the government will have to address the following issues:

- the size of the budget deficit, which is standing at about 15 per cent of GNP, and the temptations of printing more money to cover it;

- price controls and adjustments in the energy, public utilities and transport sectors; the lack of systematic restrictions placed on inter-company arrears and credits to enterprises, which in January 1993 stood at R3500 billion, well above the levels at which the central bank advanced credits in the middle of 1992;

- negative real interest rates which despite increases to 80 per cent are still well below inflation (estimates of which vary greatly);

- reducing inefficiencies in the settlements system where foreign exchange transactions take weeks to complete.

Radical reformers and gradualists disagree on the budgetary and inflationary implications of measures to be taken, on whether an evolutionary approach rather than shock therapy is more appropriate and whether convertibility should be an instrument of economic reforms or the result of sound policies. The path to full current account convertibility and limited capital convertibility is likely to be long and tortuous but, until it is achieved, foreign investors will continue to face significant exchange rate risks and will shy away from investment opportunities. It is a tough challenge for a government whose sole instrument of monetary policy so far has been the money printing press.

## 9

# Banking

### *Moscow Narodny Bank*

## THE BACKGROUND

For many years the Soviet banking system comprised three main banks: the State Bank of the USSR (also known as Gosbank USSR), the Bank for Foreign Trade of the USSR (also known as Vneshtorgbank USSR) and the Construction Bank (Stroibank USSR). In addition, the State Savings Bank (Sberbank USSR) operated under the supervision of the State Bank of the USSR, and, at times, as an integral part of it.

The State Bank operated as a central bank and commercial bank for the country's enterprises; the Foreign Trade Bank handled all external banking operations; and the Construction Bank was solely responsible for capital investment under the Five-Year Plans.

In July 1987, new banking regulations were passed and, commencing from January 1988, a system was introduced comprising six main banks:

1.  The State Bank of the USSR – its functions became limited to those of a central bank.

2.  The Bank for Foreign Economic Affairs of the USSR (Vnesheconombank USSR) – the former Bank for Foreign Trade, but renamed to reflect that its role had become rather broader than that of merely trade activity.

3.  Promstroibank USSR – developed from Sroibank but again with a broader role and involved in providing finance and credit to industry, construction, transport and communications.

4.  Agroprombank USSR – a new bank to provide finance, credit and settlement services to all agricultural sectors of industry.

5. Zhilsotsbank USSR – another new bank, providing finance for housing construction, social service facilities and the development of sports, municipal and consumer facilities.

6. Sberbank USSR – successor to the previous savings bank system which included 80,000 individual savings banks.

With the break-up of the Soviet Union in August 1991, each republic of the former USSR adopted its own banking system. In Russia, a two-tier system currently operates (see below). The former chairman of the State Bank of the USSR, Viktor Gerashchenko, is now the chairman of the Central Bank of the Russian Federation, as well as being a member of the government of the Russian Federation. To date, about 2000 commercial banks have been registered with the central bank.

## THE LEGAL FRAMEWORK

In December 1990 Russia passed laws intended to restructure its banking system. The Laws on the Central Bank of Russia and on Banks and Banking in Russia, since complemented by further enactments, were designed to introduce a two-tier system on Western lines, capable of facilitating the transfer to a market economy.

### The central bank

The Central Bank of the Russian Federation is now an autonomous institution broadly independent of the organs of state power. According to the bank's Chairman, Viktor Gerashchenko, the bank is accountable to parliament and under its immediate supervision, but operates within the framework of the economic policy which has been approved by parliament and which is being pursued by the present government.

The central bank performs broadly the same functions as its Western counterparts. Most importantly it is responsible for: regulating the money supply; maintaining the stability of the rouble; setting up a clearing scheme; and supervising the activities of commercial banks.

The law also provides the central bank with the principal levers of monetary control. It is the sole body with authority to issue bank notes and fixes base lending rates in line with government policy.

Since July 1992 it has twice a week established the official exchange rate for the rouble against convertible currencies.

### Commercial banks

Commercial banks operate on the basis of licences issued by the central bank. The licence will specify the types of activity which a commercial bank may pursue, usually covering the whole range of ordinary banking services, although insurance and commodity broking are expressly prohibited. The services provided by commercial banks include:

- maintaining accounts for clients and other banks (including foreign ones);

- issuing loans on mutually agreed terms;

- carrying out transfers and settlements with clients and correspondent banks;

- buying and selling foreign currency from and for account holders; and

- offering brokerage and advisory services.

The share of founders or stockholders in the initial capital must not exceed 35 per cent. The founders may be Russian or foreign individuals or firms and must, between them, maintain a 25 per cent interest in the bank's capital for the first two years.

Commercial banks are obliged to keep reserves with the central bank and, as noted earlier, are subject to its 'supervision'. Basically, this means that the central bank can order a commercial bank to make its records available for inspection and can require it to take certain steps should it reveal anything untoward. In early-1992, the central bank was reorganised and a special sub-division for supervising the activities of commercial banks was set up. In theory at least, individual members of staff of this department in the central bank's regional sub-divisions will be personally responsible for overseeing the operations of particular commercial banks.

## DIFFERENT TYPES OF NEW BANKS

Numerous categories of commercial banks are operating in Russia at the present time.

The first category is that of the *nationwide specialised banks* which have a network in the provinces and have developed predominantly from the specialised banks. The main banks in this category are Sberbank (Savings Bank) and Rosselkhozbank (Russian Agricultural Bank).

The second category of Russian commercial banks is that of the *specialised provincial banks*. These banks have contacts with the major enterprises and often have to lend to indebted enterprises. Their main activity is centred on regional specialisation and the finance of heavy industry.

The third category comprises the *sectoral banks*. These banks' shareholders are usually ministries and/or major enterprises. In most cases these banks have Moscow offices – eg, Tokobank and Avtobank.

The fourth category is that of the *independent banks*, such as Menatep, Credobank and Incombank. These banks invariably have mixed or private capital. Some are located in the 'new' regions – eg, Bashkortostan, Western Siberia and the Far East. The newer banks in this category (for example, Delovaya Rossiya and Vserossiisky Birzhevoi Bank) serve the new private clients. These banks place much emphasis on the quality of services provided and usually have no subsidiaries.

The fifth category is *banks with foreign affiliation*. Prior to the 1987–88 banking reform, a number of banks operated in the West with Soviet shareholders. These shareholders were primarily Soviet banks and foreign trade organisations, and the banks concerned were: Moscow Narodny Bank (with its head office in London and branches in Lebanon and Singapore); East-West United Bank (Luxembourg); Ost-West Handelsbank (Frankfurt/Main); Banque Commerciale pour l'Europe du Nord, Eurobank, SA (Paris); Donau Bank (Vienna); and Wozchod Commercial Bank (Zurich), which was later transformed into a branch of the Bank for Foreign Economic Affairs of the USSR.

These banks were known as the *Sovzagranbanki* (Soviet banks abroad) prior to the banking reform, but subsequently their shareholding has changed. For example, since Moscow Narodny Bank's activity is concentrated mainly in the Russian Republic it seems logical that its shareholders should be predominantly Russian, hence over 50 per cent of its shares now belong to the Russian central bank. Similarly, the controlling shares of Eurobank (Paris) are also held by the central bank. In the case of Ost-West Handelsbank (Frankfurt), the controlling package of shares has been acquired by Tokobank, to the extent of 80.6 per cent.

A rather more unusual bank to be established is the Russian Bank for Project Financing. Plans for this bank have been in preparation for some time. Indeed, the British Know-How Fund subsidised the feasibility study and preparation of statutory documents. The bank's main function is to finance medium and long-term investment projects. Its founders include the European Bank for Reconstruction and Development, Rosselkhozbank, Tokobank, Vozrozhdenie Bank, Delovaya Rossiya and Rodina Commercial Bank. The new bank has an authorised capital of R2.5 billion, 88 per cent of which is in convertible currency.

## CORRESPONDENT BANKING REGULATIONS

Since the new commercial banks in Russia have been operating for a relatively short period of time, it is difficult to evaluate their performance. Many such banks have only recently produced their first annual balance sheets, which cannot, of course, be compared with previous performance. However, many of the new banks represent specific branches of industry or have been set up by people with extensive experience of banking abroad. Such banks have already demonstrated their desire to establish correspondent relations with banks in the West.

The kind of information which should be sought when assessing the new Russian banks should include the following:

1.  a copy of the charter of incorporation;

2.  some indication of the banking background and experience of the bank's chairman and board members;

3.  a list of the founders/shareholders and an indication as to whether the bank is effectively controlled by a region, enterprise, co-operative, etc;

4.  details of the bank's present relations with Western correspondent banks;

5.  information concerning the granting of foreign exchange, deposit or credit lines by Western banks;

6.  information published about the bank in the local press.

Credobank, for example, mentioned earlier, has about 30,0000 clients, both legal entities and individuals. It also has 18 affiliates throughout Russia and has opened an office in Odessa, Ukraine.

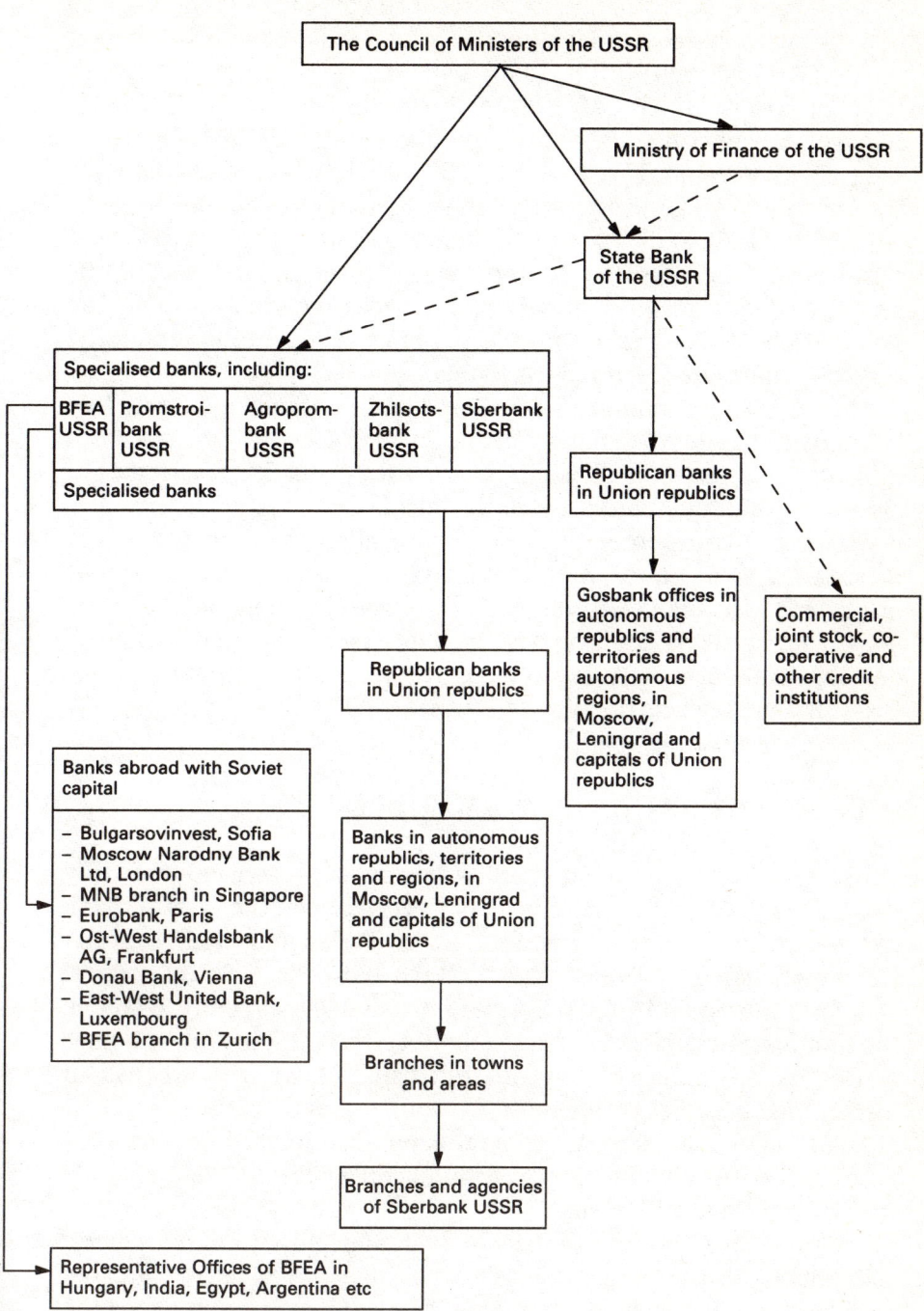

**Fig. 9.1** *The Soviet banking system, mid-1989*

Credobank has a general licence from the Russian central bank to operate with hard currency and has established correspondent relations with such foreign banks as Bank of America, Crédit Lyonnais (New York), Crédit Commercial de France, Creditanstalt-Bankverein (Vienna), Ost-West Handelsbank AG, (GFR), Deutsche Bank AG, Vereins und Westbank (GFR), Barclays Bank PLC, National Westminster Bank and Banca Commercial Italiana.

In 1991 Credobank became a member of the VISA system and since 1992 has belonged to the SWIFT international accounting system. Credobank is a member of Russia's clearing system, the Association of Russian Commercial Banks, and a founder of the Moscow Interbank Currency Exchange.

As regards the number of correspondent relationships formed by Western banks with commercial banks in Russia, these are more difficult to determine since they are rarely publicised. However, Moscow Narodny Bank, with its head office in London, has established correspondent relations with almost 100 of the newly established banks in the Russian Federation, and although this does not necessarily reflect the number of concrete business deals already concluded, it does indicate the willingness of the new banks to develop contacts with Western partners and the potential for UK–Russian business deals in the future.

## PROPOSED BANKING LAW AMENDMENTS

Banking in Russia, as mentioned earlier, is at present governed by two main legislative documents, namely the Law on the Central Bank of the Russian Federation and the Law on Banks and Banking in the Russian Federation. Numerous Western banks are already repre-sented in Russia and Crédit Lyonnais and Bank Austria were among the first foreign banks to express an interest in establishing branches in Russia, in order to carry out full banking services, instead of merely maintaining representative offices and subsidiaries. At present, banks in the West may maintain convertible currency accounts for Russian entities provided licences are duly supplied by the Central Bank of Russia.

Recently, Russia's Supreme Council aborted discussion of an amendment to the banking legislation which would have regulated foreign banks' activities but would also have supported the establishment of foreign banks' branches and affiliates in Russia. The main reason for the postponement of the discussion of the amendments was the fear that foreign banks would provide unfair competition, prior to currency stabilisation. Indeed, there has even been a move to curtail the banking activities of foreign entities in Russia. For example, International Moscow Bank is to become predominantly Russian-controlled instead of having its previous 60 per cent foreign ownership. None the less, once rouble stability and a more favourable economic climate are achieved, the number of foreign banks seeking entry into the Russian market is likely to increase.

**Table 9.1** *Russian commercial banks with a general licence*

| Name of bank | Registered no. | Chairman |
|---|---|---|
| 1. Bank St Petersburg<br>191038 St. Petersburg<br>Nab. reki Fontanki 70–72 | 436 | Yu. I. Lvov |
| 2. AvtoVAZbank<br>445038, Samarskaya obl.<br>Togliatti, ul. Voroshilova 33 | 23 | P. A. Nakhmanovich<br>(President) |
| 3. Avtobank<br>101514 Moscow<br>ul. Lesnaya 41 | 30 | N. A. Raevskaya |
| 4. Agro-Karic Bank<br>Moscow<br>Ultyanovskaya ul. 44/22 | 2057 | P. Galich |
| 5. Albank<br>125319 Moscow,<br>B. Koltevski per.3 | 340 | A. I. Kolesnikov |
| 6. Bashprombank<br>450025 Ufa<br>ul. Sverdlova 96 | 1006 | I. B. Timerkhanov |
| 7. Rosvneshtorgbank<br>103780 Moscow<br>ul. Kuznetski most 16 | 1000 | V. M. Telegin |
| 8. Vozrozhdeniye<br>103699 Moscow<br>Khrustalny per. 1 | 1439 | D. L. Orlov |
| 9. Voronezh<br>394636 Voronezh<br>ul. Ordzhonikidze 25 | 654 | G. I. Luntovski |
| 10. Vostok-Zapad<br>103879 Moscow<br>ul. Bolshaya Sadovaya 8 | 1930 | A. E. Voitenkov |

**Table 9.1** *Continued*

| Name of bank | Registered no. | Chairman |
|---|---|---|
| 11. Vostokinvestbank<br>690009 Vladivostok<br>ul. 25 October 45-a | 86 | V. E. Krupin |
| 12. Vostochno-Evropeiski<br>Investment Bank<br>113186 Moscow<br>Nagornaya ul. 22, k. 5<br>(B. Matrosski per. 1, korp. 1) | 1590 | P. E. Volgapkin |
| 13. Vserossiiskii birzhevoi bank<br>107076 Moscow<br>B. Matrosski per.<br>d.1, korp. 1 | 1538 | V. V. Soldatov |
| 14. Guta-bank<br>103006 Moscow<br>ul. Kalyaevskaya, d. 5 | 1623 | V. I. Morsin |
| 15. Dalrybbank<br>690600 Vladivostok<br>ul. Leninskaya 51-a | 118 | G. P. Belyaeva |
| 16. Dialog-bank<br>103012 Moscow<br>per. Staropanski 4 | 207 | P. V. Derby |
| 17. Eurasia<br>426057 Udmurtskaya ASSR<br>Izhevsk<br>ul. Krasnoarmeiskaya 182-a | 573 | B. S. Evdokimov |
| 18. Yenisei<br>660049 Krasnoyarsk<br>ul. Kirova 23 | 474 | V. Ya. Zabortsev |
| 19. Zapsibcombank<br>625000 Tyumen<br>ul. 8th March 2/57 | 918 | L. B. Greenfeld |
| 20. Incombank<br>117420 Moscow<br>ul. Nametkina 14, korp. 1 | 22 | V. V. Vinogradov |
| 21. Ironbank<br>113054 Moscow<br>3rd Monetchikovski per.<br>d. 4/6, stroenie 1 | 1724 | B. B. Khabitsov |
| 22. Konversbank<br>109017 Moscow<br>ul. B. Ordynka, 24/26 | 122 | N. G. Pisemski |

**Table 9.1** *Continued*

| Name of bank | Registered no. | Chairman |
|---|---|---|
| 23. Credit-Consensus<br>107005 Moscow<br>2nd Baumanskaya, 9/23<br>korp. 18 (pom.TsNIIchermet) | 1453 | A. G. Krysin |
| 24. Credobank<br>113035 Moscow<br>ul. Osipenko 15, korp. 2 | 76 | Yu. V. Agapov |
| 25. Kuzbassotsbank<br>650099 Kemerovo<br>ul. Kirova 12 | 559 | N. D. Morozenko |
| 26. Lenpromstroibank<br>191011 St. Petersburg<br>Nevski prospekt 38 | 439 | V. G. Semenov |
| 27. Lionski Credit (Russia)<br>191011 St. Petersburg<br>Nevski prospekt 12 | 1680 | J. Meriyon |
| 28. Lipetskcredit<br>398600 Lipetski<br>Pl. Plekhanova 4 | 1283 | I. A. Dmitriev |
| 29. International Joint-Stock Bank<br>103862 Moscow<br>ul. Stanislavskogo 5 | 1987 | O. A. Ilyn |
| 30. Morbank<br>103759 Moscow<br>Leningradski pr. 66, k.2 | 77 | V. A. Kapinos |
| 31. Mordovpromstroibank<br>433000 Mordovskaya ASSR<br>Saransk<br>ul. Kommunisticheskaya 50 | 752 | I. A. Gribanov |
| 32. Mosbusinessbank<br>103780 Moscow GSP<br>ul. Kuznetski most 15 | 999 | V. I. Bukato |
| 33. International Moscow Bank<br>(IMB)<br>103009 Moscow<br>ul. Pushkinskaya 5/6 | 1 | V. B. Sudakov |
| 34. Mosstroibank<br>103006 Moscow<br>ul. Chekhova 21/18 | 89 | M. I. Zhuravlev |
| 35. Most-Bank<br>117839 Moscow<br>ul. Obrucheva 34/63 | 1582 | V. A. Nesterov |

**Table 9.1** *Continued*

| Name of bank | Registered no. | Chairman |
|---|---|---|
| 36. Neftekhimbank<br>103005 Moscow<br>ul. Obraztsova 14/2 | 38 | G. V. Zhuk |
| 37. Nizhegorodets<br>603109 Nizhny Novgorod<br>ul. Dobrolyubova 7 | 239 | G. V. Andrianov |
| 38. Nizhegorodski Bankirski Dom<br>603001 Nizhny Novgorod<br>Teatralnaya pl. 2 | 1966 | B. A. Brevnov |
| 39. Novyi Symvol<br>123007 Moscow<br>2nd Silikatny pr-d, d. 8 | 370 | S. A. Chernomorov |
| 40. Orbita<br>117909 GSP-1, Moscow 49<br>2nd Spasonalivkovski per. 7/6 | 203 | F. M. Klimov |
| 41. Pervy russki nezavisimy<br>103031 Moscow<br>ul. Pushkinskaya, d.26 | 1864 | A. V. Ostroukhov |
| 42. Permcombank<br>614000 Perm<br>ul. Sovietskaya 6 | 91 | A. V. Fedyanin |
| 43. Promstroibank<br>103867 Moscow<br>Tverskoy bulvar 13 | 1449 | Ya. N. Dubenetski |
| 44. Rosselkhozbank<br>103016 Moscow<br>ul. Neglinnaya 12 | 1575 | N. P. Likhachev |
| 45. Ruskobank<br>191065 St Petersburg<br>ul. Gertsena 15 | 138 | M. A. Babich |
| 46. Sberbank RF<br>103473 Moscow<br>ul. Seleznevskaya 40 | 1481 | P. L. Zhikharev |
| 47. Sibneftebank<br>625000 Tyumen<br>ul. 8th March, 1/57 | 385 | L. F. Kin |
| 48. Stolichny<br>113095 Moscow<br>ul. Pyatnitskaya 72 | 61 | A. P. Smolenski |
| 49. Stroyinvest<br>121087 Moscow<br>ul. Zarechnaya 15/7, korp. 2 | 69 | V. V. Gruzdov |

**Table 9.1** *Continued*

| Name of bank | Registered no. | Chairman |
|---|---|---|
| 50. Tatpromstroibank<br>420106 Kazan<br>ul. Pravobulochnaya | 1723 | R. G. Mingazov |
| 51. Tatsotsbank<br>420007 Kazan<br>ul. Chernyshevskogo 18/23 | 480 | L. R. Kitaitseva |
| 52. Tveruniversalbank<br>170641 Tver<br>ul. Sovietskaya 13 | 777 | A. M. Kozyrev |
| 53. Tokobank<br>107801 Moscow<br>Orlikov per. 5 | 195 | V. K. Yakunin |
| 54. Finist-Bank<br>121165 Moscow<br>Kutuzovski pr. d. 26, str. 3 | 42 | A. V. Shcherbakov |
| 55. ELBIM-Bank<br>125047 Moscow<br>ul. 2nd Tverskaya-Yamskaya, 15 | 250 | S. L. Morozov |
| 56. Elektrobank<br>103074 Moscow<br>K-74, Kitaiski pr. 7 | 1070 | V. V. Muzhitskikh |
| 57. Yugorski<br>626440 Tyumenskaya<br>Khanti-Mansiiskaya AO<br>Nizhnevartovsk<br>ul. Lenina 25-a | 1548 | S. V. Gumelo |

Source: *Ekonomicheskaya Gazeta*, Nos. 46 47 and 49, Nov/Dec 1992.

Translation: Moscow Narodny Bank Ltd.

# 10

# Privatisation

*Frere Cholmeley Bischoff*

The privatisation of state-owned enterprises can be regarded as the main plank in the process of transforming Russia's economy, as it is the contrasting notions of the status of property which distinguish most fundamentally the command and the market systems. With commercial activity liberalised as a result of the broad deregulatory programme introduced at the beginning of 1992, the central control of production in all sectors is now viewed as the principal barrier to competition, efficiency and growth.

An ambitious agenda for privatisation was introduced in Russia during 1992, with stated aims of stabilising the economy, increasing revenue for the federal budget and laying the foundations for further moves towards a market economy, with accelerated privatisation, in 1993 and 1994. This process can be expected to produce new and potentially far-reaching opportunities for foreign investment.

The legal foundations for the privatisation process are contained in the Law on the Privatisation of State-owned and Municipal Enterprises (the Privatisation Law), adopted in July 1991 (as amended in June 1992), and a Supreme Soviet Decree on the Division of State Property (the Property Decree), issued in December 1991. This legislation is complemented by the comprehensive and far-reaching 'Privatisation Programme for the Russian Federation' enacted in June 1992. It is reasonable to assume that the measures envisaged in these programmes will establish a pattern for future efforts.

This chapter analyses the administrative structure for the privatisation programme before examining in detail the privatisation process itself and the opportunities for foreign participation.

# ADMINISTRATION

There are two main bodies involved in the administration of privatisation in Russia: The Russian State Committee for the Administration of State Property (the 'Property Committee') – known as *Goskomimushchestvo*, and The Russian Property Fund (the 'Property Fund').

These are both state agencies set up to oversee the privatisation programme, each having branches at regional and local levels.

## The Property Committee

The Property Committee performs the organisational role in the privatisation process. It is thus responsible for handling the assignment of state property to the central, regional and municipal authorities in accordance with the Property Decree. Beyond this, its primary function is to participate at every stage in the transformation of individual enterprises as well as to formulate and implement general policies where necessary. To this end, the Property Committee is empowered to issue legally binding regulations concerning specific issues of privatisation.

The Property Committee appointed a consortium of Western consultants in mid-1992 to advise on the most efficient methods of transferring assets into private hands and attracting foreign investment. The group contains several UK firms which, it is hoped, will provide know-how developed during the UK privatisations of the 1980s.

## The Property Fund

The Property Fund is the vendor of the enterprise being privatised, being responsible for supervising the sale procedure in accordance with the privatisation law and entering into the contract for the acquisition of the enterprise by the successful party. Accordingly, for a time at least, the Property Fund (determined according to the Property Decree) can be identified as the owner of the enterprise and will temporarily hold the ownership certificate for inspection by prospective purchasers.

The nomination of the Property Fund as the enterprise's owner effectively side-steps the issue of restitution, which has hindered privatisation drives in other ex-communist states. Whereas the nationalisation of assets occurred elsewhere in Central and Eastern Europe only 45 years ago, 75 years have elapsed since the Russian revolution, and few records attesting to previous ownership rights still exist. The Law on Land Reform explicitly rules out the return of land plots to their former owners and heirs. As regards other assets, though it is possible that isolated claims may be entertained, restitution is unlikely to prove an important issue in the Russian privatisation programme.

## THE PRIVATISATION PROCESS

There are various stages to the process of privatising an individual enterprise. These will be examined in sequence.

### Initiation

Under the Privatisation Law, privatisation can be initiated by a number of parties, including the Property Committee, the work-force or management of the enterprise or a prospective purchaser, who may be a foreign firm or individual. Thus the process can be originated from the top or the bottom. Application is made to the appropriate Property Committee who must arrive at and communicate a decision within one month.

Privatisation can be refused only if there is no lawful buyer for the enterprise or if the enterprise is in a sector listed in the Privatisation Programme as not being subject to privatisation. Notable examples of such sectors under the 1992 Programme are the mineral resources and power industries. In addition, the programme lists certain enterprises which can only be privatised with the permission of the central or local authorities.

However, the 1992 Programme also established a category of enterprises which are subject to mandatory privatisation. This covers enterprises seen as crucial to the development and functioning of the market infrastructure of the economy, including wholesalers, retailers, construction firms and food outlets.

### The privatisation plan

Once a decision to proceed with privatisation is taken by the Property Committee, a 'Privatisation Commission' is set up, comprising representatives of the Property Committee, the local government, the management and work-force of the enterprise concerned. The principal task of this Commission is to formulate within three months (extendable by the Property Committee to six months) a privatisation plan, tailoring the process to the individual needs of the enterprise. Thus the plan will state in particular:

- the recommended method of privatisation;
- the time-frame during which it is to be achieved;
- any proposals for the restructuring of the enterprise; and
- a notional sale price or capital fund.

Also, in line with legislation relating to the sale of land plots during privatisation, the plan should normally include information about the land on which the enterprise stands (such as its location, borders, dimensions, utilities and so forth). These details will be provided by the relevant land resources committee and other agencies.

Once promulgated, the privatisation plan is submitted for approval first by the enterprise's work-force, then the local government. In theory this should be a formality, as representatives of both these parties were present on the Privatisation Commission. However, the law provides for a procedure of redrafting and resubmission in the event of rejection of the plan, with the ultimate ruling on the matter being made by the Property Committee itself.

*Valuation*

The notional sale price suggested in the privatisation plan is derived from an assessment of the saleable value of the enterprise. On the reasoning that something is worth only what a purchaser is prepared to pay for it, this is potentially a problematic task, given that there is, by definition, no reliable existing market in Russia for trading 'assets' such as land, buildings and expertise. Questions of valuation and accounting standards are addressed in Chapter 13 but it is worth noting here that the Russian government has stated that Western advice will be sought in appropriate cases.

## Methods of privatisation

The decision on the method to be used for the privatisation of a particular enterprise is taken by the Property Committee on the recommendation contained in the privatisation plan. There are three main methods of privatisation:

- auction;
- competitive tender; and
- sale of shares.

Each method involves different procedures and will be appropriate in different cases. They will therefore be considered in turn.

*Auction*

Auctions will probably be used to privatise shops, restaurants and other small businesses as well as the assets of liquidated enterprises. The Property Fund holds the auction, with the enterprise simply being sold to the highest bidder as long as a 'reserve price' (30 per cent less than the notional price proposed in the privatisation plan) is reached.

*Competitive tender*

The use of competitive tendering will allow the Property Committee to require fulfilment by the buyer of any necessary non-price conditions. These might include an obligation to retain some or all of the work-force or to preserve the profile of an enterprise for a specified period. Accordingly, this method of privatisation is likely to be suitable for certain manufacturing enterprises or those providing basic commodities. Under the Privatisation Programme, enterprises employing fewer than 200 people with a book value at the beginning of 1992 of less than R1 million *must* be privatised either by auction or competitive tendering, so any small businesses not privatised through an auction will be put up for competitive tender. As with the auctioning process, the minimum acceptable offer will be 30 per cent below the notional price suggested by the Privatisation Commission.

*Sale of shares*

Medium-sized and large enterprises (ie those with a work-force of more than 1000 and assets of more than R50 million at the beginning of 1992) will be privatised through the sale of shares. Two stages are involved – the formation of a joint stock company and the transfer of shares therein to private owners.

To form a joint stock company, the proper founding procedure outlined in the Law on Entrepreneurial Activities must be followed. Thus a charter and other formation documents are sent for registration by the Ministry of Finance. Upon registration, the state-owned enterprise will be liquidated and its assets turned over to the joint stock company. The Property Committee, as founder, will then assign all the shares in the newly formed company to the Property Fund pending their sale to private buyers.

The transfer of shares in the newly formed joint stock company is then likely to be effected in blocks, with a certain amount being made available on favourable terms to employees (see below) and the controlling stake – up to half the firm's capital – being sold to a single investor or consortium through a tender or auction. Finally, 10 per cent of the shares will be offered to the general public.

By October 1992, every enterprise employing more than 1000 workers or with a book value of more than R150 million, excepting those in 'valuable' sectors such as defence and raw materials, was required to have formed a Privatisation Commission and submitted plans for transforming the enterprise from its existing corporate structure into a joint stock company. The Property Committee adopted various measures to facilitate and hasten this process, including the development of a model statute for joint stock companies. The aim is that the shares in these firms will be transferred from state to private ownership during 1993, or at the latest by the end of 1994.

## Buyers

The Privatisation Law provides that enterprises or shares in them may be sold only to 'lawful buyers'. These can be individuals or firms. However, Russian firms in which the central or municipal authorities hold an interest of 25 per cent or more are excluded. A likely effect of this is to rule out most existing joint ventures from participation in privatisation.

Of particular interest are the incentives available to employees of an enterprise undergoing privatisation, and the privatisation vouchers which were issued to every Russian citizen during the latter part of 1992.

### Employees

The possible degree of employee ownership in a privatised enterprise will be an important consideration for any foreign party, whether contemplating investment in the enterprise or partnership with it in a trading or other business agreement. It is commonly perceived that firms with a high proportion of worker-held equity tend to attach more importance to wage levels and job security than to long-term business strategies. In addition, the Russian government acknowledges that the encouragement of employee ownership unfairly benefits those individuals who happen to work for successful enterprises while disadvantaging those who do not. Nevertheless, political necessity and the need to prevent continued 'spontaneous privatisations' (a device whereby the work-force obtain ownership of an enterprise from the local authority without the state's approval) have caused the administration to sanction worker ownership on a large scale. Both the Privatisation Law and the Privatisation Programme offer employees substantial inducements to become involved in the ownership of an enterprise, the exact terms depending on the privatisation method used.

Where an enterprise is privatised by auction or competitive tender, benefits are available both to individual employees who put in an offer and to the work-force collectively. Individual employees (including those made redundant since 1 January 1992) are entitled to a 30 per cent discount at auctions (the maximum discount is 20 times the minimum monthly wage) or a 20 per cent discount at competitive tenders (or 15 times the minimum monthly wage). On the other hand, a limited company can be formed by at least one-third of the total work-force specifically for the purpose of bidding collectively for the privatising enterprise. This company is entitled to a 30 per cent discount on the sale price of the enterprise and can pay this by instalments over the course of 3 years (subject to an initial 25 per cent deposit).

Workers of enterprises being privatised through the sale of shares have three options:

1.  Under the standard procedure, the enterprise's workers will receive free of charge non-voting shares representing 25 per cent of the privatised enterprise's capital value, and can buy ordinary shares worth up to 10 per cent of the capital at a 30 per cent discount, once again with the right to spread the payments over 3 years (after a 15 per cent deposit). As well as this, the management are entitled to 5 per cent voting shares on favourable terms.

2.  Alternatively, the employees can vote on whether to buy a controlling stake in the firm. If a two-thirds majority of their number are in favour, 51 per cent of the newly privatised enterprise's share capital will be allocated to them. However, in such a case no discount will be available.

3.  As a final option in larger enterprises (ie those with more than 200 employees and a capital fund of between R1 million and R50 million) representatives of the work-force and management may form a group to implement over a one-year period the restructuring of the enterprise in line with a plan agreed with the rest of the employees. The members of this group can then purchase shares representing 20 per cent of the firm's capital for

their nominal value. Furthermore, another 20 per cent of the shares will be available to all the enterprise's employees at a 30 per cent discount.

Whichever course is followed, no restriction will be imposed on the resale by individual employees of the shares they have obtained. Thus, in theory at least, the door is open for prospective investors to approach representatives of an enterprise's work-force pre-privatisation with a view to arranging an advantageous buy-up of the latter's allocation when the shares are issued.

*Vouchers*

Since 1 October 1992 privatisation vouchers with a face value of R10,000 have been issued free of charge to every Russian citizen alive at that date. Notices placed at the foot of apartment buildings inform residents where thay can pick up their vouchers on production of their identification documents. Vouchers can then be freely sold for cash – Moscow has quite an active market – or used to purchase goods, services or even, under a Presidential Decree issued towards the end of 1992, land and housing.

However, despite some characteristic scepticism, most Russians have chosen to hold on to their vouchers to use them for their main function – purchasing shares in privatising enterprises. Employees are likely to gather together vouchers from their families to use in purchasing shares in the firm they work for. Otherwise private investment funds are likely to emerge to pool vouchers and bid for controlling interests in firms. However, there will be a limit of 35 per cent of the equity of any one firm which may be sold for vouchers.

# FOREIGN PARTICIPATION

The success or failure of the privatisation strategy may depend ultimately upon the extent to which foreign participation is allowed. This is because it is doubtful whether the Russian populace have sufficient savings of their own, beyond the privatisation vouchers, to invest in newly privatised enterprises. Thus some money from outside the country will have to be attracted if new owners are to be found. At the same time, there is a degree of popular opposition to the country's assets being 'bought up' on a large scale by external interests.

With this as a background, the privatisation legislation allows foreign investors to participate generally without restriction.

However, certain categories of enterprises can only be bought into with the approval of a specified body:

- Retailers, food outlets, consumer services and small businesses (with fewer than 200 employees and a total asset value of less than R1 million at the beginning of 1992) in the industrial, construction or road transport sectors can only be purchased by foreigners with the consent of the local authority.

- Enterprises involved in energy production, extracting precious and semi-precious stones or metals or radioactive ore are only permitted to attract foreign participation on approval by the government.

Also, if a foreign investor is the only bidder at an auction or competitive tender the enterprise can only be sold to such an investor after the relevant Property Fund has carried out a full valuation of it.

It is important to stress that the regime for foreign participation is likely to develop as the privatisation process gathers pace. The guidelines now in place may prove to be only a starting point, and as more foreigners become involved, may be adjusted as is appropriate.

## 11

# Foreign Investment
## *Frere Cholmeley Bischoff*

A comprehensive and broadly well-defined Law on Foreign Investments in the Russian Federation (the Foreign Investment Law) was passed in July 1991. As well as establishing the general system for regulating the flow of foreign capital into Russia, the law includes basic provisions relating to areas covered in detail in other sections of this book.

This chapter examines the overall framework for foreign investment set up by the Foreign Investment Law, and also looks at the special conditions for doing business which prevail in so-called 'free economic zones'.

## THE FRAMEWORK FOR INVESTMENT

The Foreign Investment Law is characterised by a broad lack of constraints on economic activity by foreigners on Russian territory. Thus it is provided that:

- investors may be foreign companies, individuals, states or international organisations;

- investment may take the form of any type of material or intellectual property; and

- investments may be made through forming a joint or 100 per cent foreign-owned enterprise, obtaining property rights or giving credits.

The possibility of establishing a wholly foreign-owned company is the most significant advance made by the 1991 Law. After the USSR first opened the door to foreign investment in January 1987, the only option was to form a joint venture with Soviet enterprises. Indeed it is doubtful whether alternative arrangements would in any case have been practicable during this period, as the involvement of a Russian partner, with experience of the local bureaucracy and the know-how to find reliable suppliers of raw materials and equipment, was vital if a business was to get off the ground.

However, in the developing commercial culture of President Yeltsin's Russia, outside investors can feel more confident of finding suitable contacts themselves, and will welcome the removal of restrictions on the level of foreign participation. It is now possible for Western companies to establish a wholly-owned subsidiary or branch operation in the Russian Federation, as well as participating in existing and new local enterprises.

### Investment protection

An important feature of the Foreign Investment Law is the strong protection it affords to investments made by foreign parties. However, in this respect UK investors also benefit from an Investment Protection Agreement concluded by the UK and USSR governments, and now assumed by the Russian Federation. This treaty came into force in July 1991, and follows the example of others concluded by the UK. In outline, it provides UK firms with the following guarantees:

- Fair and equitable treatment – British investments are placed on the same footing as those of any third state and will, as far as possible, receive the same treatment as Russian investments.

- Investments will not be nationalised or otherwise expropriated except in cases provided for by law and for a purpose which is in the public interest.

- In the event of lawful expropriation, the investor is entitled to 'prompt, adequate and effective compensation' – amounting to the real value of the investment immediately before the expropriation was announced.

- If Russia fails to comply with the Agreement and an amicable settlement is not reached, British investors can seek compensation through international arbitration.

Although certain provisions corresponding to these are contained in the Foreign Investment Law, this domestic legislation may be changed unilaterally and without warning. By contrast the bilateral treaty is binding under international law and, while it is still effective, can be amended only with the concurrence of both parties.

The UK/USSR Agreement is to remain in force for 15 years, and may thereafter be terminated by either country on 12 months' written notice. However, it will continue to apply to existing investments for a further 15 years. Thus British investments can benefit from the treaty's protection until at least July 2022.

During 1992 Russia became a signatory to the convention for the Multilateral Investment Guarantee Agency (MIGA) – a member of the World Bank Group. But as yet the MIGA Convention has not been ratified by the Supreme Soviet. This organisation has been insuring investment projects in developing countries since 1988, and also offers promotional and advisory services. MIGA is currently involved in a number of projects in the Central and Eastern European region, and has advised the Russian authorities on how to create an attractive investment climate.

Once the Convention is ratified, MIGA will be able to offer long-term political risk insurance to eligible investors for qualified investments. Coverage can extend to currency transfers, expropriation, war and civil disturbance and breach of contract.

### Income and profits

The dismantling of central planning mechanisms in the Russian Federation has enabled businesses there to move towards basing their operations on ordinary supply and demand considerations. Thus the Foreign Investment Law specifically provides that foreign enterprises can freely determine the price and terms of sale and delivery of their products on a contractual basis in the Russian market. Payments received in local currency can then be deposited with banks licensed by the Russian central bank to maintain such accounts and used to finance purchases and other outgoings on Russian territory.

Special rules apply to profits in convertible currency derived from exports. Although the Foreign Investment Law states that such monies are 'fully owned' by firms with foreign capital, there is a general requirement that they be paid into accounts opened at authorised banks in Russia. Moreover at the time of writing all enterprises, including those with foreign participation, are obliged to sell 50 per cent of their hard currency receipts from exports to central funds at the market exchange rate. This latter obligation may even be increased to 100 per cent as the central bank attempts to bolster its currency reserves in order to stabilise the exchange rate of the rouble against the dollar.

After payment of taxes and any other fees due, foreign investors can freely transfer remaining profits, dividends, royalties and other receipts to other countries. This must be done in foreign currency, so any surplus roubles should be exchanged on the domestic market (foreign investors can attend currency auctions for this purpose). The guarantee of profit repatriation is fundamental to the Foreign Investment Law, and is also contained in the UK/USSR IPA mentioned above.

## FREE ECONOMIC ZONES

The Foreign Investment Law sanctions the creation on Russian territory of free economic zones (FEZs). These are regions in which special regulations are in force designed to attract foreign investment and stimulate business activity generally, thus providing an engine for the overall development of the national economy.

Ten FEZs have so far been set up, St Petersburg (formerly Leningrad) being an example of particular interest. The procedure followed involved the local authority drafting regulations to be applied in the FEZ, which then came into effect through ratification by the Russian central government. Thus national laws are still fully applicable on the FEZ's territory, but must, if necessary, be read in the light of more liberal measures in force at the local levels. A law specifically on FEZs, to be enacted in the near future, is expected to confirm this situation.

Foreign investors in FEZs can expect to enjoy the following privileges:

- simplified procedures for establishing and registering companies;

- tax benefits, such as a tax holiday or a reduction of up to 50 per cent on profit taxes.;

- enhanced property rights (including long-term leases with the right to underlet) and lower ground rents;

- low import and export duties and streamlined customs formalities; and

- straightforward border controls for foreigners.

Beyond these, the principal advantage of investing in one of these zones is the fact that administrative matters will be dealt with by identifiable branches of the local authority. As a result, the red-tape and bureaucracy still associated with the central bodies is avoided.

# 12

# Investing in Oil

*Frere Cholmeley Bischoff*

The Russian oil industry is potentially a very attractive area for Western investment. The country has estimated reserves of 2500 billion barrels – a base capable, as the government recognises, of generating a wealth of hard currency. Moreover for some years oil production has been dropping as machinery has become depleted and investment declined. Without foreign capital there is a danger that output may fall below the level of domestic demand.

However, the amount of finance required for many projects means that a strong legislative base is necessary if such investment is to be attracted. Recent laws have been aimed at introducing a Western-style investment framework and licensing system. This chapter examines these laws and highlights some of the aspects of the Russian oil industry which will affect a foreign investor.

## THE FRAMEWORK FOR INVESTMENT

The key principles governing foreign participation in the Russian oil industry are contained, as with all areas, in the 1991 Foreign Investment Law. However, in March 1992 a Russian Federation Law Concerning Subsurface Resources ('the Subsurface Resources Law') came into effect, establishing a basic structure of rights and obligations for all producers in the minerals sector.

In addition, legislation specifically relating to the oil and gas industries is to be passed shortly. This is expected to enhance the Subsurface Resources Law and deal particularly with matters such as pipeline transportation. Russia is a signatory to the recent European Energy Charter and has thus shown a commitment to liberalising opportunities for foreign investors in this field.

## Contract basis

Prior to the enactment of the Subsurface Resources Law, Russian legislation envisaged foreign investment in the oil industry as possible only on a concession basis. The new Law, however, explicitly provides that arrangements may be founded on any of the following formulae:

- concessions;
- production sharing; or
- service contracts (with or without risk).

It can be anticipated that production sharing agreements may be the most appropriate model for the Russian oil industry while the economy is undergoing transition to a market system. From the host country's point of view, production sharing agreements are likely to ensure a reliable flow of oil on to the domestic market and allow Russian companies access to Western techniques and development technology. For the foreign party, production sharing is an attractive option while the economic and political situation remains uncertain.

## Royalty payments

The Subsurface Resources Law requires producers to pay royalties to the host country for the right to extract from Russian deposits. Such levies may take the form of monetary payments but, as already observed, will more usually comprise a share of the output. The first payment is made on conclusion of the contract, with subsequent payments commencing when commercial production begins.

The amount of the royalties will depend on various factors but will probably be in line with international norms. Some guidance can be obtained from the terms of the contract concluded in early 1992 by Elf Aquitaine to explore and develop in a large area of the Volga estuary. Under this agreement Elf will be prospecting at its own risk then, on discovery of viable deposits, sharing output beyond the first seven million tonnes on a sliding scale. Russia will receive 60 per cent of the first 50 million tonnes, increasing to 85 per cent above this level.

## Central and regional government

Before the Subsurface Resources Law was passed, investors in the Russian energy sector encountered a number of problems arising from disputes between central and local authorities regarding control over the nation's resources. The new Law makes some effort to resolve such difficulties by specifying the responsibilities respectively enjoyed by federal, regional and local bodies.

However, the Law states that ultimate control over the state's oil reserves will be exercised jointly by central and local government. Thus any contract should be entered into by all such bodies. This, indeed, was the case with the Elf Aquitaine agreement.

In addition, the law provides a formula for the division of royalties between federal and regional funds. For development in most areas, the state's share of the output should be distributed as follows:

- 50 per cent to the district or city budget;

- 25 per cent to the budget of the region or autonomous republic;

- 25 per cent to the Russian Federation budget.

## THE LICENSING SYSTEM

Prospecting for and extracting of oil in Russia can only be carried out if a licence for such activities has been obtained. Licences are issued jointly by the regional and central government bodies, the latter through the Ministry of Ecology and Natural Resources of the Russian Federation.

Detailed provisions on the structure and procedure of the licensing system are contained in the Subsurface Resources Law and a draft Statute on the Procedure for Issuing Licences. The following is an outline of the main principles.

### Obtaining a licence

Licences for exploration and the development of oil fields are generally granted through competitions and auctions publicised in the mass media, though in certain cases they may be obtained through direct negotiations. Competitions are used where conditions are to be attached to the licence. The Law requires the central and local authorities to agree on the methods to be used for granting a licence in a given case.

To participate in a competition or auction a standard form written application should be submitted containing the applicant's registered name, address, citizenship and so forth, as well as details of the planned operations under the licence. A fee is levied for registration of the application, payable in hard currency by foreign entities.

Under the auction system the licence is awarded to the highest bidder. In a competition, the winner will be the applicant which proves it is in a position to fulfil all the required conditions. The legislation contains various provisions aimed at ensuring procedural fairness for the issuing of licences, and rules out discrimination on the basis of national origin. However, it is not clear on what basis a licence will be awarded should more than one candidate fulfil the conditions for 'winning' the competition. It may perhaps be supposed that in such a case, a licence will go to the party which offers more in negotiations conducted with the authorities.

## Contents of the licence

The licence is the basic document certifying the right of the holder to carry out operations on a given site. Thus it will contain full details of the activities to be pursued and the rights and obligations of the licensee when conducting such activities. In particular it will include the following:

- the date of commencement and period of validity of the licence;

- specification of the boundaries of the territory on which the activities are to take place;

- the agreed level of extraction;

- the agreed proportions for distribution of output together with the time and procedure for such payment;

- the types and amounts of taxes to be paid and the procedure for paying them;

- obligations regarding safety practices for work and the protection of the environment.

In addition, the licence will contain any special terms of the contract in question.

## Termination of the licence

Licences for exploration and development are generally issued for a fixed term of 25 years from the date of issue. However, this period may be extended on the initiative of the holder for five-year periods until the potential for commercial exploitation of the field is exhausted. On the other hand, the licence can be terminated early on renunciation by the holder.

The Subsurface Resources Law envisages several cases in which the licence may be suspended or terminated early by the relevant authorities. Principal among these are the following:

■ where the holder does not commence production within the period fixed in the licence and at the specified volumes;

■ where the holder violates the fundamental terms of the licence;

■ where the holder systematically breaches established rules for resource development;

■ should 'emergency circumstances' arise – the Law does not define these beyond giving the examples of natural disasters and military actions.

However, if the facts which cause the licence to be terminated or suspended cease to exist, the licence may be reinstated, with the length of time for which rights were suspended ignored as regards the total period of validity of the licence.

## SPECIFIC ASPECTS OF THE RUSSIAN OIL INDUSTRY

Although the Subsurface Resources Law and other legislation improves considerably the climate for foreign participation in the Russian oil industry, there remain a number of characteristics of the market of which a potential Western investor will wish to be aware. On the whole, they are part of the legacy of the current system and by-products of the transition process. Principal among them are the domestic pricing system, the foreign trade regime and the structure of state administration.

### Prices

Oil and other forms of energy were not included in the price liberalisation which took place in January 1992. Instead oil prices were administratively raised to levels designed to cover production costs, with Russian enterprises permitted to sell a proportion of their output at free prices through oil exchanges. As high inflation has led to regular increases in prices for materials and technology, it is doubtful whether the fixed price genuinely facilitates self-financing.

It is not entirely clear whether, and if so at what stage, it is intended to remove all administrative controls on oil prices. The original proposal was to adopt a programme of gradual increases to world price levels, but a Presidential decree of September 1992 instead introduced a complex system under which fixed pricing was abandoned, but a progressive levy is imposed on producers in respect of price increases above R4000 (about $9) per tonne. Also a limit of 50 per cent of production costs is set on such producers' profit levels.

## Foreign trade

With the possibility that production may not satisfy domestic consumption, conditions for the export of oil from Russia remain unpredictable. A government decree of November 1991 suspended all export licences until the beginning of 1992 to protect supplies for the winter. There is a risk that similar measures may be introduced should such a situation be repeated.

In addition, a tariff on the export of oil at 26 per cent per tonne (estimated to equal $5 a barrel) was brought in in 1992. However special legislative measures mean that an exemption from this tax for long-term foreign investors may be negotiable.

## State administration

There is some doubt as to the competences of the various government departments charged with overseeing the Russian oil industry. Responsibility is loosely divided between the Ministry of Fuel and Energy and the Ministry of Ecology and Natural Resources. However another body, Rosneft, is overseeing the re-structuring of most (though not all) Russian oil enterprises. Since Rosneft is not answerable to either Ministry, interested Western investors may find themselves having to deal with at least three agencies, particularly if a joint venture is being considered.

## 13

# Valuation and Accounting Issues

## *KPMG Peat Marwick*

The future of Russian accounting is very much on the drawing board. Regulations still do not differentiate between the preparation of accounting records for computing a company's taxable income and those based on generally accepted principles for assessing profitability. A lack of understanding of the function of accounting in a market economy may lead reformers to perceive developments in accountancy as secondary to sound macroeconomic policies, privatisation or the setting up of a banking system.

Too many detailed regulations on the mechanics of keeping financial records have made, and will continue to make, accountants and reformers pay more attention to form rather than substance and distract from potentially more critical areas such as asset valuation. However, it is becoming apparent that accountancy is an essential part of the arsenal of reform laws: from a passive function in collating and providing figures for central planners, accountancy will have to become a tool of management which will enable managers to exercise judgement about production, cost and pricing, devise business strategies and improve performance.

## THE ACCOUNTING ENVIRONMENT

Financial information as an instrument of management is taken for granted in market economies, but it was neither relevant nor required in the former Soviet Union. In a planned economy, accountancy focuses on recording the implementation of production objectives. The preparation of reports in a set form and the use of a unified chart of accounts facilitates the collation of the statistical information required by central planners.

Profitability is not the key management criterion: set production targets, subsidies and fixed prices distort any real measure of performance. Input and output are measured in quantitative terms: the output for this plant will be so many tonnes and to achieve this output it is to receive so many tonnes of raw materials, so much energy and it will use so much labour.

The main purpose of keeping accounting records is to determine the entity's tax obligation and not to give a true and fair view of its financial circumstances. Its balance sheet, therefore, is in effect its tax return and any changes in the tax laws must be integrated into the calculation of income.

Now that the command economy has crumbled away, many businesses are limping along with antiquated plants, obsolete machinery and nobody to buy their goods. Stock and work in progress are difficult to value. They owe and are owed enormous amounts of money and their operating results are unreliable. In these circumstances, it is hard to attach a price tag to companies or restructure them. They face an uncertain future and probably liquidation.

## ACCOUNTING REGULATIONS

Uniform regulations and procedures on accounting are prescribed by the Ministry of Finance. The latest version is contained in the *Instructions on the Use of the Plan of Accounts for Financial and Business Accounting of Enterprises* which became effective as of 1 January 1992. These regulations apply to all enterprises, associations and legal entities conducting economic activity in Russia. They also apply to enterprises with foreign participation, joint ventures and companies wholly foreign owned. The regulations describe how enterprises must maintain their books and compile their financial statements.

Generally, double entry bookkeeping is used, and all accounting material must be in Russian. The rouble is the basic unit of account. Transactions denominated in foreign currency must be converted into roubles for accounting purposes at a rate set by the central bank. The financial year is the calendar year and income and expenditure must be accounted for in the period to which they relate. Losses can be carried forward for five years for tax relief purposes.

In addition to these statutory requirements, companies with foreign participation may keep accounts for their own purposes according to the regulations of their country of origin. This ensures that they record financial information, costs, earnings and profitability in a manner which is familiar to them.

### Financial statements

Enterprises which carry out double entry bookkeeping (excluding banks and agencies supported out of the state budget) must use the prescribed chart of accounts. The chart details the title of each account that has to be set up. Russian law requires separate accounts for each business activity.

From the standpoint of the investor, Russian financial statements do not contain all the information that usually serves as a basis for financial decisions and estimates. There is no requirement either to give information on leaseholds and assets purchased under instalment purchase plans, or to disclose the market value of investments if different from their carrying value, or associated company and inter-company receivables and payables. Statements tend to conceal negative book value, poor earnings history and tax debts. Liabilities and commitments such as environmental pollution go unrecorded. The readability of the balance sheet is hampered by its length.

## VALUATION

The value investors give to investments and businesses is based on comparison with similar transactions or other investment opportunities. Also the means of valuing must be identical. Western approaches to valuing assets are stretched in post-communist economies: in the past no one tried to put a value on stock, work in progress or machinery.

A major problem is that Russian managers will tend to put forward inflated values for the assets being sold, or which are to form part of their contribution to a joint venture. They will stress value in terms of jobs, output, hard currency earnings and revenue from taxation (because the state is the shareholder). Foreign investors interested in a joint venture or buying into a company will look at future earnings in relation to the risks attached to the investments and the contributions that they will have to make in order to achieve these earnings.

The principal adjustments to financial statements will usually arise in connection with:

- the rates of depreciation and valuation of fixed assets;

- the elimination of overhead costs form stock and work in progress (particularly in the manufacturing sector);

- the provisions against slow moving and obsolete stock and valuation of stocks;

- the provisions against bad and doubtful debts and the evaluation of debtors; and

- the classification of various funds which represent the net assets of the business.

### Fixed assets

As a general rule, assets are valued at historical cost and this value is maintained in the books. Historical cost does not require judgement on the part of accountants. Fixed assets are depreciated in accordance with their useful lives and there is no subjective estimate of what this may be. Rules exist for calculating depreciation and the rates of depreciation are usually low. Many enterprises invest substantially in repair and maintenance expenditure each year to ensure that older plant and machinery continues to be operational. To take inflation into account assets were mandatorily revalued in July 1992 but with arbitrary coefficients.

A joint venture may decide on its own depreciation policy in the manner agreed and set out in its foundation documents.

There is a question mark over the valuation of land. As long as it belonged to the state or municipality (therefore to nobody in particular), it had no intrinsic value.

### Stocks

Stocks are valued at purchase price but it is necessary to enquire in detail as to how stocks are valued and what overheads are capitalised in stock since general overheads are often included in inventory valuation. There will often be considerable amounts of working capital tied up in stocks. Stock levels tend to be high because goods were produced with scant regard for demand, while obsolete stock is retained in the balance sheet at unrealistic values. Provisions are rarely made against obsolete stock and, if they were, they would materially affect the business's trading results.

### Debtors

Under current practices, bad debts are not booked until they are finally confirmed. As a result very low (or no) provisions have been made. Traditionally, whether the debt was recoverable was not particularly relevant to Russian managers. The state, as the shareholder in most enterprises, would have eventually issued credits to cover the debts, but the state is no longer in a position to do so. Enterprises are generally illiquid and debts take a long time to be paid. The introduction of bankruptcy laws means that debt-laden enterprises will go out of business. Managers will have to pay more attention to the credit standing of their clients and improve their credit control procedures.

### Reserves

The net assets of a company are reflected in several funds, which are the equivalent of its share capital and reserves. Various employee and other funds are accounted for below the line or through special reserves. The profit after tax is divided up – partly to be retained in the enterprise and partly to be used for the benefit of employees.

### Forecasts

A valuation is only as sound as the underlying information on which it is based. Past earnings should not be used as a guide to the future potential of the business. The levels of inflation experienced over the past year make year-on-year comparisons futile and there is no requirement for using price indices to give a clear picture of a company's affairs in a hyperinflationary economy. Reliable future earnings forecasts are difficult to produce as assumptions will have to made about inflation and the exchange rate. In the absence of a market, assessing opportunities will prove difficult, even after having restated the accounts into a comprehensible format.

## AUDIT REQUIREMENTS

The statutory audit of enterprises is centred on checking that all transactions have been recorded correctly in the books and that the records conform with laws and regulations. The verification of the financial statements of enterprises for tax purposes is conducted by organisations accredited by the Ministry of Finance. All enterprises (with the exception of enterprises with foreign participation) must file quarterly and annual accounts with the tax and statistical authorities; enterprises with foreign participation must file their annual accounts by 15 March with the same bodies (and 15 March for representative offices and branches).

A draft law on audit is being devised under the sponsorship of a UN working party. It is expected that it will come close to international practice.

# 14

# Property
## *Frere Cholmeley Bischoff*

Russian property law is currently in a state of great upheaval. The legislation necessary to enable the transfer of Russia's land from the ownership of the state to the ownership of private individuals is inevitably extensive and, though major steps have already been taken, complete and effective mechanisms for conveying real estate are not yet established. This chapter examines the developing framework for obtaining rights in Russian land and outlines the conditions for using property as security.

## OWNERSHIP OF LAND

The principle of private ownership of Russian land was first established by a Property Act passed in December 1990. This law established the basic rights of a property owner, including the right to use property for entrepreneurial purposes, the right to dispose of property and the right to full compensation in the event of expropriation.

### General provisions

The basic laws on land ownership allow state-owned land to be transferred by a local Soviet of People's Deputies (with or without payment) to Russian individuals, but not normally foreigners or companies. Thereafter land can only be sold in four cases:

- retirement;
- on receiving land by inheritance;
- on moving elsewhere to set up a farm;

- if the sale proceeds are invested in a service, retail, building or other enterprise.

It can be seen that, although these provisions prevent speculative dealing in property, their effect is also to limit severely the possibilities for Russians to become landowners.

While the emergence of an active property market will be impossible until a new Constitution is introduced, certain initiatives have been launched to simulate the initial purchase by private parties of state land. Of particular importance are the provisions relating to land transfers tied in with the privatisation programme. This process, and a pilot scheme for land auctions operating in Moscow are described below.

### Land purchases during privatisation

In the summer of 1992 comprehensive regulations were laid down concerning the sale of plots of land during the privatisation of state-owned enterprises. The main points of this legislation are:

- Land is sold by any organisation authorised by the appropriate Soviet of People's Deputies.

- An enterprise's privatisation plan should include details of the site it is situated on, including its location, borders, dimensions and the utilities serving it.

- The buyer of an enterprise being privatised through an auction or competition can purchase the land on which the enterprise stands.

- Joint stock companies formed by enterprises undergoing privatisation through the sale of shares are obliged to buy the enterprise's plot once all the shares owned by the state or the local authority have been sold.

- An application to purchase the enterprise's land is immediately registered, and within one month the seller and the buyer should conclude a purchase contract. Within one further month the local authority will issue the buyer with the title to the plot of land concerned.

- Land for general use in populated areas (including roads, squares, parks, etc), as well as agricultural land and areas which are rich in natural resources, are not available for private purchase.

In addition to these provisions, the regulations allow the new private owners of an enterprise to purchase other sites for expansion or additional construction projects. Appropriate sites (ie those not subject to any other property rights) will be advertised by the local authority, and can be bought through an auction or competitive bidding. In line with the general principles of privatisation, a competitive tender will be held if specific conditions are to be attached to the use of the land, otherwise the property will be auctioned.

Since the Russian privatisation legislation (examined in detail in Chapter 10) allows foreign companies and individuals – in certain circumstances – to purchase enterprises or shares therein, the regulations on the sale of land plots open the door to foreign ownership of Russian real estate. Although the possibilities for subsequent resale are very limited, this represents a break with the general regime, but is as yet confined to the peculiar circumstances of privatisation.

### Pilot land auctions in Moscow

Under a Presidential decree issued in October 1992, Russians residing in the Moscow region are to be given the chance to purchase land plots for constructing individual houses. Available plots (which will only be in Moscow's Ramensky district) are to be auctioned during 1993 with the express aim of gauging market interest generally. The Moscow housing market has already proved very active, with over 100,000 flats in the capital purchased by their occupants since restrictions on the private ownership of buildings were first lifted.

## OTHER RIGHTS IN LAND

As well as ownership, Russian law recognises two other types of right in land: a right of use (permanent or temporary) and a lease.

### Use

Instead of transferring land into the ownership of private parties, a local Soviet can grant a permanent or temporary right of use. In practice, this right is commonly granted to companies, including those wholly or partly foreign owned. Russian individuals would normally instead obtain a 'right to possession' of the land, which lasts for the lifetime of the holder and is inheritable. Foreign individuals cannot be granted a right of use.

The terms of use of the land granted depends largely on the agreement concluded with the local Soviet. In particular, consent will be needed before any building or installation can be erected. However the right itself entitles the holder to compensation for the value of any 'improvements' made at their own expense.

There is some scope under the law for private landowners, users or lessees to grant a right of use to a third party. In general this is only possible for a three-year term.

### *Lease*

Any firm or individual, whether Russian or foreign owned, can lease a plot of land from the local Soviet. This can be for a maximum 50-year term, though the lessee has a preferential right to renew the lease on its expiry. In addition, the legislation on land purchases during privatisation allows the new private owner of an enterprise to lease the land on which it stands with a right subsequently to acquire it outright.

The conditions of a lease depend entirely on the contract concluded between the parties. The law imposes a general duty on the lessee to maintain property in good repair, and assigns ownership of improvements to the lessee with a right to compensation on termination of the contract. However the parties can contract out of the conditions if they so wish.

As with the right of use, the law offers some possibility to private individuals to act as a lessor. However this is currently very limited, and is unlikely to occur in practice.

## FORMALITIES

Since the transfer of land plots became possible in Russia only very recently, few of the formalities associated with the buying and selling of property in Western countries are as yet established. However, rudimentary land taxation and registration systems have been introduced, and are outlined below.

### *Land tax*

Since the beginning of 1992 a 'standard land price' has been payable on any transfer and a flat-rate land tax levied annually on most owners, holders and users of Russian land (rents are payable under a lease). The key features of this system are:

- Tax assessments are drawn up first within a month of land being transferred and thereafter annually.

- The amount of tax payable depends on the size and location of the land concerned.

- Enterprises estimate their own tax bill, with responsibility for its correctness and prompt payment lying with the directors.

- The amount due should be paid in two equal instalments, by 15 September and 15 November. Interest at a rate of 0.2 per cent daily is payable on late instalments.

### Registration

In common with most Western systems, Russian law recognises that a register should be maintained of land transactions so as to certify and protect the interest of the landholder. Since the initial sale or other allocation of state-owned land is effected by the local Soviet, this body also maintains the register. At present, the entry records the official document issued by the local Soviet on a grant of ownership, inheritable lifetime possession or right to permanent use of land, or the agreement in approved form concluded on the grant of a lease or right of temporary use. A more sophisticated land registration system will be necessary as land dealings become more commonplace, and more specific provisions relating to this area may be included in the expected new Land Code.

## PROPERTY AS SECURITY

One of the major legislative advances made in 1992 was the enactment of a Law on Pledge. Previously the possibilities for securing credit under Russian law were very restricted and, consequently, opportunities for enterprises to raise finance for investment very limited. The new Law was developed with expert Western assistance and is based on concepts which will be recognisable to those familiar with English law in this area.

### Basic principles

#### Contractual supremacy
In line with basic market principles, the Law on Pledge allows a debtor and creditor to determine their own conditions in the

agreement they conclude. Usually, the law steps in only if the contract is silent on a given point. One fundamental precept which the parties cannot alter is the right of the debtor to fulfil his obligations and cancel the security at any time.

### Property which may be used as security

Generally, the law allows any property which a party can lawfully dispose of to be used for securing a loan. This includes land, buildings, businesses (including their fixed and working capital and, like a floating charge, assets being circulated and processed), rights and other interests. Rights under a lease can be pledged without the lessor's consent unless the lease itself provides otherwise.

The object used as security can usually either be retained by the debtor or transferred to the creditor's custody. In either case the party with possession of the property is obliged to insure it to its full value (at the debtor's expense) and to take all necessary measures for preserving it. If the property remains in the hands of the debtor, it can be transferred for temporary possession or use to a third party, although in the event of a lease the creditor must be notified.

### Multiple security

Property already used to secure one obligation can generally be used to secure others unless the preceding agreement stipulates to the contrary. However, creditors have priority according to the date of their agreement, so a subsequent creditor will usually wish to ensure that the secured property has sufficient value to satisfy his claim in addition to earlier ones. Accordingly, the Law provides that the debtor must notify the creditor of the nature and amount of any existing obligations guaranteed by the same property.

### Realisation

If the debtor has not fulfilled his obligations by the deadline stipulated in the security agreement, the creditor can ordinarily seek an attachment order in court. The secured property can then be sold and, if the proceeds do not cover the debt, the creditor can recover the shortfall by attaching other (unsecured) property of the debtor – though in this respect the creditor has no priority over other unsecured creditors. If the sale proceeds exceed the amount owed, the difference is returned to the debtor.

## Procedural requirements

### Contract

The Law on Pledge requires that security agreements are in writing and contain the following conditions:

- a full specification of the kind of security involved;

- the essence and amount of the secured obligation;

- the deadline for fulfilment of the obligation; and

- the composition and value of the secured property.

Other formalities may be necessary, depending on the nature of the property used as security. Thus an agreement secured by circulating assets should determine their form and overall value as well as specifying their location and potential substitutes. Also if rights are used to provide security the contract must identify the party who is himself under the obligation to the debtor.

As a general rule, security agreements need only be notarised if the underlying obligation is itself subject to such certification (by law or agreement between the parties). If so, the same notary should be used. However, any mortgage agreement (ie a security of land) is required by the Law to be duly notarised.

## Registration

An agreement using as security property subject to state registration must also be registered by the same body. The agreement is then considered effective only from the moment of such registration and is otherwise invalid. The registering body will issue a certificate to both the debtor and the creditor, and is obliged to supply any interested party with excerpts from the register on request. A state duty is payable in advance for all these operations connected with registration.

## Record book

Whether or not the agreement is subject to state registration, companies and registered entrepreneurs are obliged to keep a record of their secured obligations. Within 10 days of a security's creation details of the kind and object of security involved and the amount of the obligation guaranteed should be entered in this record, and any interested person must be allowed to inspect it. The debtor is liable in full for any loss caused by entries being made late or inaccurately.

## Release

When a security agreement subject to registration is fully or partially fulfilled, the debtor can demand that the creditor issue him with a document confirming this position. These should then be forwarded to the registering body, which must immediately make the appropriate entry in the register.

## 15

# The Fiscal Framework

## *KPMG Peat Marwick*

Clarity of tax legislation is essential in providing a stable environment for foreign investment. A number of laws were adopted in the last quarter of 1991 which provide an outline but not clear guidance on tax issues. Laws and regulations remain largely untested. Often they result from compromises between those who want higher rates of tax and a wider taxable base and those who insist that lower rates are necessary to enable local entrepreneurs and foreigners to invest. Consequently, the only constant investors can expect is constant change.

There are three broad levels of tax: federal, republic and local taxes. Federal taxes are applied uniformly throughout the territory of the Russian Federation and include:

■ the enterprise profits tax;

■ individual income tax;

■ taxes on the income of banks and insurance companies; and

■ VAT and excise duty.

The republic taxes include:

■ the tax on the use of resources;

■ the business property tax;

■ forestry income tax; and

■ payments for water usage by industry.

Local taxes include:

■ the land tax; and

■ the individual property tax.

The State Tax Inspectorate was created in December 1991 to take over tax administration from the Ministry of Finance. It is a centralised agency responsible for collecting all governmental revenue except customs duties. It is in the process of restructuring and modernisation. One of its departments – the Main Administration of Tax Investigation – is in charge of uncovering tax evasion and violations of tax legislation. All taxpayers, whether they are enterprises or individuals, must register with the tax authorities.

## TAXES ON RESIDENT COMPANIES

Two laws, one on the income of enterprises, the other on their profits, were debated at the same time. The first was proposed by parliament and adopted on 20 December 1991 whereas the second was initiated by the government and adopted on 27 December 1991. However the implementation of the Income Tax Law was suspended until some unspecified time. It seems unlikely that it will ever come into effect.

### Tax on the profits of enterprises

Although the Profits Tax Law was originally conceived as a temporary measure, there have been more instructions implementing it than the Income Tax Law which was supposed to replace it. The Law is applicable to all legal entities engaging in business activities, including companies with foreign participation. Profits are taxed at a basic rate of 32 per cent. A higher rate of 45 per cent applies to certain activities such as brokerage, stock exchange activities and wholesale trading. There are no specific incentives for foreign investors registered after 1 January 1992. However there are some incentives available to small enterprises and employers of disabled persons and reliefs for investments which increase production or make for the protection of the environment.

Profits are defined as gross receipts from the sale of goods and services less costs incurred in obtaining the income. All entities must file separate returns for each type of business activity with the tax authorities by 15 March following the year-end. Advance payments from entities with foreign capital are due quarterly.

### Taxes on payroll and social security

Every month, employers must contribute 39 per cent of the payroll to the various social security funds (28 per cent to the Pension Fund, 5.4 per cent to the Social Insurance Fund, 2 per cent to the Employment Fund and 3.6 per cent to the Medical Insurance Fund).

# TAXES ON NON RESIDENT COMPANIES

### Companies with a permanent establishment

All companies registered abroad, which engage in economic activity in Russia through a permanent establishment, must register with the tax authorities of the area where the permanent establishment is located within a month of commencing activities. They must do so whether or not their activity will be taxable. Failure to register may be viewed as an attempt to avoid paying tax. Tax is levied only on the portion of income which is attributable to the permanent establishment.

### Companies without a permanent establishment

Companies which are not incorporated in Russia and which do not have a permanent representation in Russia, are liable to tax on some sources of income which are paid by a Russian entity, or which result from property rights in Russia. The rates are 15 per cent on dividends and interest and 20 per cent on income from copyrights, licences and rental fees. Tax is withheld by the paying entity. Foreign legal entities, entitled to total or partial relief under tax treaties must give written notice to the State Tax Inspectorate within a year.

# INDIRECT TAXATION

### VAT and excise

VAT and excise taxes were introduced on 1 January 1992 to replace the turnover tax and sales tax.

Excise taxes are levied on alcoholic beverages, tyres, tobacco goods, passenger cars and other luxury articles. The rates vary from 14 to 90 per cent. The tax base is the non-regulated excise inclusive sales price of goods. Russian enterprises, including those with foreign investment and branches of foreign companies, must collect and pay the tax into the state budget. Excise duties are not payable on exports.

VAT is to be paid into the state budget by all Russian entities, including those with foreign investments, private businesses, branches of foreign companies and by foreign companies not incorporated in Russia engaged in commercial activities. The tax is assessed at various stages in the production of goods and services whether sold for cash, disposed of on a barter basis, or within an enterprise or by an enterprise to its own employees. The taxable base is the sales price excluding the tax itself but including tariffs. Intra-CIS sales are taxed at the point of origin. Exports out of the CIS are not liable to VAT. Imports are taxable, but this measure is still largely untested. The top rate of 28 per cent was reduced to 20 per cent for all goods as of 1 January 1993, except a very limited number of foodstuffs such as macaroni, cheese, and cereals which are taxed at the rate of 10 per cent.

### Customs duties and export taxes

The legislation relating to international transactions is still in a state of flux. Export and import duties are payable to the State Customs Committee.

Goods such as oil, gas, minerals, tobacco and vodka are subject to export duties when transported outside Russia. Rates vary from 30 to 60 per cent. Goods which are used in barter transactions are subject to higher duties. Export duties must be paid before or when the goods are presented at customs control. Payment is in roubles.

All enterprises are liable to import duties. Import tariffs vary according to the category of goods. Basic rates are paid by nationals and enterprises of countries enjoying most favoured nation status, which includes the UK, the EC and EFTA countries. Developing countries pay 50 per cent of this rate, but an exemption applies to the least developed countries. Other countries pay 200 per cent. Import duties are payable either in roubles or in hard currency.

## TAXES ON THE INCOME OF INDIVIDUALS

Earnings from employment subject to taxation in Russia include all earnings, bonuses and other forms of payment or reward connected with the employment including benefits in kind. Income tax is computed during the year and is withheld by the employer. Each monthly payment is a payment on account and the final settlement is made at the end of the year. Individuals who do not obtain income other than from employment are not required to submit a return. If they have another source of income they must declare it before

1 April of the following year. The individual income tax rates for 1992 are set out in Table 15.1.

| Table 15.1 *Income tax rates, 1992* | |
|---|---|
| *Taxable income* | *Amounts of tax* |
| Up to R200,000 | 12% of the taxable amount |
| R200,001–R400,000 | R24,000 + 20% of the amount in excess of R200,000 |
| R400,001–R600,000 | R64,000 + 30% on the amount in excess of R400,000 |
| over R600,001 | R124,000 + 40% on the amount in excess of R600,000 |

Employees must also contribute to the pension fund at the rate of one per cent of their salaries.

### Taxation of expatriates

Foreigners are liable to Russian income tax if they remain in Russia more than 183 days in a calendar year or if their salary is paid directly by a Russian enterprise or a permanent establishment of a foreign enterprise. Foreigners expecting to become residents must register with the tax authorities within 30 days of their arrival. They are also required to report their world-wide income. The taxable income of expatriates is determined in the same way as for Russian nationals and the rates are the same. However they must estimate their taxes due and pay 75 per cent of this estimated amount in three equal parts.

When incomes of foreign individuals are recalculated at the current rate of exchange, most of their revenue falls within the highest tax bracket (40 per cent). However, because incomes, if received in hard currency, must be converted into roubles on the day they are received using the rate set by the Central Bank of Russia, and payments take place much later, the effective rate is much lower due to inflation.

The high dollar to the rouble rate of exchange makes it almost impossible for expatriates to obtain the large quantities of roubles necessary to pay income tax in cash. In 1991, the individual amounts of expatriate tax averaged R20,000. In 1992, the amounts will be in the millions of roubles for every earning foreigner. The Moscow Tax Inspectorate has recommended to the Ministry of Finance that payments should be allowed in hard currency but so far this has not been accepted.

### Taxation of non-residents

Income other than from employment received by non-residents from sources in the Russian Federation is subject to a withholding tax of 20 per cent unless treaties provide for lower rates or on the basis of reciprocity.

## TAX TREATIES

As Russia considers itself a successor state of the Soviet Union, treaties entered into by the latter are still in force and will be honoured. However, it is expected that most double taxation treaties will be renegotiated. This includes the one signed with the UK in 1985.

## 16

# Contract Law

*Frere Cholmeley Bischoff*

The basic legal principles relating to the conclusion and performance of contracts under Russian law are to be found in the USSR 'Fundamental Principles of Civil Legislation'. These were adopted in 1991 to form the basis of modern civil codes for Russia and the Soviet Union's other constituent republics. Although due soon, Russia's Civil Code is yet to be revised and the existing Code, which goes back to 1964, is now outdated. Accordingly, it was decided in the middle of 1992 that the Fundamental Principles are to apply in the meantime. This chapter outlines the basic concepts of Russian contract law and highlights some of the provisions relevant to product quality and consumer protection.

## BASIC CONCEPTS

The new Russian law reflects a general shift away from legal regulation of economic relationships towards allowing the parties to determine their own agendas. The law is concerned principally with defining when an agreement exists and providing remedies for the injured party on its breakdown.

A businessman looking to commence trading in Russia will find the basic concepts of Russian contract law broadly similar to English law:

- A contract is concluded at the point when both parties reach agreement on its essential terms – ie on the subject-matter and on any matter which either party clearly identifies as fundamental.

- Written contracts may be concluded either by exchanging documents each signed by the other party or by jointly signing a single document.

- Courts will construe the wording of the contract according to its literal meaning or, if this is ambiguous, in line with the contract's general purpose.

- Damages are payable for non-performance or inadequate performance.

# SALE OF GOODS

Some of the principles of Russian contract law particularly relevant to the sale of goods are:

- Advertisements, price lists and other information are generally non-binding invitations to negotiate, on the basis of which prospective purchasers can make offers.

- An offer made with an indication that there is a time-limit for acceptance cannot be revoked before then.

- The seller is responsible for safe delivery unless the parties agree to the contrary.

## *Product quality*

A comprehensive regulatory framework relating to the protection of consumers' rights is already in place under Russian law. The basic provisions in the Fundamental Principles are complemented by a detailed Law on the Protection of Consumers' Rights passed in February 1992.

The Law places an obligation on manufacturers to ensure that their products function properly for the entire period agreed with the purchaser or, in the absence of such agreement, for ten years. Producers are also required to provide service and repair facilities throughout this period, and may therefore wish to include 'guarantees' limiting their responsibility to a shorter period, as is common in the West, to avoid having to maintain support services for products long since discontinued.

Retailers are obliged to ensure that their merchandise is up to specification and is fit to be used for its common purpose. They must also supply the purchaser with information on various aspects of the product (eg how it should be used and how long it should last) and are, of course, liable if it does not conform to the terms in the contract. The door is thus open for consumers to claim relief if they were assured in a shop that a given item could be used for a certain purpose (even if this is not its usual purpose) only to discover later that this was not the case. On the other hand, a retailer is not responsible for defects which he brings to the attention of the purchaser before sale.

The buyer of a defective good can demand:

- repairs to the product or reimbursement of the costs of repair;

- an appropriate reduction in the purchase price;

- replacement of the item with an identical one;

- exchange of the item for a comparable one, with a commensurate reduction of the purchase price; or

- annulment of the contract and a full refund.

## SERVICE CONTRACTS

A number of statutory terms are implied into contracts for service under Russian law, in much the same way as English law. A service must be carried out within the time-limit fixed by contract or, if this is not specified, within a reasonable time. If the work done is not of a satisfactory standard, the customer can require that this is put right, or can ask for reimbursement of the cost of putting it right or a simple reduction of the price paid.

# 17

# Competition
## *Frere Cholmeley Bischoff*

A free market economy requires competition. As old command mechanisms are dismantled, effective competition rules are an important complement to price liberalisation and privatisation in ensuring that state-owned monopolies do not become private monopolies able to charge customers non-market driven prices. Indeed in many ways a coherent competition policy is especially vital in Russia as, given the size of the economy and interdependency of many sectors, foreign products are likely to take some time to become established on the market and to become rivals for locally-produced goods.

The Law of the Russian Federation on Competition and Restricting Monopolistic Activities on Goods Markets (the Competition Law) sets out to achieve precisely these objectives. Similar in approach to US anti-trust and EC competition rules, its aims are essentially twofold: to ensure conditions for creating goods markets and to ensure their effective functioning by preventing, limiting or arresting monopolistic activities and unfair competition. The former function is to be performed by encouraging the break-up of monopolistic state-owned suppliers and promoting the emergence of new private ones. The latter function, on which this chapter will focus, involves prohibiting unfair and anti-competitive practices and regulating takeovers and mergers.

## THE ANTI-MONOPOLY COMMITTEE

The Competition Law establishes an Anti-Monopoly Committee (AMC) to implement and enforce the competition rules. In performing this role the AMC is granted extensive powers, comparable to those of the EC Commission. These include:

- The right to require enterprises to provide information and documentation relevant to its investigations, and a right of access to premises to inspect 'all necessary documents'.

- The power to issue mandatory 'instructions' requiring enterprises to cease practices which violate the law and to restore the status quo ante, including if necessary the annulment or amendment of contracts and the payment of damages for any losses incurred.

- The right to fine enterprises and their officials for breaching the law or failing to comply with an instruction.

- The power to order the compulsory division of enterprises holding a dominant position and/or whose actions restrict competition, providing such separation is organisationally and/ or territorially feasible.

- The right to cancel the registration of enterprises – in particular those formed with the unlawful participation of government officials.

- Authority, in tandem with other appropriate organs, to prohibit or suspend enterprises' foreign trading operations.

Non-compliance with a directive of the AMC is also an offence under the Criminal Code, punishable by a fine and a ban on holding certain positions or engaging in certain activities.

### Jurisdiction

The Competition Law has elements of both territorial and extra-territorial jurisdiction. It regulates activities of firms and individuals on Russian territory, and also governs actions by Russian entities outside the Russian Federation which have the effect of restricting competition on the Russian market. In this respect it is in line with the EC competition rules. What remains to be seen is whether the Russian law can be interpreted so as to include an 'effects doctrine', thereby regulating agreements between non-Russian concerns outside Russia which affect competition inside Russia's borders (as developed in the EC in the 'Woodpulp case'). Another, related question of particular importance to firms opening offices in Russia is whether the AMC will assert jurisdiction over a foreign-based parent company in relation to anti-competitive acts of its Russian subsidiary (a policy elaborated by the EC in the 'Dyestuffs case').

# ANTI-COMPETITIVE PRACTICES

## *Abuse of a dominant position*

Restrictions on the activities of dominant suppliers are of great importance in the current conditions, as foreign companies move into Russia and consequently a number of new goods are introduced to the consumer market.

Under the Competition Law an enterprise potentially occupies a dominant position if its share of the market for a particular product is 35 per cent or more. If such is the case, dominance is assumed unless it is proved that the enterprise was unable to influence competition in that market, either by restricting others' access to it or otherwise impeding their commercial activities.

Accordingly much will hinge on what constitutes the 'relevant market'. A market can, of course, be divided both geographically and by product. The Russian Federation contains several geographical markets – in the autonomous republics, regions and areas. As regards product markets, the important question is what the consumers in the area supplied regard as identical, similar or substitute goods.

It is important to stress that to hold a dominant position on a given market is not in itself prohibited. What the law seeks to prevent is the *abuse* of such a position by restricting competition or frustrating the interests of others (consumers or fellow suppliers). Abuse can include:

- suspending supplies of a product so as to create a shortage or an increase in prices;

- imposing on a purchaser unfair contractual terms;

- forcing acceptance of conditions unrelated to the subject matter of the contract (such as requiring a buyer to enter an unrelated agreement);

- discriminating between purchasers on arbitrary grounds, thereby placing them at a competitive disadvantage; or

- obstructing other producers' access to or exit from the market.

## *Cartels*

A cartel arises if two or more enterprises agree to adopt a certain practice which results, or may result, in preventing or restricting competition. Agreements such as these are potentially very common in Russia as enterprises in a particular branch ministry have customarily joined together in trade associations. The Competition Law prohibits cartels between both competing (or potentially competing) producers who between them hold a dominant position; and a buyer and supplier, one of which occupies a dominant position.

Generally, a cartel agreement may take any form – it might, for example, be simply an understanding. The Competition Law gives as examples agreements which:

- fix prices;

- provide discounts or bonuses;

- divide markets by area, product, suppliers or consumers;

- restrict access to the market or drive from it other producers or purchasers; or

- prevent the conclusion of contracts with certain suppliers or consumers.

### Exemptions

The prohibitions on some activities regarded as *prima facie* anti-competitive may be lifted if it can be shown that their effect was in fact the reverse. The law requires it to be shown that the actions promoted, or will promote: the saturation of the market; improvements in the quality of the goods; and increased competitiveness, particularly on the export market.

## CONTROL OF MERGERS

The AMC exercises preliminary control over:

- Proposed mergers to create a concern with a capital value over R50 million.

- Stock purchases by a firm with at least a 35 per cent share of a given market in one of its competitors.

- The acquisition of a controlling interest in an enterprise occupying a dominant position by any firm or individual.

The AMC is authorised to prevent any of the above if they may lead to a substantial restriction of competition and/or (in the case of mergers) a dominant position being held.

Clearly the net here is quite broad. Once again, there is no need for the AMC to show that the dominant position will be *abused* – its existence is enough for the proposed merger to be blocked. In fact neither of the grounds need be established beyond doubt, their *possible* consequence being sufficient in itself. On the other hand the AMC may give the go-ahead even if the above grounds are made out, if it believes that quantitative and qualitative improvements on the market may result and export potential may be enhanced.

The parties involved in a proposed transaction should obtain the approval of the local branch of the AMC in advance. The following should be supplied:

- a letter requesting consent to the merger;

- information about the basic activities of the enterprises concerned;

- each party's share in the relevant goods market; and

- a copy of the draft merger agreement.

The AMC should report its decision within 30 days (though a longer wait may be expected in practice). If it refuses to allow the proposed new venture, the AMC is required to give its reasons.

## UNFAIR COMPETITION

The general deregulation of economic activity in many Central and Eastern European countries has often led to established suppliers falling victim to the unscrupulous business practices of 'new entrepreneurs'. To help safeguard against this, the Competition Law lists a number of activities which are prohibited as constituting 'unfair competition'. These are:

- Passing-off – ie, representing one's own goods as someone else's by wilfully using the trademark, company or product name, or copying the design, packaging or appearance of the product of another firm.

- Comparative advertising – crudely contrasting one's own product with another.

- Spreading false, inaccurate or distorted information capable of damaging another enterprise or harming its business reputation.

■ Misleading the public regarding the nature, method or place of production, consumer properties or quality of goods.

Also protected are 'know-how' and commercial secrets. Provided it has an actual or potential value (because it is unknown to third persons) and cannot lawfully be accessed freely – and necessary measures are taken to protect its confidentiality – the owner of technical or productive information is protected against others obtaining, using or disclosing it without his consent. Any person who infringes this right is obliged to pay damages. However, a party who obtains the information independently and *bona fide* is entitled to use it freely. It is worth noting in this connection that any material of this nature obtained by the AMC in the course of its investigations must be kept secret and, if this duty is broken, damages are payable.

# 18

# The Labour Market

*KPMG Peat Marwick*

## CULTURE

Russian employees are the product of 70 years of top-down hierarchical work and social environments. Jobs used to be for life and, officially, unemployment did not exist. However, bloated structures masked the extent of overmanning. Absenteeism was endemic as workers took time off to buy essentials. Workers did not need to work hard. Initiative was frowned upon and even penalised. Now the times of full employment are over as economic reforms take their toll. Adjustments will take time: although output has dropped dramatically, unemployment has grown at a much slower pace, which implies a drop in productivity. However, even now, not everybody believes that free enterprise will revive the motherland or that making money is not a dirty game. Workers will refrain from taking responsibilities and this will create misunderstandings. Attitudes towards foreign investors are often ambivalent. One response is to dismiss these attitudes as an overhang from the past, but it is very difficult to recruit a new team which will start working as a single coherent whole. Patience as well as rewards are required to encourage new attitudes.

### Skills

The labour force is generally well educated and achieves high rates of literacy. However, the school system applied a very rigid curriculum based on discipline and narrow ideological views. Within the framework of central planning, it was difficult to match educational profiles with job specifications due to the increasing complexities of the economy and there is a shortage of skilled labour. The changes now occurring have brought demands for new skills and vocational training is encouraged. The highest proportion of skilled workers is to be found in the defence industries which accounted directly or indirectly for up to 25 per cent of the labour force employed in enterprises which are unable to switch to the civilian market on their own. A shortage of housing is a major hindrance to labour mobility.

The underdevelopment of services is one of the most striking features of the economies of Eastern Europe. Although there has been some movement towards employment in services as in Western countries, the process has been much slower than in the West. Over 20 per cent of the population is still employed in agriculture and forestry (excluding seasonal labour which used to be allocated to farms during harvest time). Industry accounts for 30 per cent and construction 10 per cent.

### Management

Output was the stuff of which glorious statistics were made. Achieving the plan or better still exceeding it put you in a good place in the race for favours – a party card for example. Management skills were strictly limited to this context: it was often safer not to make any show of initiative. Managers who have survived from the old days are tarnished by years of working under communism and present a powerful conservative lobby.

Now that effective state control of state-owned enterprises has collapsed, managers have not generally responded by adopting market orientated pricing, investment or marketing strategies. Instead, they have sought to compensate workers by increasing wages and prices. They know instinctively that one of the outcomes of privatisation will be to separate the winners and the losers, especially when bankruptcy laws come into effect. They also know that the old command system is dead but would probably be happy with a cosy world of state contracts and a monopoly supply niche. Managers of state companies often want new credits and subsidies to alleviate what they perceive as the annihilation of Russia's industrial base or, if their firms are making money, they will be keen to privatise them on the quiet and to allocate the shares to themselves.

Training will be necessary to help managers become self-confident and able to pick up from a constant flow of information what is relevant to evaluate performance and costs.

### Entrepreneurs

For decades, private economic activity was frowned upon. The advent of *perestroika* did not change attitudes because of the identification of enterprise with the black market or indeed gangsterism. Lack of accountability was the stock in trade of its practitioners. Russia is attempting to relegate its feudal system resulting from decades of social and economic engineering and dominated by an amorphous, all-encompassing state, to the dustbin of history. Foreign capital will only provide a relatively small part of what is needed. Entrepreneurs will have to build capitalism without capital and without even the memory of capitalism, without banks, insurance companies and building societies. It is estimated that there are about 46,000 private enterprises in Russia.

Russian entrepreneurs tend to be impatient capitalists, not yet used to the idea that trading and business relations are built over time and involve some degree of mutual trust. Their goals, perhaps dictated by circumstances, tend to be temporary, with each deal seen as a one-off on which they expect to see a big profit margin. They seek to realise value rather than put capital back into their businesses.

### Expatriates

Generally, Western companies tend to put expatriates in key functional positions in their new ventures. Expatriates represent a major cost and a major investment. Their role and objectives should be clear from the start but flexibility should be allowed. Permanent revolution will probably be the order of the day and they will need to be capable of imaginative solutions when faced with circumstances over which they have no control, such as changing legislation or supplies failing to turn up. Expatriates must be self-confident and tolerant. They should also be pedagogues so as to transfer skills and bring out the best in the local staff and develop local talent for the future. Careful consideration should be given to their contracts, the tax and social security implications and timing of their transfer.

## THE PROFESSIONS

The professions have suffered from a visible culture shock as they found themselves attacked on all fronts by their Western counterparts which have set up offices in Russia and give advice on what should be their area of expertise.

## Lawyers

The majority of Russian lawyers who have established themselves in private practice are either advocates or in-house lawyers. So-called legal consultants are totally unregulated.

Foreign investors often complain that, although Russian lawyers can draw up documents, they have little commercial awareness and it is difficult to get timely and comprehensive answers. Russian lawyers complain that foreign lawyers are not acquainted with local laws and do not understand the business environment. A few early associations of Western and local firms have subsequently fallen apart. However, it is worth remembering that the legal vacuum within a tangled business environment combined with a lack of understanding of and even disrespect for the rule of law, means that contracts which may have taken months to negotiate may flounder and will not be worth the paper they are printed on. This could happen whether dealing with Russian or foreign lawyers.

## Accountants

What the English call accountants will probably have the title of economists. They would have a degree in economics and ten years' accounting experience. What the Russians call accountants will be closer to our bookkeepers and often low down the company hierarchy and low paid. The chief accountant occupies a prominent position since he is responsible for the correctness of the financial statements. He also signs most notifications to the authorities.

The word audit is also the source of semantic confusion: an audit is simply an examination of accounts for tax compliance purposes. Russian auditors advertise their services in the press, but do not expect them to check whether your company accounts give a true and fair view of its financial situation.

A proper regulatory framework is being devised for the accountancy profession in line with accountancy professions in the Western world. Regulations are being drafted to define terms precisely. A draft law on auditors looks into the qualifications that individuals must possess to call themselves auditors.

## Scientists and engineers

Russia presents a striking paradox: it has inherited from the Soviet Union both strong research capabilities and a backward economy. Official Soviet statistics used to boast that there were 1.5 million scientists in the USSR, which is about a fifth of the world total, working in more than 5000 establishments. The technological gap between the West and Russia does not originate from an inability to think in innovative ways: Soviet science was highly speculative and abstract. The failure of Soviet science was in not making use of research results and in an inability to jump from new ideas into production or their diffusion. Only a very small proportion of ideas found their way into production. Research was wholly financed out of state budgets with results handed over gratuitously. Scientists were not sensitive to their economic environment and the economy was not sensitive to scientific advances. Today, science and technology is in disarray, research projects have been dropped and salaries have plummeted. There is a fear of a brain drain of highly skilled specialists: very low Western salaries are attractive and there is a high demand for engineers, physicists, chemists and mathematicians. Much hope is placed on foreign investment around poles of excellence such as space and defence research, but there too new markets have to be found.

## EMPLOYMENT PRACTICES

### Recruitment

Employers are now free to hire and fire. However, there is no pool of ready-made people with all the necessary skills you require, whether managerial, technical or linguistic. For an employer, the choice is very often limited either to people with no experience but who can be trained or staff with experience but set in their bad habits. In any event, training and motivation of staff will be essential. Most jobs are still awarded on the basis of nepotism and by word of mouth, through personal contacts. New employment bureaux exist which try to apply similar procedures as in the West such as psychometric and other tests. Advertisements in newspapers also provide new ways of hiring people. These are usually well answered: but allow time to sift through all the applications. It is also worth conducting an ongoing search and keeping files on possible candidates.

### Wages

Salary levels have mirrored the changes in society at large and now vary greatly. While the minimum monthly salary is around R2225 and the average R8500, some joint ventures and foreign companies are paying up to 30 times that amount for skilled personnel with language capabilities. Payments usually combine both a rouble and a hard currency element. Hard currency payments may represent anything between 20 and 100 per cent of the rouble salary. However, according to current legislation it is expressly forbidden to make direct hard currency payments to Russian nationals. Ways are found to circumvent this prohibition such as vouchers to be used in hard currency stores. It is important to keep track of wages paid for a particular job as the pool of skilled staff is small and they may leave if dissatisfied.

## LABOUR RELATIONS

So far, Russians have been stoic, not to say resigned in the face of growing hardship. Strikes and stoppages occur but are usually settled by significant increases in wages. Authorities and managers have been unwilling to face up to the social costs of restructuring. Output has plunged but very few workers have been made redundant. Even so, the government expects unemployment to soar from under a million to more than five million. This more than low wages and high prices, the government fears, makes the possibility of strikes by workers faced with group sacking and civil unrest very real.

Much has been done: training programmes and unemployment centres have been set up, but their functioning remains untested. There are talks of labour intensive public work programmes, but there will probably be little finance for an active labour policy from a cash-strapped government.

# 19

# Employment Law

*Frere Cholmeley Bischoff*

The principal aspects of the employer–employee relationship in a Russian enterprise are governed by a collective agreement negotiated between the administration and representatives of the employees, and individual contracts concluded between the parties. Minimum standards on various factors are fixed by legislation, and agreements between the parties are subject to these. This legislation, except as regards a few matters, also applies to non-Russian employees permanently resident in the Russian Federation.

## THE COLLECTIVE AGREEMENT

At the root of labour relations in a Russian enterprise lies the collective agreement. This is a contract negotiated between the employers and representatives of the employees (in major concerns often the trade union) outlining the important conditions affecting employment such as pay levels, length of the working week, guarantees, compensation and so forth.

Thus, one of the first tasks for any new employer will be to formulate an acceptable collective agreement. Indeed the privatisation regulations, for example, require that a new collective agreement be concluded within six months of an enterprise's transfer into private hands.

## THE INDIVIDUAL CONTRACT

In line with the collective agreement, the employer will enter into an oral or written contract with the individual employee. Recent legislation has substantially increased the importance of the individual employment contract, particularly as regards procedures for settling disputes. So the document should be carefully drafted – as in the West.

### Term

The agreement between the parties may be for:

- an indefinite period;
- a fixed period; or
- the time required to fulfil a specified task.

The employee may be hired for an initial probationary period (maximum six months). In practice, such a trial period tends to be from one week's to one month's duration.

### Pay

There is a minimum wage fixed by Russian law, but this tends to lag behind inflation and is anyway set very low. Pay scales, intervals and so on are determined by individual enterprises and are contained in the collective agreements. It is worth noting that, in late-1992, many state enterprises switched from monthly to weekly payments in order to help their employees' cash flow.

Under current conditions, Russian employees cannot generally be paid in hard currency, and wages over R3600 per month are not deductible by businesses for tax purposes. The lack of such constraints on foreign employees' pay levels has led to a situation where foreign and local staff often receive very different salaries for doing the same work. While such differentials may simply be the result of the freeing of the labour market, their persistence beyond the short term may result in legislation envisaging equal pay for equal work being enacted.

### Social fund contributions

The foreign investment law provides for enterprises with foreign investments to make payments to state social insurance for local and foreign employees, and to pension funds for local employees. In 1992, 5.4 per cent of the wage fund was payable to the Social Security Fund and 31.6 per cent to the Russian Federation Pension Fund. Payments towards pensions of foreign employees are transferred to the respective funds in their places of residence in the currency and under conditions exercised in those countries.

## Hours

A 40-hour, 5-day working week is normal in Russia. Lengths of shifts are fixed by the enterprise itself, and hours worked should be recorded in a daily or weekly register.

Flexible working hours are allowed for certain categories of workers. The positions involved should be specified in the collective agreements. Overtime is not permitted other than in exceptional circumstances.

## Holidays

Employees are entitled to a minimum 20 days paid holiday per year. Short unpaid holidays may be requested by an employee with a good reason.

## The labour book

Upon commencement of employment, the employee should provide his employer with his labour book. This carries details on the employee, the type of work performed, commencement and termination dates.

# TERMINATION

Russian employment law provides that the employment contract may only be terminated if one of eight specified bases for termination exist. These bases are:

1. mutual agreement;

2. expiry of a fixed-term contract;

3. military conscription of the employee;

4. imprisonment of the employee (or other penal sentence inconsistent with his/her continued employment);

5. transfer of the employee with his/her consent to a different enterprise;

6. refusal of the employee to transfer his/her place of work together with the business (provided the employee's position and earnings

were to be unaffected by this move) or to continue working following changes in working conditions;

7.  termination by the employee;

8.  termination by the employer.

Of these, the final two require further explanation.

### Termination by the employee

An employee under an indefinite-term contract may terminate by giving two months written notice unless there are reasons to justify shorter notice of at least one month. An employee under a fixed-term contract may generally only terminate before time in the event of illness or disability, or if the management breaches the employment agreement, the collective agreement or the employment law itself.

### Termination by the employer

The law envisages several grounds justifying dismissal by the employer. These can be broadly categorised as redundancy, retirement, capability and conduct.

#### Redundancy

Employees who are to be dismissed as a result of the liquidation of the enterprise or as part of a reduction in staffing levels should be given at least two months written notice. However, in the event of large-scale redundancies the employer is required to give written notification at least three months in advance to the employment services and appropriate trade union bodies, giving details of the number and categories of employees likely to be affected and the time-scale during which the dismissals are to take place.

When selecting those to be made redundant, the employer is obliged to have regard to various factors, including the qualifications, productivity, length of service and number of dependants in the family of the employee.

#### Retirement

Employees become entitled to a full pension on reaching the age of 60 (for men with 25 years service) or 55 (for women with 20 years service). On their becoming so entitled, the employer can terminate the employment contract.

#### Capability

Where an employee's qualifications or health leads to his/her performance being inadequate for the position held, the employer is justified in dismissing him/her from that position.

*Conduct*

The employer may also dismiss an employee for any of the following reasons:

- Persistent non-compliance on the part of the employee with obligations under the contract or internal regulations, without good reason. To justify dismissal on this ground, a disciplinary procedure involving warnings and reprimands should have been followed.

- Absence from work for more than four months due to temporary incapacity or for over three hours of a working day without good reason.

- Arrival at work in a drunken state or otherwise intoxicated.

- Theft from the place of work (confirmed by law enforcement bodies).

## SETTLEMENT OF DISPUTES

Any dispute arising between the employer and the employee is heard before the Commission on Labour Disputes of the enterprise, the Trade Union Committee of the enterprise, or the District or City People's Court.

### The Commission on Labour Disputes

Except in cases referred by law directly to the courts (see below), the Commission on Labour Disputes is the mandatory body for the initial hearing. The Commission contains equal representation from the trade union and management. Application is made by the employee concerned to the Trade Union and the case will be heard within five days. The Commission reaches its decision on the basis of agreement between its members.

### The Trade Union Committee

In the event of the Commission on Labour Disputes failing to reach agreement, or should the employee wish to appeal against its decision, he/she may apply to the Trade Union Committee for a further hearing. Such applications should be made within ten days and the case heard within a further five days.

### The People's Court

The local People's Court hears appeals from the decisions of the above bodies, on application within nine days by the employee concerned or the management (in the latter instance on questions of law only), and any case involving an enterprise where no Commission on Labour Disputes exists.

In addition, the law refers directly to the court for first instance hearing cases involving reinstatement against dismissal or amendment of the date and reasons for dismissal, or compensation sought by the administration against employees for damages sustained by the enterprise.

The court has jurisdiction to order the reinstatement of a worker dismissed unlawfully or without regard to proper procedures, and compensation of up to three months average earnings.

# 20

# Defence Conversion

## *Frere Cholmeley Bischoff and Brown & Root*

As a reflection of the historical priorities of the Soviet Union and the capacity of a command economy to divert resources towards those priorities, a huge percentage of the Russian Federation's productive capacity, when compared with Western countries, is engaged in the defence and related industries. It has been estimated that 50 per cent of the country's industrial output is from these industries alone.

The reduced emphasis on these sectors following the end of the Cold War means that the factories involved can now switch to producing consumer and, especially, high-technology goods (indeed many have already been sidelining in such fields for some years now). This process, known as 'conversion' is expected by the government to form the bedrock of Russia's economic recovery and, in 1993, R250 billion (half the projected investment credits for the year) are being set aside to support it.

Early in 1992 the legal framework for the programme was enacted in a Conversion Law, which specifically provides that the principal aim of converted enterprises is the production of goods able to compete on the world market. This chapter is intended to provide a brief outline of the basic legal principles involved; the capabilities of the military industrial complex; the prospects for successful conversion, and the difficulties involved.

## THE CONVERSION PROCESS

Since all enterprises in the defence sector are currently state owned, the startling point in the conversion process is inevitably the Russian Federation Defence Ministry's assessment of the state's long-term military needs, based on the policy of the government. In the light of this assessment, a conversion programme is developed and sent to the relevant enterprises.

Thereafter, primary responsibility for the organisation of the conversion rests with the enterprise itself, under the supervision of the regional co-ordination council and the central Ministry of Industry of the Russian Federation. The Conversion Law provides for various measures to facilitate the transition process:

- the establishment of a Federal Conversion Fund to provide financial assistance;

- the retention for employees of various privileges enjoyed by them as a consequence of working in the defence industry, together with the creation of certain advantages for those made unemployed as a result of the conversion;

- the availability of tax benefits for the enterprises concerned.

Subject to various restrictions (imposed to protect state security and strategic interests), the converted enterprise is free to export equipment and material not needed for civilian production and to import new technology and component parts. The Conversion Law specifically envisages the marketing of intellectual property. Special centralised funds for financing research and development may be established, to which payments up to a certain level are tax-deductible.

Any unit of the enterprise (eg shop, branch, etc) which becomes fully converted can establish itself as a distinct legal entity if its labour collective (a body comprising representatives of management and employees) so decides. A fully converted legal entity may then apply to be privatised, again at the initiative of the labour collective.

It is at this point that foreign parties may wish to get involved. The Conversion Law provides for the full participation of foreign investors in the privatisation of converted military industries. However it is clear from the Privatisation Law that this can only be done after the permission of the central authorities, in the form of a licence, has been obtained.

## THE CAPABILITIES OF THE MILITARY INDUSTRIAL COMPLEX

The Russian military complex consists of a great number of factories, strategically positioned throughout Russia. There is a concentration around St Petersburg, and many positioned around the Ural mountains, where they were moved to safety during the advance of Hitler. Of course, these factories were highly secret until recently and would have had few Russian visitors: certainly none from the West. In the past few years, however, many have opened their doors to potential Western investors. Western visitors are welcomed very courteously to such factories, and the Russian management is usually delighted to demonstrate the technical capability of the workshops. Quite often a camera is permitted, provided that the Western visitor observes the protocol of requesting permission for each picture.

Within the communist system, engineering design and research and development were carried out at separate institutes – some of which became world-class centres of excellence – that were usually linked to particular manufacturing enterprises. The expertise of the manufacturing enterprise is therefore solely related to manufacturing processes and know-how. If a manufacturing organisation believes it will benefit by working with a Western company in order to develop a new, non-defence product, then the people may have difficulty in coming to terms with working with anyone other than their own design institute. Nevertheless, there are Russian managers who do understand that such a move may be beneficial, or possibly the only way to save their enterprise.

In the past, the enterprise produced a deliberately limited range of products that it was not required to understand – for example, parts of a warship. The shift from making a small range of highly complex parts to making less complex non-military products is great.

Often, the technical capability of the plants is very great indeed. Complex machined aluminium castings made to a very high quality; beautiful titanium welds with no blemish detectable; huge shafts; three-metre diameter propellers being machined fully automatically from bronze castings. Such components are being manufactured throughout Russia.

Although the range of military components in each enterprise may have been limited, often the processes and techniques used in an enterprise were many and varied. For example, at the propeller factory, all the processes were undertaken on the same site, from making the moulds to casting, to machining. This ensured that the monthly quota of manufactured items would not be jeopardised by the failure of another factory to deliver fittings.

The machinery in the factories ranges from sturdy older Russian-designed presses to modern CNC machines imported from Germany, because even in the communist era, selected imports continued. In some cases, Russian-made machine tools were adapted to accept Western computer control technology. The overall level of automation is probably less than in the West, but certainly modern computer production techniques were understood and used where necessary.

The skill levels of the engineers and technologists in the manufacturing enterprises and institutes which form Russian military industrial complex are high. Currently this expertise is costed at much lower prices than equivalent skilled people in the West, even though this differential may not last for very many years.

## THE PROSPECTS FOR SUCCESSFUL CONVERSION

For successful conversion, an enterprise will first need to identify suitable non-military products. These may be, for example, consumer goods, transport equipment such as non-military ships or locomotives, oil and gas equipment, or environmental equipment. The military factory personnel tend to be reluctant to turn to consumer goods and make 'only saucepans', although an electronics factory may be interested in a high-tech product such as a video disc. Transport equipment is certainly a distinct possibility for some complexes, although the investment cost to achieve a conversion is likely to be very high, and the market for such high-value goods uncertain. Oil and gas equipment such as pumps and valves made to demanding standards offers a good possibility, and so does environmental equipment, which may include items which have not been produced before, such as scrubbers for coal-fired power plants.

The conversion of defence factories to the manufacture of goods for the domestic market, where payment is in roubles, will be very slow and Western companies are unlikely to be able to achieve much business success in assisting with this process. However, there are good possibilities if conversion is for the manufacture of a product which will be sold to Western investors in Russia or exported for hard currency. An example of the first is oil and gas equipment; large Western companies are seeking work in Russia in this area, and as the market expands, they will increasingly look to source components from local sources that meet the rigorous standards of the industry. A Russian defence factory is unlikely to be able to meet the standards in the required time-frame without Western assistance. Such assistance may include the supply of a valve design under licence; supply of some Western manufacturing machines; detailed information on American or Western European design standards; and certainly considerable assistance and training with quality control, production planning and general management.

Products for export offer similar opportunities for Western companies, and it is likely to be the Western company, not the Russian enterprise, which selects a product that will achieve successful export sales. A Western company will not necessarily have to make substantial investment in the Russian enterprise, although this is what the Russians will initially expect. A Western company that can identify a suitable defence-conversion product, secure a market for that product where hard currency payments will be made, and arrange finance to cover the time delay, will be able to develop business for the supply of Western know-how and equipment. For such a project to be successful, it will be necessary to develop the export market first, so that the majority of the new product is concentrated in export sales until the pay-back for the project set-up costs is complete. Thereafter, the enormous domestic market will be available to develop.

## THE DIFFICULTIES

As mentioned above, a common difficulty at any factory relates to the identification of suitable non-military products. Generally, the defence factories have manufactured to the state's demands and have had no responsibility for making choices that affect their own future. They have had no need to make judgements on the likely business success of alternative products. They do not know how to achieve a balance between high quality and low price, and may choose to cut back on the paint finish specification to save costs, then wonder why no one wants to buy a product that looks awful. Many factory directors recognise that they must 'walk before they can run', and for export they expect to aim at relatively simple products first.

The Russians must realise that they need to work to meet a demand, not to make products to fill a warehouse and try to sell them later. It is evident that some of the managers in the Moscow offices which were formerly responsible for defence procurement, have difficulty with this mind-shift. They make statements like, 'If you give us a guaranteed order for a particular valve, we will set up a production line ourselves, and guarantee the quality.' They do not understand why a Western company will not guarantee the purchase of the total factory output. It is almost certainly to a Western company's advantage to go to a Russian factory direct, ideally selecting one where the senior managers are prepared to absorb Western ideas quickly.

Although the engineering skills in these factories may be very high, complementary skills are often lacking. Ideas of management such as project planning, cost control, 'just-in-time' and quality control may be novel. There may be no people trained in marketing, or none who are skilled at international negotiations. Further, the engineers themselves may find transferring their skills to the manufacture of civilian products to be quite difficult. Training will therefore be high on the agenda.

A further widespread problem is the assurance of a supply of quality raw materials. In Russia, defence factories used to be in a privileged position, receiving the very best raw materials. Unfortunately, it seems that such supplies may not now be guaranteed. Another difficulty is related to the ownership of the enterprise. Some factory directors themselves know that they used to belong to the Ministry, but have no clear idea to whom they are responsible.

Perhaps the problem that seems to be most difficult to solve is that of arranging finance for defence conversion projects. New plants making quality exportable products will ultimately earn enough to repay a loan. First, however, it is necessary to find an institution that is willing to put forward a low interest rate loan to the factory, against the background of the risks mentioned above. The involvement of a large Western company with a reputation for quality and for completion of projects, will lessen the risk, but there is unlikely to be any hard guarantee forthcoming from the enterprise or from the Russian government that will be sufficient to cover the loan if, for any reason, the product is not made and sold.

Without doubt there are many opportunities in defence conversion in Russia for Western companies that are bold and clever enough to find a way through the difficulties. The military complex has vast potential to generate wealth, with access to high-quality personnel and cheap raw materials. The supply of business ideas, project finance and overall management expertise from Western companies could turn a difficult situation into a successful outcome for both parties.

## 21

# Distribution

## *ALM Consulting*

Since the beginning of the economic reform programme, the Russian government has assigned great importance to the development of the internal trading system, recognising free trade as a key factor in the liberalisation of the economy. The centralised distribution of material resources severely limits production and hinders price stabilisation – as well as producing marked price differentials by region or branch.

Currently all internal trade is carried out through one of three channels:

- the state distribution system;

- direct exchange between enterprises; and

- newly created market structures.

Of these, the command distribution structures continue to predominate, with purchases for state needs in 1992 accounting for 50 per cent of the whole.

## THE STATE DISTRIBUTION SYSTEM

Among the most important elements within the state distribution system are the various committees of the Ministry of Trade and Resources, 26 republican 'wholesale-intermediary' (*optovo-posryed-nicheskii*) firms, 73 'commercial-intermediary' (*kommyerchyestvo-posryednicheskii*) companies, and departmental and local coordinating organisations, including several large agencies such as Agrosnab and Rosnefteprodukt. These bodies are staffed by the most experienced personnel and own the vast majority of the country's warehousing facilities.

Thus the trading activities of individual enterprises are generally regulated by uniform organisational structures – a reflection of the monopolistic nature of the system. So, for example, larger enterprises can operate without go-betweens and principally work with specialised, independent wholesale-intermediary firms. Smaller producers and users, on the other hand, use the services of the wholesale traders and outlets which operate as sub-divisions of the territorial commercial-intermediary companies.

Since this trade monopoly is of an artificial nature, founded on the links fixed administratively between users and producers and specific suppliers, the government has recognised that the most expedient way of breaking it up is by liquidating the constituent units of the state distribution system and setting up a network of trade enterprises: wholesalers, warehouses, depots and co-ordinating storage facilities. (Given the shortage of warehousing on Russian territory, wholesalers may be divided into trading – intermediary – and storage enterprises.) However for the foreseeable future a system of state purchases will be maintained for a category of users to whom a supply of resources should be guaranteed. Among these are the army, health service, schools, the Interior Ministry, cultural facilities and other branches of budgetary financing as laid down by sectoral government programmes.

### Direct exchange between enterprises

Many Russian enterprises are still some way off coming to terms with the new market environment. Currently, disorientated by the chaotic economic situation, spiralling inflation and payments crisis, and without developed sales and marketing services, they tend to rely on direct links with other enterprises both upstream and downstream. Such links can be supported by barter and other operations unconnected with ordinary trading at market prices. In 1992 direct links accounted for over 55 per cent of all turnover.

## MARKET STRUCTURES

Since the beginning of the reforms, some trading has been carried out through private market mechanisms – namely commodity exchanges, brokerage firms, or trading houses.

### Commodity exchanges

By the beginning of 1993, 400 commodity exchanges had been

registered on Russian territory. However the actual turnover of goods through these exchanges is not great, accounting for only 1.5 per cent of the overall figure, and supply and demand on the exchanges tends to be unpredictable. Thus, though the range of goods on offer can be quite wide, this is frequently a matter of chance.

Another problem is the general lack of experience among traders. Attempts to introduce the use of forward and futures contracts have met with little enthusiasm, owing to an absence of guarantees for their fulfilment and a broad lack of interest among producers for long-term agreements while inflation remains high.

## Brokerage firms

In 1992 more than 20,000 intermediary concerns, along the lines of brokerage firms, were registered in Russia. Although the size and turnover of these operations vary considerably, all of them lag far behind state wholesale-intermediary enterprises in this respect. However their merit lies in their versatility and flexibility.

A current trend, as recognisable market dynamics emerge in the economy, is for private intermediaries to switch from simple brokerage to dealing-type (account trading) operations. Compared with 1991 this type of trading was less oriented to export-import operations in 1992, as such activities became markedly less advantageous.

Russian government experts believe that brokerage firms will soon begin to break up long-standing economic links between state enterprises. However this will depend on such firms developing their own storage facilities.

## Trading houses

Alongside brokerage firms in the private division of the wholesale sector are 'trading houses'. These are generally larger than brokerage firms, specialising basically in dealing operations with imported goods (especially organisational technology and foodstuffs).

# 22

# Transport

## Dr Michael Bradshaw, University of Birmingham

Russia, which accounted for 74 per cent of the USSR, is now the largest country in the world, covering an area of 17,075,400 square kilometres and spanning 11 time zones from the outpost of Kaliningrad in the west to the Pacific gateway of Vladivostok in the east. As the geographical successor to the Soviet Union, Russia retains most of the geographical challenges posed by size, continentality and latitudinal position.

The transportation system was planned and developed by the state, with control centralised in Moscow. The planners in Moscow boasted of a 'united transportation system' which stressed complementarity not competition. In theory the various modes of transportation were integrated to provide an efficient transportation system. The reality was somewhat different – duplication not integration. The tendency of individual production ministries to develop their own transportation systems, the existence of separate ministries for each transportation sector, and the continuing dominance of the railways have left a transport system ill-equipped to meet the needs of a market economy.

The modal mix of the Russian transportation system reflects the priority attached to rapid industrialisation. The railways remain dominant. The dominance of heavy industry and ever-increasing distances between resource-producing and resource-consuming regions means that the railways remain the most logical means of meeting transport needs. Railways are also well suited to the harsh Russian climate, traversing regions where road building would be prohibitively expensive.

In 1990 the railways accounted for only 34 per cent of total Russian freight in terms of tonnage, but 55 per cent of total ton/kilometres. Automobile transport, by comparison, accounted for 46.5 per cent of total tonnage, but only 1.5 per cent of ton/kilometres. The average hauling distance in the Soviet Union in the late-1980s was 950 kilometres for rail and 20 kilometres for road. These statistics suggest that the railways monopolise long-distance hauls and that most road hauls are short distance. The oil and gas pipeline system is also a major carrier, accounting, in 1990, for 8.8 per cent of total tonnage and 27.5 per cent of total ton/kilometres. This reflects the fact that the major oil and gas producing regions are in West Siberia, a great distance from major markets in European Russia and export markets in Europe. The spectacular development of the West Siberian oil and gas fields resulted in the 1970s in the construction of the world's largest pipeline system. In 1970 the average hauling distance by pipeline in the Soviet Union was 80 kilometres; by 1988 it had increased to 2350 kilometres.

## RAIL

According to the IMF report on the Soviet economy, more than half of the world's railway freight (by ton/kilometres) and more than 25 per cent of its railway passenger kilometres were carried by the USSR Ministry of Railways. The Ministry has now been broken up and Russia now controls its own railways, but has also inherited all the problems. The railways have been operating at close to capacity and are suffering from neglect. They are now seeking Western investment to help them modernise; for example, a high speed rail link is to be developed between Moscow and St Petersburg. However, many of the less glamorous lines in Siberia and the Russian Far East, in particular the Baikal–Amur mainline, will continue to be very costly to maintain. If the Russian economy succeeds in restructuring and the share of heavy industry declines, the railways may soon find themselves short of customers. At present the collapse of inter-republic trade has already led to a reduction in freight movements (down 8–10 per cent during 1991).

## ROAD

While the railways have been controlled by Moscow, road transport was the responsibility of republican-level ministries. This helps to explain the relative neglect of the road system, particularly long-

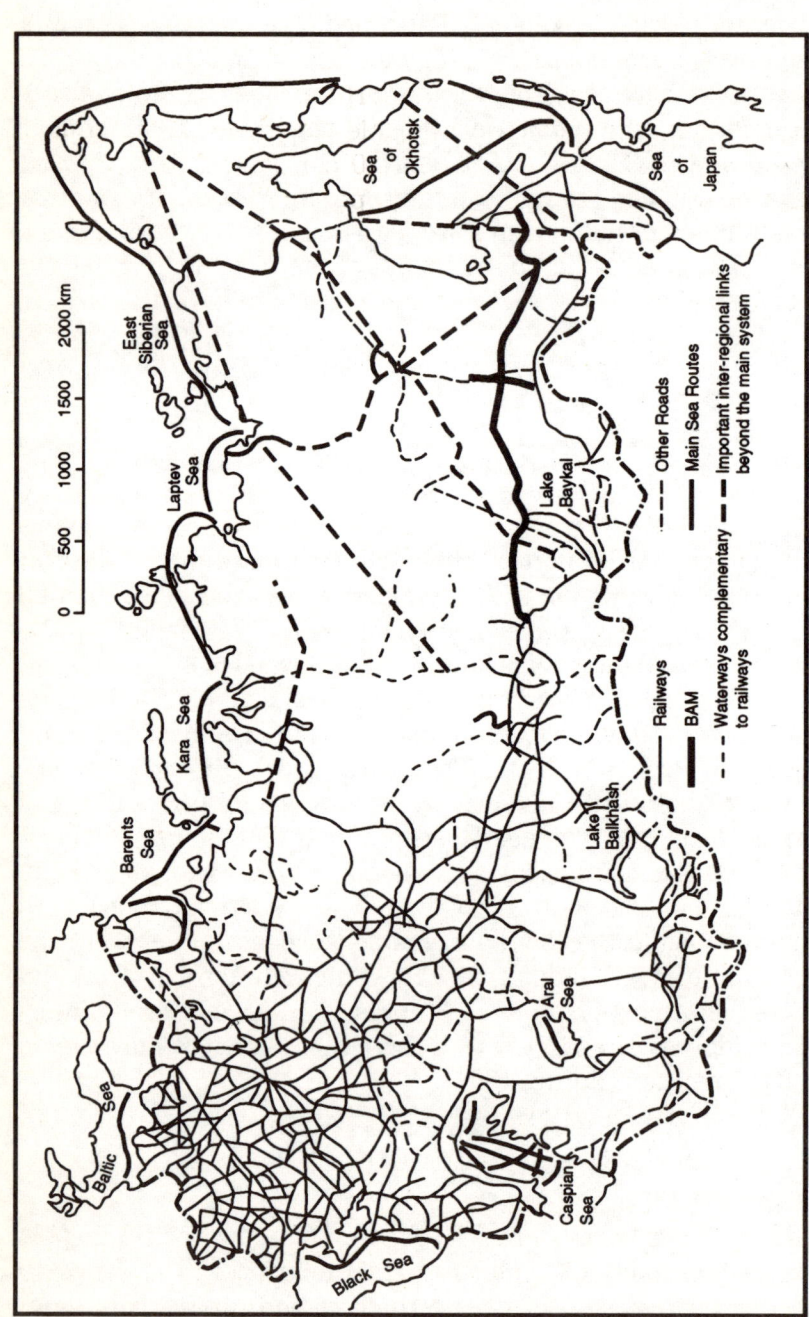

* BAM = Baikal – Amur mainline railway

**Map 22.1** *Transportation system in Russia*

Source: Bater, J H (1989) *The Soviet Scene*, Edward Arnold, London, p237.

distance haulage. In the late 1980s, the total length of the road network in the USSR was 1,586,416 kilometres, in the US the network was 6,233,308 kilometres and in the UK 352,292 kilometres. In 1988 Russia had a road network of 849,500 thousand kilometres, 619,800 thousand kilometres (73 per cent) of which was paved. A low level of car ownership means that most of the population relies upon the public transportation system. Most enterprises run their own freight operations, but the vehicles available to them are outdated, inefficient and unreliable. Only about 10 per cent of the trucks are specifically designed for cold weather operations.

## AIR

Prior to the break up of the Soviet Union, Aeroflot was the world's largest single network. It is now not only breaking up into new 'state' airlines, it also faces the prospect of international competition on internal routes and a radical shake-up of the aviation industry that supplied its aircraft. There are now a number of Western joint ventures providing specialist air services for Western customers operating in the former Soviet Union and Western companies are also interested in investing in the Russian aerospace industry.

Aeroflot carried 132 million passengers in 1989. At that time the airline was still divided into 31 regional departments, paralleled by the regional directorates of the USSR Ministry of Civil Aviation, responsible for the 200 or so airports used by Aeroflot. Despite this extensive network, Aeroflot was unable to satisfy passenger demand – every year 30 to 40 million requests for domestic airline tickets could not be satisfied. As with the road vehicle park, the aircraft at Aeroflot's disposal are outdated. Soviet aircraft are two to three times less fuel efficient than their modern Western counterparts. Such inefficiencies could be ignored when fuel was plentiful and cheap. Now the price of fuel in Russia is soaring and is in short supply. Spare parts are also hard to find and many airports are littered with cannibalised aircraft (it has been suggested that only 40 per cent of former Aeroflot aircraft are still operational). The airline system is desperately in need of modernisation.

## WATERBORNE TRANSPORT

Merchant shipping and inland river transport are of limited significance to the Russian economy: first, because the policies of self-sufficiency have tended to reduce participation in international trade; second, because many of the rivers run north–south, while the dominant traffic flows have tended to be east–west; and finally, because the harsh climate means that the rivers are frozen for long periods. From the 1960s onwards there was a gradual opening up of the Soviet economy; increased participation in foreign trade and the support of client states in the Third World increased the need for merchant shipping. On 1 January 1989, the Soviet Maritime Shipping Companies owned 2827 vessels totalling 22.8 million dwt.

None of the ports in the former Soviet Union is particularly large and they have tended to concentrate on general cargo and bulk goods, reflecting the structure of Soviet foreign trade. There is a low level of containerisation (this is true of the entire transport system). Russia now finds itself dependent upon ports in other newly independent states, such as the oil terminal of Ventspils in Latvia. This will lead to the expansion of facilities at St Petersburg providing access to the Baltic, Novorossiysk in the Black Sea and Nakhodka-Vladivostok on the Pacific coast.

During the Soviet period a great deal of money was spent, in large part for strategic reasons, to expand operations along the northern sea route. The western sector is now kept open year-round using nuclear-powered icebreakers. The eastern sector has a limited navigation season, but provides a vital link to mining settlements in the Russian north. It is difficult to see how these high cost operations will survive marketisation. The nuclear icebreakers now spend much of their time taking Western tourists to the North Pole!

For a country the size of Russia, an efficient transport system is crucial to economic prosperity. It is clear that Russia's transport system is in trouble and in desperate need of modernisation. It is to be hoped that the inadequacies of the system will not act as a barrier to economic restructuring and marketisation.

# 23

# Telecommunications

## *CIT Research Ltd*

Russia *should* be on the verge of a telecommunications boom. But that is cold comfort to the thousands of western businesses, large and small, currently trying to cope with the totally inadequate telephone system. Not to mention their Russian trading partners, for whom easy access to one of the basic tools of commerce – telecommunications – remains difficult and costly.

With the demise of Soviet central control, telecommunications, along with other utilities, is now the responsibility of each republic. This means, in theory at least, that each of the new states has a separate infrastructure and range of services. In practice, of course, because these have been designed and operated centrally for decades, it will be a while before any of the republics can reconfigure their networks to exploit their new autonomy. Russia (and more importantly Moscow) is, then, in a fortunate position in having been the hub of the old system, in terms of both the CIS and the Russian Federation.

The ministers responsible in each state have established a Regional Communications Committee, to ensure the continued co-ordination of both postal and telecoms services. Dr Bulgak, who is the Russian Telecommunications Minister, is the current chairman of the RCC.

The Russian Federation is due to enact new telecommunications legislation – part of its complete overhaul of the body of laws inherited from the former Soviet Union. Until this legislation is ready, the industry is governed by the terms of a general decree (dated September 1991). This makes all telecoms activities subject to the regulation of the Ministry of Communications, Information Science and Space. Anyone wishing to provide a service must hold a licence from the Ministry, which has issued a two-page application form for a communications licence.

At the moment, the Ministry is all powerful in Russian telecommunications. But, in the extremely fluid political conditions, it is tending to produce new regulations as it deems necessary, and some of these may subsequently be found to be of dubious legality.

Centralisation of decision making in Moscow is also creating considerable bottle-necks in settling telecoms disputes which would previously have been sorted out locally.

There are not, as yet, any moves towards the constitutional separation of telecoms *regulation* from telecoms *operation*, as there have been in Western Europe. In practice, there is some effective separation, as various operating entities of the telecoms ministry take part in joint ventures to partner US and European companies entering the market. If Russia wishes eventually to become a member of the EC, it may try to develop its telecoms service industry in line with the policies advocated by the EC Green Paper on telecoms. On the other hand, its geography and size, plus the fact that much of the current investment in telecoms is coming from the US, may mean that it leans more towards the American framework for regulating the provision of services.

## NETWORK AND SERVICE DEVELOPMENTS

### Local telephone systems

At the start of 1992 there were about 33,500 local exchanges in the Russian Federation, with a total capacity of about 22 million numbers. Most of these are on crossbar exchanges (roughly 15 million numbers or 70 per cent of exchange capacity). Work on introducing digital transmission has been going on since 1986, and about half the transmission system is now digital. However, only a small proportion of the lines between local exchanges and trunk switching centres are fibre optic. About 30 per cent of telephones installed are in businesses (6.5 million telephones versus 15 million in homes in 1992). The Ministry reports an increase of 1 million lines during 1992, slightly exceeding its stated target of 800,000. There are about 15 phone lines per 100 of the population. At a household level, about 25 per cent of homes have telephones, though urban areas are obviously much better served than rural ones. There is a waiting list for residential telephones of over 10 million.

As of 1 June 1992 tariffs were increased for Moscow's 400,000 telephone subscribers. Installation charges for domestic customers went up to R3000 and the monthly line rental increased to R42, while for businesses the increase was R120,000 and R1500 (for international direct dial) respectively.

Besides those in homes and businesses, there are about 225,000 public telephones in Russia, but only 20 per cent of these can handle long distance calls. Call boxes are inclined to be fault prone, partly because of people's attempts to force the wrong coins into the slots – possibly a result of shortage of metal coinage (a familiar problem in all hyperinflationary economies). The charge is currently 15 kopecks, but this is due to be increased, and tokens may also be introduced.

All of this adds up to a rather modest telecoms provision for a large population. A fact well recognised by the telecommunications ministry. It has announced plans to install about 40 million new exchange lines in the years up to 2000, and to replace all remaining step-by-step exchanges with digital ones in the same period. All of this, of course, depends on finding the large investment required.

Still, there are projects afoot. Most of these concentrate on the Moscow metropolitan area, and target foreign businesses and the diplomatic community requiring international direct dialling services. While this does little to improve the situation for under-communicated Russian businesses and households, it does at least ease things for the staff of overseas companies, making contact with their home base less frustrating and time consuming.

A new commercial telecoms service has been launched by Comstar, the Russian-British joint venture between GPT (with financial support from the UK government) and the Moscow Telecommunications Network. On-demand voice, fax and datacoms are available for the first time over the same network following the launch of a new Business Services Digital Overlay Network.

In addition the Comstar joint venture has established a prepaid and credit card payphone network in Moscow, initially targeting the main tourist areas. Comstar aims to have 100,000 phone lines by the end of the decade. Rouble revenues are being reinvested in a factory which will begin making telephone handsets next year.

Another digital overlay network has been established by Newbridge Soviet Telecom (a joint venture between Newbridge Networks and Moscow Telephone Company). Newbridge plans similar ventures in Minsk (Belarus) and St Petersburg.

Sovintel, a collaboration between MTLCC (Main Trunk Lines Control Centre of the Russian Telecoms Ministry) and Sovinet (itself a joint venture between GTE and San Francisco/Moscow Teleport), has yet another digital overlay network using a combination of microwave, fibre optic and satellite transmission technology to bypass the existing Moscow telephone network.

Macomnet (a joint venture between Andrew Corporation and Moscow Metro) will use the metro infrastructure to establish quickly a fibre optic network in key areas of Moscow. Operating as a 'carrier's carrier', it will provide a managed digital transport service using Northern Telecom SDH equipment. Early availability of the Nortel equipment is enabling Macomnet to start operation of the network in Spring 1993.

In a more grandiose project, the Russian government has announced a fibre optic communications network in the Moscow area. Named the Integrated Communications Network (ICN), it will support a switched digital network offering voice, data and cable TV services. The network, which will be domestically constructed using Russian manufactured equipment, will cost an estimated R8 billion, and will be controlled by Moscow Telecoms Company (MTC), which will act as a holding company. The first lines were due to be installed at the end of 1992, and construction is expected to take five years to complete. The government has (with the help of private investors) provided R3 billion of start up capital. The Moscow network will, it is hoped, be linked to a network of high capacity fibre trunks which will connect the Baltic area in the north with Nakhodka in the east, and extend as far as the Crimea (Ukraine) in the south. A memorandum of understanding has been signed by Russia's Intertelecom, KDD of Japan, Korea Telecom, and two Danish telecommunications companies which will be involved in providing parts of these main trunks.

Elsewhere in Russia, local access to telephone services is even more archaic than in Moscow. Other places do not enjoy the density of overseas residents and businesses that can provide the initial support to telecoms infrastructure investment. However, there is some progress. St Petersburg and Minsk have been targeted by Newbridge for digital overlay networks for large customers. Also, the free zone of Kaliningrad has attracted France Telecom, which has contracted with Zimland Telekom to help modernise the telephone network there. Yakutsk, in north eastern Siberia, has also announced a major telecoms upgrade, ordering 10,000 lines from Ericsson.

### Fibre optic trunk systems

Most of the long distance network in Russia is still using analogue transmission systems. There are few, if any, fibre trunks. In addition to copper wire and microwave, the Russians make considerable use of satellite communications, on the Molniya and Gorizont (Horizon) systems.

Some 1.2 billion trunk calls are made annually. About three-quarters of these are connected automatically. There are extensive plans to install fibre optic trunk circuits between major cities in Russia, but these have not yet been implemented due to lack of investment and CoCom restrictions. The latter have now been eased, and exports of fibre technology will be allowed for domestic Russian systems of up to 156 megabits per second.

At present, only 1 per cent of total telephone calls in Russia are international (40 million annually, most made by government officials or staff of foreign companies). They use a combination of wireline and satellite links. The sole international exchange in Moscow (capacity 1500 circuits) is to be supplemented with new exchanges in St Petersburg and Vladivostok.

Among the long distance cable projects, the one that has attracted most publicity – TSL or Trans-Soviet Line – was led by US West. A second consortium, comprising 10 Russian financial and other institutions, is planning its own transnational fibre optic cable link. The 'Russian TSL' plan is to use mostly home-made equipment (saving on cost), though the hope is to use Western equipment in about 25 per cent to 30 per cent of the project. Construction of the first 100 kilometres of the line is scheduled to take place in April and May of 1993, running between Moscow and either Novgorod or Samara.

Overseas investors have turned their attentions to constructing the fibre links into Russia from various parts of the world. A new submarine fibre link is under construction between Copenhagen and Kingisepp (in the St Petersburg region), provided in a joint venture between Telecom Denmark and Great Nordic. Simultaneously, new switching centres are being constructed, along with a digital microwave relay line between Kingisepp and St Petersburg, and St Petersburg and Moscow.

Deutsche Bundespost Telekom's plan for a US$60 million fibre trunk between Germany and Russia initially had problems with CoCom rules on laser technology. The cable, known as TEL (Trans-European Line), should run between Frankfurt and Moscow, with possible spurs to other East European countries. Italy, too, is building a combined overland and submarine fibre optic link from Moscow to Palermo via Istanbul. Two international gateways are to be installed in Moscow and Rostov.

KDD, Korea Telecom and two Danish telecoms companies in collaboration with Russian long distance carrier, Intertelecom, are also laying high-speed high-capacity optical fibre links between Khabarovsk, Japan and Korea. The project could be complete by 1995 and could cost ¥20 billion (US$150 million). The existing cable between Japan and Russia, established in 1969, has a capacity equivalent to only 60 lines.

### Satellite systems

On the satellite front, the commitment of the former Soviet Union to the space race in the 1960s and 1970s gave it a formidable base of rocket and spacecraft technology. Satellite is therefore one of the few communications sectors where Russian enterprises can be said to parallel Western operations, at the technical, if not at the marketing level.

The Minister of the telecoms ministry for the Russian Federation, Valdamir Bulgak, is keen to see expansion of the satellite capacity serving the Russian Federation, citing 'the low level of terrestrial infrastructure development'. While rejecting proposals for massive new 18-tonne Polyot platforms, he has supported the development of new generations of smaller communications satellites. Satellites are used for communication between Moscow and republican, territorial and regional centres. Since 1980, the geostationary Horizon (Gorizont) satellites have been put into operation. About 70 per cent of all satellite channels are currently used for communications inside Russia. This system at present has little support for any possible mobile-based applications. The Gorizont series carries domestic and international TV as well as telecoms.

Intersputnik is offering low prices in an attempt to build up its customer base. The organisation has undergone a major transformation in the last three years. In 1991 it adopted dollars for its bookkeeping, and then used part of its earnings to establish a new capital base of US$1.5 million. It is looking to recruit new members other than the existing current and former communist countries. Intersputnik leases Gorizont satellites from the Russian government to provide telephone, television and data transmission services to its members and other customers. Both AT&T and CNN have used the service whilst DBP Telekom uses the membership that used to belong to East Germany. Intersputnik is an international body and not a Russian one. It is now offering entire transponders covering either Europe or Asia from as little as US$1.25 million for a five-year contract. A new generation of satellites, the Express model (more stable than Gorizont), will be available from 1994. Intersputnik will have total control over 20 transponders on the two Express satellites, and hopes to be able to attract business clients who use small satellite dishes.

An interesting collaborative venture in this area is SovCanStar, which includes Canadian partners. The principal Russian partner, NPO-PM, will provide two self contained platforms, based on the existing Loutch design, while the communications payload will be provided by the Canadians. To be positioned at 145 degrees east and 14 degrees west in 1995/96, they will offer both Pacific and Atlantic coverage – though the latter slot is not ideal for the US eastern seaboard, as the angle of the beam is rather low and the operators would prefer a more westerly location.

In another satellite space segment venture, ANT (part of Bosch), MBB (Daimler Benz), Dornier (also part of Daimler Benz) and DBP Telekom set up a project in 1991 under the name Romantis. It envisaged three communications satellites to provide three million telephone lines and possibly TV transmissions. The satellites would be built in Germany and launched in Russia.

Another system has been announced recently which envisages three satellites with combined coverage of the CIS and Asia-Pacific regions. Partners here include a Hong Kong consortium, GIS, a Philippines company, and a Russian company, NPO-Lovochkin. It is not clear whether the latter is a rival to, or a part of, NPO-PM.

There is no doubt that communications channels to and from the CIS will expand substantially, with satellite providing interim solutions as terrestrial networks and cable systems are developed. However, with the possible lengthy time-frames involved in the rollout of wireline systems, the importance of satellite may well be sustained, especially as new mobile networks penetrate undeveloped telecoms markets.

### Long distance and international telephone services

Intertelecom is the Russian long distance carrier, but it has been facing some difficulties recently with the political changes. Made up of the long distance carriers of the constituent republics, it now finds some of its members reluctant to continue funding the organisation, since each republic now has autonomy over its telecoms provision. With the republics now providing their own links, the accounting and billing structure between republics is confused and uncertain. Intertelecom's joint venture with Cable & Wireless (C&W) (see below) may provide a lifeline in these troubled waters.

To increase the availability of international circuits, US West is financing and operating three new international gateway digital switching systems, with equipment built by a Croatian firm, Nikola Tesla, under licence from Ericsson. The three switches are being installed in Moscow, St Petersburg and Kiev (Ukraine), and were due on stream by the end of 1992. US West's investment is relatively modest, at US$18 million over two years. However, the company will receive 16 per cent of the revenues switched through the systems for 15 years of operation. The new switches will add 23,000 circuits (15,000 in Moscow and 4000 each in St Petersburg and Kiev) to the 1200 existing international circuits from Moscow.

Meanwhile, a number of joint ventures have been established to service the fast growing demand for long distance and international telephony. Table 23.1 gives brief details of the main long distance and international services available or planned in Russia.

### Telegraph/telex and data communications

Russia has an extensive telegraph network. It is primarily used for document exchange between state offices (with an estimated 180,000 organisations connected), plus other state organisations and enterprises. In 72 Russian cities the system is interconnected into the international telex network, but all of this traffic must currently go via Moscow.

Still, this apparently crude network has formed the platform for a joint venture between Sprint and the Russian telecommunications ministry, providing datacommunications based on X.25 packet switching. Services offered include transactional communications and credit card verification for retailers (mainly hard currency stores).

C&W may also become a significant player in data networking via its Sovam joint venture, with the Russian IAS and SFMT in California. Sovam Teleport (a joint venture between IAS and SFMT) has been sending data from Moscow since 1984. Customers include news organisations, Coca Cola, Du Pont and Barclays Bank. C&W's limited £4 million investment should cover the cost of upgrading transmission facilities and expanding into other CIS cities. The new joint venture is offering electronic messaging and packet switched data services.

France Telecom, via Transpac, has set up a joint venture (Sovpac) with the Ministry and PEPI, an association of transport companies. The aim was to develop an X.25 network and operate related value

**Table 23.1**    Principal long distance and international telephone services

| Name | Owners/joint venture partners | Services offered |
|---|---|---|
| Metropolitan Communications | Intertelecom 50% Cable & Wireless 50% | Currently examining the communications feasibility of long distance and international telecoms within the Tyumen oblast (Russia's major oil field), the 'Golden Ring' of towns surrounding Moscow, Moscow itself and St Petersburg |
| EDN Sovintel | MTLCC (Main Lines Trunk Control/Russian Ministry) 50% Sovinet 50% (Sovinet is a joint venture between GTE International Services Corp and San Francisco/Moscow Teleport Inc) | International direct dial services in Moscow via a new international gateway switch – capacity 20,000 simultaneous calls. Service points are Expocenter and four of the main international hotels in Moscow. Sovintel is making use of the Iskra military network (fee for connection c US$600) |
| Vostoktelecom | Interdaltelecom 25% KDD 37.5% Nisho Iwai Corp 37.5% | International direct dial service between far Eastern Russia and Japan via satellite. Coverage will include Vladivostok, Khabarovsk, Yuzhno-Sakhalinsk, Irkutsk and Yakutsk, offering direct links between these cities as well. The service is targeting Japanese government institutions and Japanese corporations |
| Astelit | Astra (Russian) 50% Italcable 25% Telespazio 25% | International direct dial services via satellite. The service currently links the Moscow business centre, Tecnopark, with the earth station at Fucino, near Rome. A similar service is planned for St Petersburg |
| Combellga | Comincom (Russian) 69% RTT and Alcatel-Bell Telephone combined 31% | International direct dial service in Moscow |
| Comstar | GPT Moscow Telecom Network | International direct dial service in Moscow |
| Baltic Communications | C&W 40% SFMT 3 regional telcos (St Peterburg) | International direct dial service in St Petersburg |

added services. The experimental network had a Transpac node in Moscow and four concentrators in St Petersburg, Riga (Latvia), Odessa (Ukraine) and Vladivostok.

An MCI Communications gateway for the city of Ekaterinburg is being marketed by local company AEA. The AEA Information System is a package of services including electronic adverts, electronic catalogue shopping and E-mail, and will be offered over the country's telegraph lines. So far, the network has around 200 subscribers in 50 cities in the CIS.

Russian-based Infokom offers 2400-baud data links from Moscow via a leased line to Finland, where it connects with the Infonet world-wide managed network service. Another company, Relcom, uses the same route through Finland to offer international datacommunications services. It has created a 'network of networks' with over 50,000 users, rather like the much larger US-based Internet operation. E-mail services can also be obtained via Glasnet, an offshoot of the Institute for Global Communications, which will accept payment in roubles.

### Mobile communications

Until the advent of new cellular networks, there were only about 20,000 users of radio telephones in the entire country, using the Altai system, available in 90 Russian cities. New cellular ventures have been established in Moscow and St Petersburg, usually by the local telephone companies in partnership with firms like Nokia, Bell Atlantic, Belle Mead, Millicom and US West. These were among the first ventures in Russia to attract Western investors, targeting the market formed by the staff of overseas companies trying to establish trading ventures in the CIS. These users can pay dollars, and are desperate to get access to a reliable telephone service, as often as not using the cellphones from their desks rather than in mobile mode.

The two operational services in Moscow (MSS and AMT) are analogue and use the 450MHz band. Nokia and Moscow Telephone Network (MGTS), under the joint venture company AMT, opened the first public mobile telephone network in 1991. The rival MSS consortium consists of Moscow City Telephone Network, US West, Millicom, Eye Microsurgery and the State Communications Design Institute.

St Petersburg's system, Delta Telecom, has 2000 subscribers with an ultimate capacity of about 50,000. The system connects directly to an international gateway switch, allowing customers to dial international calls more easily than via the regular telephone network.

The Russian Ministry of Railways is setting up a cellular telephone network based on its extensive hard-wired network and radio relay stations. Existing radio relay facilities will be used as nodes in the planned cellular system. The preliminary stage of the project has been completed.

The military still has a significant influence over telecommunications projects in the CIS. Until recently, frequencies in the 800MHz range were reserved for military and civil aviation purposes. Applications to provide 800MHz cellular services in Moscow were rejected outright by the ministry on this account. But in May 1992, a state-owned company, Vimpel, announced it had been awarded a licence to test a cellular service at around 850MHz conforming to the AMPS standard. Vimpel is a major supplier to the military. The licence is only experimental, but if tests demonstrate that interference is not a problem, the company expects to receive a full licence soon. Vimpel has formed Euronet, a 50/50 joint venture with a US company, Plexsys International, to build the network.

### Equipment supply

Telecoms equipment in Russia – whether infrastructure or customer handsets, etc – is, not surprisingly, antiquated by most Western standards. A major programme of upgrading has now started, though to date this has tended to be a 'cherry picking' exercise (concentrating on a few key areas of high traffic) rather than a clearly thought out strategic investment plan.

AT&T has a joint venture to supply digital transmission equipment to improve domestic and international long distance links in Russia. AT&T describes the initial investment as 'relatively small, a few million dollars'. Siemens, too, has set up two joint ventures to manufacture digital telephone exchanges. Alcatel is expected to start manufacture of digital exchanges in Russia in 1993 or 1994.

Minnesota Mining & Manufacturing Co (3M) has formed a joint venture with a Russian telephone equipment maker and the Russian government to produce wire connectors and other telecoms products in St Petersburg. The US company's investment exceeds US$10 million.

Northern Telecom has received its first order, valued at just under US$1 million, for Synchronous Digital Hierarchy (SDH) transmission equipment in Russia.

## OUTLOOK

In all, Russian telecoms has already come a long way. The last three years have seen almost as much movement as the previous 20. But with several major Western players committing to service and applications ventures, plus long-term funding from the London-based European Bank for Reconstruction and Development, the market could now really take off. There is enormous potential for equipment sales. Some sources put the figure as high as US$20 billion a year by the end of the decade. Perhaps about 20 per cent of this will be imported, with the rest manufactured in Russia and other CIS republics, mostly under joint ventures.

Estimates of current (1992) annual service revenues run to some US$20 billion equivalent. This may seem high, but represents only 15 per cent of the comparable value of the business in the US and 10 per cent of that in Western Europe. By the year 2000, however, it may all look rather different. To build a modern telecoms service industry, with all the advanced, high added value services we are used to in much of the West, you need large numbers of heavy telecommunications users. In practice this means banks, insurance and other financial services, plus major retailing, transport, travel and hotel chains. With the growth of these sorts of enterprises, demand – particularly for mobile and datacommunications, as well as for long distance and international services – will expand strongly.

In real terms the service market could more than quadruple by the end of the decade. An annual equivalent figure of approaching US$100 billion might thus be achieved. Most Western companies have invested in international gateway exchanges, as these are potentially the most lucrative, though some people feel the investment may be profitable only in the short term. Companies willing to service the Russian domestic market, and to commit for the long run, could well win out in the end.

As for users, the infrastructure is, as yet, wholly inadequate to meet the demand. As with all markets, the new operators are 'cream skimming' in the early days. Unless you are a big user with a regular requirement, and can afford to make your own arrangements with one of the new Western-backed companies, you can expect to try, try and try again. You should also pray that the party you're trying to reach is at the other end when you finally do get through!

*Part III*

# Options for Western Companies

# 24

# Strategies for Market Entry

## *KPMG Peat Marwick McLintock*

In a trading context, of all the countries of Eastern Europe, the former Soviet Union is usually considered the most difficult. The obstacles are as daunting as the opportunities are challenging: the distribution system is chaotic; the infrastructure is deficient; the currency is not fully convertible; the banking system is collapsing; the economy and productivity are in decline; and inflation is galloping. Doing business can be a test of patience and a drain on resources.

Despite these difficulties, UK companies, both small and large, have found new markets for their products and new sources for goods and raw materials. They have also made, to a limited extent, investment commitments. The sheer size and potential wealth of Russia continues to attract newcomers and keep the old hands working at the pump. Between January and November 1992, UK trade with the former USSR (excluding the Baltics) was as follows: exports (FOB) £404 million and imports (FOB) £604 million (source: East European Trade Council). These figures are, of course, a poor reflection of trading levels reached prior to the break-up of the Soviet system, but indicate that the market is not dead.

In the telecommunications sector, GPT has recently won a $45 million contract to supply System X digital exchange equipment for the Moscow telecommunications network – a network desperately in need of modernisation in view of the current two to three year wait for a telephone line on applying through the normal channels.

British Airways has taken a 31 per cent participation in Air Russia. Air Russia is set to provide an air service between Western Europe and the Far East via Moscow from 1994, provided a reputed US$85 million financing package involving the World Bank and the EBRD is finalised. These routes are regarded as having tremendous potential.

Despite the current economic and political situation, companies dare not risk holding back when their competitors are moving in. BAT Industries has recently opened joint venture negotiations with Yava, Moscow's largest cigarette factory and is looking at two further Russian cigarette plants with joint ventures in mind. It simply cannot allow Philip Morris or RJ Reynolds to steal the show – possibly for good. The same thinking applies to Coca-Cola's reputed $12 million investment into the Russian market to regain lost ground from its arch rival, Pepsi Cola.

Of course, it is much harder to win market share when the market is mature than when it is in the process of being created. There is a 'window of opportunity' and the opportunities need to be investigated to properly assess the risks involved.

## TRADING

The Soviet Union never ranked as a giant in international trade. Trading between the UK and what was the Soviet Union suffered a 40 per cent fall between 1990 and 1991. There are no figures available for Russia alone, but trade will suffer further declines as prior trading relations within the Soviet Union and Comecon, based more on administrative convenience than from sound economic relations and are now collapsing. New trading relationships will provide a springboard to future investments, allowing insights on potential partners, the quality of their goods and their reliability.

A number of possibilities exist:

- trading through ex Foreign Trade Organisations (FTOs);

- trading with Russian companies directly;

- trading with joint ventures which is becoming a substantial factor in the trading market;

- selling to companies opening hard currency shops in big cities: there are about 200 hundred such shops in Moscow alone, although however the new Prime Minister, Mr Chernomyrdin, has expressed a clear wish to eliminate internal trade in dollars in Russia.

The future of the FTOs is uncertain but because of their experience in the international trade arena, a high proportion of trade still goes through them. They are changing fast with regard to the products they handle and the services they offer. Many are being transformed into joint stock companies.

### Direct sales to Russia

Businessmen have a vision of a market starved of consumer and other goods. However, without banks, insurance companies, trade financing possibilities and a clear legal framework, transactions are difficult. The majority of exports is considered uninsurable and where cover is offered, it is on very restrictive terms. The effects of liberalisation of foreign trade were somewhat offset by the imposition of heavy export tariffs, and although there are enterprises with hard currency to spend, it is difficult to identify them. Small amounts of currency are sold through auctions to finance imports. However, as compulsory sales of hard currency begin to bite, opportunities may be reduced even further. A move to greater convertibility would open up the field.

Think about the cost of setting up a country-wide dealership. Check the distribution and transport arrangements. Make sure your distributor or agent is able to deliver. Also investigate the possibilities of having your product put on the priority lists of imports with the Ministries. Remember that CoCom restrictions still apply to Russia and that export licences may be required for some high-tech exports.

## MARKETING

Although it may seem obvious, it should be pointed out that, because Russia is only now beginning to develop a market infrastructure for its economy, the process of marketing a product there is something of an unpredictable exercise. The kind of considerations on which companies base their marketing policies in developed market economies either do not yet apply or simply cannot be gauged. It is still the case, to a great extent, that consumers have to go and find goods and not the other way round. However the experience of many Western firms supplying consumer goods to Russia is that promoting product awareness can prove very advantageous. In this connection mounting some form of an advertising campaign and participating in trade fairs can play an important role.

Russia's embryonic advertising industry is still very much finding its feet, and many campaigns are extremely amateur compared to those launched in developed market economies. This is partly due to lack of experience and partly, of course, because the economy remains largely monopolised – therefore for many enterprises a sophisticated marketing drive is simply not necessary. However, Western influences are already having an impact, and there can be no doubt that the standard of advertisements in Russia is now improving rapidly.

None the less, it seems unlikely that many private advertising agencies will emerge for some time yet. The main body which specialises in providing such services to the import-export sector is the state-owned Sovero concern. This organisation helps in the marketing both of Russian goods abroad and of foreign goods imported into Russia. Either independently or through Russian marketing firms, Sovero gathers data, conducts research and provides the materials necessary to assist its clients in marketing their products or services.

### Trade fairs

One of the most important inlets into Russia for Western business-men is participation in trade fairs and, even if not personally exhibiting, merely visiting can bring about useful contacts in specific industries. Unlike other East European countries which endeavour to cover all economic sectors in one event, Russia concentrates on specialised events.

The former Soviet Union's largest exhibition centre was the Exhibition of Economic Achievements (VDNKh). However, in view of the transition to a market economy, this exhibition centre is to be transformed into an open joint stock society. It has been decided that the centre will remain a state institution, on account of its unique historical and cultural value, but the portion of its shares held by the Federation cannot be less than 51 per cent.

It is believed that this centre will be the largest not only in Russia but in the world, accommodating trading houses, stock exchanges, commercial banks and trade fairs. These reflect both regional and sectoral interests.

Numerous exhibitions, conferences and trade fairs are held regularly, mostly in Moscow and St Petersburg, although increasingly in other major towns in Russia as well (see Appendix 3).

## IMPORTING FROM RUSSIA

Companies and individuals are now free to trade directly but there is not much experience nor many marketable goods on offer. Most of the goods which are attractive to Western buyers, such as commodities, are those that require licences. Enterprises, operating as they were in a vacuum, have little knowledge of competing

Western products or of Western market requirements. The quality of the product is often poor and so is the packaging. Timeliness of deliveries may also be an issue. Transport arrangements and export licences should be checked.

## Countertrade

Given the absence of a convertible rouble and the shortage of hard currency, countertrade is a possibility to be explored. Past deals involving Western companies have included spare parts for whole vehicles, shoes for oil, consumer goods for timber products and soft drinks for vodka. If you are offered payment through a countertrade arrangement, find out if the goods on offer face market restrictions in the West, such as import quotas as well as export restrictions. Countertrade deals can be extremely complex and, if you are dealing with goods with which you have no previous experience, or if you don't want to make use of them yourself, it is advisable to seek advice or use a trading house.

## Representatives

Representative offices are not entitled to conduct trade on their own behalf – their purpose is to handle business on behalf of the parent company. A representative office is not therefore for those who want to set up an independent operation on the Russian market. It remains an attractive option for foreign companies which service the foreign community, such as banks and insurance companies or to test market with the possibility of transforming it into a 100 per cent owned company at a later stage.

## Projects

Exports of capital goods and projects to Russia may be dependent upon the provision of finance in the form of officially supported export credits. ECGD (the UK government department which provides guarantees to facilitate the provision of finance for such exports) has only a limited capacity to cover business in Russia and such cover is intended to be devoted primarily to substantial projects which will be self-financing in hard currency terms. During President Yeltsin's visit to London in November 1992, certain projects were identified as priorities for ECGD support. Assuming these go ahead they will utilise most of the available cover. The prospects of ECGD support for other projects are not good.

## AID PROGRAMMES

A number of programmes for providing finance to assist Russia's economic transformation have been initiated over the last few years. These are targeted mostly at core sectors (food distribution, energy, transport, communications, financial services, human resources and support to small enterprises) on the basis that a properly functioning infrastructure is necessary if capital investment throughout the economy is to be attracted.

The European Bank for Reconstruction and Development (EBRD) was founded specifically to work for the promotion of democratic market economies in Eastern Europe. As a hybrid of a merchant and development bank, support can be offered both to private sector and infrastructure projects. Finance is provided on a commercial basis through loans, equity or guarantees and underwriting, and the minimum funding required of the bank must be ECU5 million.

Proposals submitted to the EBRD should demonstrate the following:

- good market prospects;

- significant capital commitment;

- reliable technology;

- improved competitiveness;

- high investment returns;

- sound financial basis of the borrowing enterprise;

- environmental viability.

The International Bank for Reconstruction and Development (IBRD) is part of the World Bank, the largest global aid organisation. The IBRD provides funding to specific chosen infrastructure projects, involving the conclusion of contracts for specific products or services with individual suppliers. In the last few years the East European countries have become increasingly important in the World Bank's activities, and Russia became a member during 1992. Accordingly, a number of projects in Russia can be expected in the coming years.

Another agency of the World Bank is the International Finance Corporation (IFC). This organisation provides funding, usually in the form of share capital, to private ventures in developing countries among its members. The IFC has become closely involved with the Russian privatisation process, assisting in the arrangement of pilot privatisation schemes in Nizhny Novgorod and Volgograd. This may lead in the long term to Russia's becoming a major target for IFC funding.

# INVESTING

Direct investment by foreigners in the eyes of Russians is preferable to importing as the government's ability to borrow from abroad has almost been exhausted and very little investment capital will be forthcoming from local sources. Foreign investment brings in new technologies and managerial expertise. The obstacles to investing are well known: the legislative framework is incomplete, contradictory and changes frequently. Several autonomous republics and regions have sought legislative independence and have enacted laws which conflict with federal laws and decrees. To this must be added the instability of fiscal policy and political volatility. The question of whether foreign investors can own land has yet to be resolved. There is no proper mechanism in place to protect investments, while the debt moratorium also severely restricts the number of financial institutions willing to invest in Russia.

Despite all of this, two reasons for investing are often put forward by existing investors: to establish share and get brands established before competitors do; and to take advantage of the low cost base for products destined to Western markets. The first reason will take time to materialise and, as for the second, the overhead costs may be lower but with import tariffs, export taxes and compulsory surrendering of currency, this may be a view which is fast becoming obsolete. In any event, objectives must fit within your overall strategy.

Investing is not just about identifying a good project or a particular need. Potential backers are risk-averse and hesitant. The few who are willing to do so insist on watertight schemes and viable projects with sufficient returns (for example, commodity production which will be sold on the world market). Not all opportunities involve distant and doubtful profits. Smaller firms may piggy back on larger projects and offer specialist services with good profit prospects involving little upfront investment.

Be systematic in your evaluation of opportunities. Do your homework and prepare a feasibility study and a proper financial analysis of the project. Think of environmental implications and of the domestic/export markets. Export markets are essential if you want to generate enough revenue for repatriation of profit purposes. Cut down on hard currency costs and find locally sourced inputs. If possible phase investment and in any event, seek proper advice.

### Joint venture?

Russian managers are very keen to establish joint ventures as a way of freeing themselves from state control and gaining access to Western technology, know-how and money. Until recently, Western companies could only make direct investments under the USSR 1987 Joint Venture Law which limited their participation to 49 per cent of the equity. Often, very little formal research is done and deals rely on chance encounters with managers of enterprises or a minister. But have a long hard look at the documentation that is available:

- Check whether the enterprise you are dealing with is state owned, a co-operative, or a municipal entity.

- Have a look at the enterprise's charter to see what is the company entitled to do and how it is managed.

- The registration forms will tell you who is entitled to sign on behalf of the enterprise.

- Check the terms on which the land, buildings and non-property rights, such as licences, have been granted to the enterprise concerned and that the company has been authorised to transfer them to the joint venture.

- Find facts from suppliers and local authorities which will help you determine the size of the company's inputs, and from its customers ascertain the quality of its products and its reliability.

Make sure that you are in agreement on interpreting historical information and that non-commercial considerations such as employment and the environment have been taken into account. Show an understanding of your potential partner's priorities, which may be different from the ones you set out to achieve, particularly if your objectives are weighted towards entering the Russian market rather than producing for export. The feasibility study must be understood by all participants in the joint venture. It should specify the timing and evaluation of capital contributions. This will help avoid one of the major problems which bring joint ventures into continuous conflict or even cause their termination. Clear all details before signing the deal.

### Wholly-owned subsidiaries?

The joint venture route is not for you if you are afraid of interference, intransigence from or being swindled by a potential partner. And a lot of the advantages given in favour of joint ventures such as local knowledge and market access are often overstated. Contacts may have gone and markets may have all disintegrated with the demise of the USSR. A number of companies which started out as joint ventures are buying out their partners.

But setting up a wholly-owned subsidiary does not preclude the need to understand local conditions. Make sure you hire staff who understand local demands and expectations as well as yours, who are familiar with official bodies, local authorities and suppliers and who can keep their ear to the ground for legal and regulatory changes.

### Buying a company through privatisation

The pace of acquisitions by foreign investors in Eastern Europe has mirrored the speed and efficiency of the privatisation procedures which have had a very limited scope in Russia. It is still unclear what role foreigners will be allowed to play. Various methods will be used for the disposal of various types of enterprises. These are open to foreigners except for small-scale enterprises where permission from the local council is required and defence, mineral and energy industries. If the method chosen to privatise a company includes a voucher auction, foreigners may purchase these on the secondary market.

Privatisations involving a foreign investor may be viewed as a hostile takeover by the management and work-force, intent on preserving jobs, in particular their own. This calls for open dialogue during the planning phase. Beware of the fact that assets tend to deteriorate in net value very rapidly before a sale takes place: assets are sold off and debts accumulate.

### Location

Moscow is the capital and therefore has attracted most attention. St Petersburg is Russia's largest port. Kaliningrad, Russia's only ice-free port on the Baltic is an enclave among what are now foreign countries. Free trade zones are being set up (for example in Nakhodka). Vladivostock is also attracting interest. Other possibilities include the southern industrial towns running along the trans-Siberian railroad and the Volga corridor. Costs vary between major centres in the Russian Federation depending on the availability of raw materials, labour, consumer prices, transportation and distribution infrastructure.

# 25

# Agencies and Distributorships

*Nicholas Louis*

The Russian market still operates in a very different way from the West. As a result, the expectations of both manufacturers and local dealers or representatives are very different. This chapter looks at various aspects of the relationship between a Western producer and the agent or distributor in Russia.

## ENTERING THE MARKET

The initial foray into Russia often occurs after an introduction to the country by a business associate, a press report or even the success there of a competitor. Often a large company may have ignored Russia completely, when suddenly the sales of a particular division take off and a corporate decision is taken to develop the market. However, long-term sales are not achieved overnight and maintaining contact with the end-user is crucial for the success of the business.

The first direct contact with the market is usually through the Commercial Department at the Embassy in Moscow, or a recommended trading company. Sometimes the same producing company will have different divisions working through different agents. Indeed 'Russian' goods may even end up being re-exported to third countries in competition with local suppliers. Thus it is important to ensure from the start that the market is clearly defined and the appointed agent has the experience required for the particular job. Both foreign and Russian companies should be considered, but it is worth bearing in mind that foreign companies are often treated with greater respect by the consumer. Many

Russian-registered or Russian-owned firms choose exotic or foreign-sounding names.

Very high local taxation is another major deterrent to manufacturers trading directly. It can be advantageous to supply either semi-processed goods or sub-assemblies to qualify for the status of local production. In this case the import taxes on finished goods may be avoided.

## SECURING AN AGENT

Often the success or failure of an operation in Russia depends on the ingenuity of the agent finding his way through the red tape. Many products, such as consumer electronics or automobiles, depend on a strong dealer network and technical back-up service. Qualified labour is at a premium, so the best service should be expected from dealerships with a strong team of capable technicians under good management, rather than from an organisation with sufficient capital investment in maintenance equipment and outlets, but run to low Russian standards. It should also be borne in mind that, though Russia is learning the rules of Western trading very quickly, there is nothing that can substitute years of experience. It frequently may be advisable to concentrate initially on a single product or product line, rather than risk the outcome of a sales operation with a dealer who is eager, but new to the game.

Commonly, a Russian-registered company specialising in a craft such as basket-weaving or pottery ends up trading in computers or cars. So, since all companies are obliged to register the type of business they intend to carry out, it is worth checking their company statutes to see whether they can act as agents or dealers for particular products or services in the first place. In any event, the help of a local lawyer should be sought, as should that of an accountant or auditor. With the rouble still not freely convertible, it is also worth considering the question of repatriation of profits and the security of any investments.

When negotiating, sales figures, such as market experience in other ex-East European markets is of disproportionate value. A single sale concluded at par, or even at a slight loss, may pave the way to a much larger deal in the future.

An agency agreement may be concluded on the standard terms of the producer, or negotiated separately. In many areas Russian commercial legislation still lags behind other countries, so it may be safer to insist on the governing law of the domicile of the foreign company. It is common for a local agent to seek exclusive representation. Exclusivity could be granted for a limited period subject to renewal based on performance. The start-up cost to the agent may be much higher than elsewhere and results, though slow in coming, may be to a scale reflecting the vastness of the market. Frequently a single contract justifies many months of painstaking work and even companies with years of experience trading in Russia are oblivious of the size of demand for practically everything.

## BUILDING A PROFILE

Huge resources are often spent on advertising and promoting a new product in developed markets. In Russia it was traditionally the case that only inferior goods which could not be sold otherwise needed advertising. However the change to a consumer-oriented society is now slowly taking place, with the person in the street gradually becoming brand-conscious.

Billboards advertising consumer electronics, soft drinks and cars are now mushrooming in great numbers around Moscow, but in regional centres and even some republican capitals the old slogans extolling the merits of the socialist system are very much in evidence. Much of the current television and radio advertising time is taken up by the dozens of commodity exchanges and commercial banks, which are of no relevance to most of the audience. The same story is true of the press, where the target of an advertising campaign often cannot be pinpointed. Advertising of pet food, for example, even has a negative effect, with people complaining that there is not enough food for themselves and their families, let alone their cats and dogs.

Brands which have been produced locally under licence for a number of years certainly stand a better chance than 'unknowns'. However the appeal of the Western way of life is very strong, and several television advertising campaigns aimed at the younger generation have achieved remarkable results.

With the stability of the political system still in doubt, the future of the country's economy now seems clear – there is no way back. The consumer has come of age.

# 26

# Export and Import

*ALM Consulting*

## ABOLITION OF FOREIGN TRADE MONOPOLIES

Until recently the state had a monopoly on foreign economic activity on the territory of the former USSR. This meant that the government, through various organs and ministries, regulated and controlled all aspects of conducting business with foreigners. In outline, a foreign party would deal with the Foreign Trade Organisation (FTO) representing the industry or sector concerned with the proposed transaction. The FTO would then contract itself with the Russian enterprise doing the buying or selling. Thus supplier and purchaser would have no direct contact.

This position changed only slightly during the *perestroika* years. Reforms designed to dismantle the state's trading monopoly went some way towards this aim, but were characterised above all by unpredictability and bureaucratic red-tape. Only in November 1991, in a Presidential Decree On the Liberalisation of Foreign Economic Activity on the Territory of the Russian Federation, was a genuine move towards free trade principles and a reliable customs procedure signalled. Most importantly, the Decree removed the requirement that enterprises wishing to supply or purchase from markets abroad be specially registered for this purpose.

## EXPORT AND IMPORT OPERATIONS

### Registration

Since 1 July 1992, registration has been necessary only for exporters of the following 'strategically important' raw materials:

- crude oils and oil products;

- natural gas, oil gases and other gases and hydrocarbons;

- electric energy;

- hard coal, coke and coalite;

- commercial timbers, sawn timber, pulp and board;

- ferrous and non-ferrous metals, and their ores, alloys and waste;

- mineral fertilisers, ammonia, methynol;

- inorganic acids;

- furs;

- grain; and

- oil-seed meal.

To export any of these products an enterprise has to be registered by the Ministry of Foreign Economic Relations. There is a detailed application procedure for such registration, with the following basic documents required:

- A written application for registration, containing a brief description of the enterprise's field or business and an indication of the type of goods to be traded.

- Notarised copies of the foundation documents and the enterprise's certificate of registration (in the Companies' Register).

- A letter from a Russian bank confirming that the enterprise is solvent, holds both rouble and hard currency accounts with it and has an account at a foreign bank.

- A list of contracts from the previous year – indicating the main contractual terms, prices and the volume of export – signed by the enterprise's managers and certified by a stamp.

On the basis of the documents provided, the Ministry's Registration Commission will draw up a report on the application and the Deputy Minister will reach a decision within 60 days. Registration can be refused if there is evidence that the enterprise has breached currency, financial or customs regulations, has disregarded foreign laws and thus caused economic and political damage to Russia, or engages in unfair business practices (for example by arbitrarily refusing to provide intermediary services to raw material producers or by undercharging for exports with a view to dumping). However, this list is non-exhaustive and the Ministry is not obliged to give its reasons – the law only requires that a refusal be 'justified'.

If the application is approved, the enterprise is entered in the Register and sent a certificate signed by a Deputy Minister and certified by the Ministry's official stamp. It can then commence export operations involving raw materials. The certificate is valid for a year and will be renewed annually unless the enterprise has acted improperly (in the senses mentioned above as justifying non-registration). The certificate can also be revoked at any time for up to a year if any such actions come to light (though obligations commenced under existing contracts can be performed in full).

Registered exporters operate subject to certain conditions. In acting as a middle man, contracts must be concluded on a commission basis, on pre-defined terms. The maximum intermediary commission which can be charged for exporting crude oil is 0.8 per cent, and for oil products, etc and natural gas 1 per cent. The other percentages laid down are 2 per cent (electric energy, coal, ferrous and non-ferrous metals, etc) and 1.5 per cent (all other controlled raw materials). Payments and currency sales relating to ore export operations involving the 'strategically important' raw materials have to be effected through the bank settlement accounts notified by the exporter at the time of registration.

For enterprises with foreign capital of 30 per cent or more, the registration requirements sit uneasily with the provisions of the Foreign Investment Law of 1991. This grants such enterprises the right to export their products without licences. Clearly this is an area which requires further clarification, but in practice foreign companies producing the controlled products for export are registering with the Ministry for External Economic Relations.

### Export duties

All enterprises, regardless of their place of registration and their form of ownership, are generally obliged to pay duties on the export of goods from Russia. These are collected by the State Customs Committee before or at the time a good is presented for customs control. The rate of the duty is denominated in ECUs and levied in roubles calculated according to the exchange rate quoted by the central bank at the time.

The list of goods subject to export duties, and the rate of the tariff itself, change frequently. In the summer of 1992 the duty on some commodities was reduced, but on crude oil it was doubled. Generally, the rates are between 20 and 35 per cent on the world market price for the good concerned. However, both the number of goods taxed and the amount of the duty are expected to be reduced at the beginning of 1993, with a (perhaps over optimistic) view to their being completely abolished in the long term.

Since 1 January 1993 goods exported as part of a barter deal are taxed at a rate 50 per cent higher than the base rate. The customs authorities can defer payment of export duty for up to 60 days against a bank guarantee or by permission of the Russian Finance Ministry. However, in such cases a deferment charge is levied either of 0.2 per cent per day payable in roubles or, with the consent of the Finance Ministry, of 0.01 per cent per day if the whole amount due is paid in convertible currency.

## Import duties

A principal concern of Western companies looking to export products to the Russian market are the duties charged on their import into the country. These are subject to frequent and sudden change, but the basic structure of the tariff was laid down during 1992.

### Exemptions

Under the system in operation at the end of 1992, the following categories were exempt from import duties:

- foodstuffs;
- medicines and raw materials for their manufacture;
- printed matter, including books and newspapers;
- children's clothing and accessories; and
- medical, surgical and healthcare equipment.

In addition, all goods originating from 'least developed' countries (various African and certain Asian countries) are completely exempt from import duties.

### Tariff rates

The basic rate of import duty is 15 per cent of the customs value of the good. This is calculated in ECUs and payable either in roubles (at the central bank exchange rate) or hard currency at the option of the importer. It will be collected by the customs authorities when the customs declaration is presented.

Certain products attract a higher rate, notably: beers and wines (20%); sparkling wines, televisions, video equipment (25%); alcohol (30%); and spirits (100%).

Most of these rates were increased considerably during the second half of 1992 and may be varied again in 1993. Goods originating in 'developing countries' (mostly South American and Arabian countries) are taxed at one-third of the normal rate.

*Duty frees*

Individuals can take into Russia goods worth up to US$10,000 in their luggage with a maximum of 5 litres of spirits and 1000 cigarettes. Cars, however, are taxed at a rate of ECU 0.1. per cubic centimetre of engine cylinder volume.

## Currency receipts

The Russian government's efforts to make the rouble convertible have entailed the maintenance of a number of constraints on the free use of hard currency. To prevent enterprises transferring hard currency revenues abroad – which would lead to insufficient supplies of hard currency on the internal market for maintaining a stable rouble exchange rate – all export revenues in hard currency must be entered into accounts at authorised banks on Russian territory.

Since enterprises are also obliged to sell 50 per cent of currency received from exports (less expenses, such as customs duties, transport and insurance costs – ordinarily 30 per cent to the currency reserve of the central bank and 20 per cent directly on the domestic currency market), two parallel accounts should be opened: a transit currency account and a current currency account. When received, all foreign currency is held initially in the transit currency account. If the amount received exceeds $500 the enterprise should within 14 days instruct the bank to effect the 30 per cent compulsory sale. The money will be taken from the transit currency account at the rate quoted when the hard currency was originally received and forwarded to the central bank. The 20 per cent compulsory sale must also be effected within 14 days and the remaining funds are transferred to the current currency account. In two cases the 30 per cent sale to the central bank is not necessary: if the amount received is less than $500, or if the enterprise concerned has foreign capital. In such instances, the entire 50 per cent compulsory sale is made on the domestic currency market.

These measures were introduced in the summer of 1992, as efforts were being made to establish 'internal convertibility'. However, it proved impossible to maintain a stable rouble exchange rate, and a more exacting regime may be imposed in 1993. Russian enterprises are likely to be required to sell all foreign currency receipts, but more favourable provisions may be applied to companies with foreign capital.

## SIGNING CONTRACTS

The Russian Civil Code provides that foreign companies can enter into contracts in Russia in the course of external trade without any special permission. However, the law lays down certain requirements for any foreign trade transaction involving a Russian party:

- The contract must be in writing.

- The contract should be signed by two representatives of the Russian organisation – either directors or deputy directors, or a person empowered to sign by a power of attorney executed by a director.

- The names of the parties, the purpose of the transaction, a description of the goods and the price agreed between the parties must all be specified in the agreement.

- Any bill of exchange or other promissory note issued by the Russian party should also be signed by two persons – any director, deputy director or the firm's chief (or senior) accountant is empowered for this purpose, as is anyone in whose favour a power of attorney has been executed by both a director and the chief accountant.

A general point to note in respect of all contracts is that Russian commercial law remains somewhat undeveloped, and accordingly the agreement should be meticulously drafted and exhaustive in its inclusion of points agreed between the parties.

## CUSTOMS PROCEDURES

The Russian customs authorities are charged with ensuring that customs laws are observed, import and export mechanisms operate effectively, border controls and formalities are complied with and drugs and other contraband do not enter the country.

A new Customs Code is awaiting enactment by the Russian parliament. This will increase to 600 the number of checkpoints in operation on Russia's borders, reflecting the new position in trading relations with the other republics of the former Soviet Union. The new Code is expected generally to streamline customs procedures and minimise the number of formalities to be observed.

The basic document to be presented to the border control on any foreign trade transaction is the 'customs declaration'. This must state the following:

■ the full names and addresses of the exporting and importing organisations;

■ the full name and particulars of the authorised bank through which settlements with the foreign partner are to be effected;

■ the forms of such settlements; and

■ the date on which currency payments are receivable.

# 27

# Intellectual Property
## *Frere Cholmeley Bischoff*

Laws on intellectual property govern the rights to, and use of, intangible property such as inventions, designs, trade names and creative works. In market economies, such laws give exclusive rights to the author or owner of intellectual property in the form of patents, trade marks, copyrights, etc. Thus a certain degree of market monopoly is given as a reward for creative effort. In the socialist planned economy context, various state rewards were necessary to encourage innovation, but the above principles were irrelevant. There was no specific intellectual property law in the sense understood in the West.

The drive to create a market economy in Russia and the wish to attract foreign technology have made it necessary for Russian law to offer the appropriate safeguards and rewards for intellectual property owners. After a number of false starts, various new laws in the area were passed towards the end of 1992. Most importantly, these include up-to-date patent and trade mark laws. A copyright law is expected to follow shortly. This chapter takes a detailed look at the basic elements of legal protection for the various forms of intellectual property.

## PATENTS

In Western capitalist systems patents function, in general terms, as the essential rewards for technological innovation in industry – ie R&D and invention. A patent confers official specification of a particular invention, and the patent owner (the inventor or his legal successor) obtains the exclusive right to use, assign or grant licences under that invention for a specified term.

Until recently, in the republics of the now-defunct USSR, patents were available only for a few categories of inventions, and were anyway of limited use and relevance in the socialist system. However, a new Patent Law of the Russian Federation (the Patent Law) was passed on 23 September 1992 and is, at the time of writing, awaiting the President's signature. This Law seeks to establish a patent system along Western lines.

### Mechanics of the present system

*Patentable inventions*

A patent may be granted for an invention if it is new and involves an inventive step, and is capable of industrial application – exactly as in English law. Computer programs and scientific theories are *not* patentable.

*Duration*

A patent will be valid for 20 years from the date of filing. However this period may be reduced on application by the patent holder, and will be terminated early if the annual duty for its maintenance is not paid. Also the patent may be invalidated at any time if it is successfully contested – on the grounds that the protected object does not meet the requirements of patentability, or that there were discrepancies in the original application document or the patent itself.

*Ownership of the patent*

A patent will generally be issued to the author of the invention (or his assignee). An exception arises where an invention is developed in the course of employment, in which case the right to obtain a patent belongs to the employer unless the labour contract specifically provides otherwise. If the employer then patents the invention, assigns the right to obtain a patent to another party, decides to keep the invention secret or is unable to obtain a patent for reasons within his control, the inventor-employee is entitled to remuneration equal to the amount of profit derived by his employer (or which would be derived were the invention duly exploited). If the employer takes none of these actions within four months the employee-inventor can obtain a patent in his own name, but his employer will be entitled to use the invention on payment of royalties.

*Nature of the rights conferred by a patent*

The patentholder has the exclusive right to use the invention, and to prevent others from using it. He is also free to assign the patent or grant a licence contract on such terms as he thinks fit.

A patent is infringed if there is any manufacture, use, import, sale, offer for sale, etc of the invention without the patent holder's consent. The Patent Law lists various acts which are not regarded as infringing the exclusive right of the patentee – most important among them being the use of the protected object for private purposes without obtaining profit.

## Licensing

As mentioned above, the patent holder may grant licence contracts to third parties, thus transferring the right to use the invention to one or more other persons. Key features of this system are:

- licences may be exclusive or non-exclusive;

- there is no limit to the amount of remuneration the licensor may negotiate;

- licence agreements must, like assignments of patents, be registered at the patent office – otherwise they will be invalid.

A patent holder may alternatively file at the relevant patent office an 'open licence' (ie a statement of his willingness to grant licences to anyone). For this the patent renewal fee will be reduced by 50 per cent.

## Compulsory licensing

The Patent Law provides for compulsory licensing when there has been no or insufficient use of a patented invention for a period of five years after the patent was granted. Interested persons may require a patent holder to grant them compulsory non-exclusive licences for limited use of the invention on terms determined by the Supreme Patent Chamber.

This system ensures that Russian industry may benefit from new technology and is in conformity with the provisions of the Paris Convention for the Protection of Industrial Property (1883). Similar measures exist in most patenting countries.

## Application procedure for a patent

The following procedure for application is laid down in the patent law:

- A patent application must relate to one invention or a group of very closely linked inventions.

- The application must be in the Russian language or, if not, translation into Russian must follow within two months.

■ Russian citizens may apply for patents and deal with the Patent Office directly, whereas foreign nationals and enterprises must act through Russian patent agents registered with Rospatent.

■ The application will undergo expert examination and, during this time, information will be published about the patent applied for.

■ A patent will be officially granted upon entry in the State Register of Inventions.

Further procedural requirements may be laid down as necessary by the Patent Office.

*Enforcement of patent rights*

In general, jurisdiction over disputes regarding patent ownership is exercised by the ordinary Russian court system (including *arbitrazh* and the arbitration courts). Such cases may involve, establishment of authorship and patent ownership, conclusion and performance of licence contracts, and violation of the exclusive right to use the invention – the Patent Law specifically provides for damages to be payable to the patent holder by the patent infringer.

The Law also sets up a new, specialised Supreme Patent Chamber to hear petitions on certain matters. Principally this forum is to function as a body of final appeal regarding complaints concerning the patent application. If an applicant considers his invention to have been unfairly refused a patent, he has the right to file a reasoned appeal with the Chamber of Appeals of the Patent Office (Rospatent). The decision of the Chamber may in turn be appealed in the Supreme Patent Chamber, whose decision will be final. A third party could also challenge the granting of a patent in the same way.

## Other patentable works

An unusual feature of the Russian Patent Law is that it covers not only inventions but also 'utility models' and industrial design. For certain purposes the terms and conditions of patentability vary according to the designation of the protected object. The main features of these systems are examined below.

*Utility model*

The utility model is a concept intended, roughly speaking, to offer some limited reward and protection for enterprises which develop in situ new machines or goods which, though new, are not necessarily 'inventive'. A patent for a utility model is valid for five years from the date Rospatent receives the application – though this can be extended for up to three years more on request. The compulsory licensing provisions of the Patent Law come into operation if a utility model is not used, or is insufficiently used, within three years of the patent being granted.

## Industrial designs

The protection offered by the Patent Law to industrial designs in Russia is relatively straightforward, and is in close conformity with Western legislation on the subject. The author of an industrial design will be granted a patent for the term of 10 years, with the possibility of a further extension of 5 years.

To be patentable, the essential features of an industrial design must establish the aesthetic and/or ergonomic characteristics of the object's exterior. They may be features of shape, pattern, configuration or ornament, or a combination of all of these. As with an invention, the design must be new, original and applicable in industry.

When applying for a patent for an industrial design the author must include with his application to Rospatent, photographs, and also general drawings if necessary, to explain the features of the design. The scope of the patent, if granted, will be determined by the essential features of the design thus depicted.

## Inter-state aspects

In December 1991 the Russian Federation, together with Armenia, Belarus, Moldova, Tadzhikistan and the Ukraine signed a 'Provisional Agreement', pending a full Convention, for the Protection of Industrial Property throughout these countries. Industrial property is defined as covering rights to inventions, designs, trademarks and service marks.

This document is open for signature by all the other former Soviet republics. It creates a multinational organisation based in Moscow, with the aim of ensuring the equality of intellectual property rights and co-ordination of policy in the signatory states, while leaving each of them free to determine their own laws.

The key aspects of the agreement are as follows:

■ A new patent office for the organisation is created to accept and examine patent applications.

- The office will issue patents (for inventions and industrial designs) in the form of 'inter-state protection documents', which will have equal effect in all the signatory states.

- An Inter-state Patent Court is to be established for hearing and settling disputes regarding the issuing and effectiveness of the protection documents.

- Previously issued legal protection documents valid in the ex-USSR will still be effective in the signatory states.

- The USSR's prior international obligations in respect of industrial property will be observed in all the states.

- The agreement sets out the participating states' ultimate goal – harmonisation of legislation and conformity with international law in the field of industrial property.

An important aspect of the Agreement, however, is the machinery it contains for its own entry into force. It will be effective once three of the signatory states have confirmed: the validity of existing USSR legislation on their territories; the enforceability of previously owned USSR legal protection documents on industrial property rights; and the appointment of a representative and deputy to the Administration Council of the new body.

As yet none of these conditions have been met, and it seems likely that a new impetus is needed for the Agreement to come into force. This may occur once more concrete and clearly defined structures have been developed on the foundations of the Commonwealth of Independent States (CIS). Once effective, the Agreement has force provisionally for one year only, though this may be prolonged on agreement by the signatories. The experience of 1992, when most countries of the CIS were in something of a patent vacuum, suggests that the issue of creating a system to co-ordinate intellectual property protection should be addressed with some urgency.

### The international aspect

The USSR joined the (1883) Paris Industrial Convention in 1964, and Russia has inherited the obligations of the former Soviet Union under this agreement. Thus equal, non-discriminatory treatment is guaranteed for foreign nationals under the Russian patent system, as is the principle of 'Convention Priority' whereby an application in one member country gives a 12-month priority period in which to apply in any of the others.

Russia is also bound by the 1970 Patent Co-operation Treaty and the 1971 Strasbourg Agreement on International Patent Classification.

### Problems of the present situation

Despite the passing of a comprehensive new Patent Law, there remain a number of problems relating to patent enforcement, and intellectual property protection in general, on the territory of Russia. Most important is the question of the competence in the intellectual property sphere of the legislatures of Russia's 20 constituent republics. The Patent Law failed to come into force in the spring of 1992 after it was ruled unconstitutional on the grounds that intellectual property law was not within the federal jurisdiction. This difficulty was then ironed out, with the eventual version of the Patent Law providing that the Russian republics may pass their own patent legislation on the basis of the federal law. However, given the unpredictable nature of relations between the centre and the republics, further problems related to this issue cannot be ruled out in the future.

### Soviet patents

The Russian Supreme Soviet Resolution passing the Patent Law contained a number of provisions relating to the validity of documents issued by the Soviet authorities protecting rights to inventions and industrial designs before the break-up of the USSR. In general, such documents will be recognised for the remainder of their validity period. However, they are effectively now governed by the new Russian Law, and can accordingly be challenged under that Law on the grounds outlined above.

The Resolution specifically grants to holders of non-expired 'author's certificates' (a document issued by the Soviet authorities under which the right to an invention passed to the state, in return for payment to the inventor of certain remuneration) and certificates for industrial designs the right to petition for the cancellation of the documents and simultaneous issue of a Russian patent for the remainder of their protection validity period. However, in these circumstances any person lawfully using such an invention or industrial design protected by USSR documents may continue to do so without having to conclude a licensing agreement.

# TRADE MARKS

The proper functioning of a market economy requires that consumers act rationally in choosing between different products available for them to purchase. To do this they must be aware of any significant difference between those products. In broad terms, a trade mark allows a consumer to associate a particular good with particular attributes, and a manufacturer to distinguish his product from those of others. Thus effective trade mark recognition and protection are essential components of a market economy.

The Russian Federation enacted a new Law on Trade Marks, Service Marks and Appellations of Origin (the Trade Mark Law) in September 1992. Like the Patent Law, this seeks to introduce a Western-style system of legal protection in the area, and can expect the confidence of prospective foreign investors.

## *Protection of trade marks*

Legal protection of a trade mark is established upon its entry in the State Register of Trade Marks and Service Marks (the Register) in the name of its owner – who may be a company or an individual engaged in business activities. Registration is acknowledged by the issuing of a certificate.

### *Registrable designations*

Any verbal, pictorial, three-dimensional or other designation, or a combination of designations, can be registered as a trade mark. Also, any colour or collection of colours can be registered as part of the trade mark.

The Trade Mark Law lists a number of grounds for refusing registration of the trade mark, most of which are broadly comparable to the conditions existing under Western systems. Most importantly, registration of a designation may be refused if:

- it is in general use for denominating a certain type of product;

- it may give a false or misleading indication to the consumer regarding the nature of the product or its manufacturer; or

- it is the same as, or confusingly similar to, a trade mark already registered or filed by another party in respect of analogous goods.

### *Duration*

A trade mark is protected for 10 years from the date Rospatent receives the registration application. This period may be extended for 10 years at a time on application by the owner during the year preceding its expiry, or within six months of its expiry on payment of a fee. The renewal is entered on the Register and marked on the certificate held by the owner.

Registration may be terminated early in any of the following instances:

- On request by an interested person, if it is shown that the trade mark was not 'used' (see below) for five continuous years following the date of its registration or immediately preceding the filing of such request.

- If the conditions of registration are no longer fulfilled – for example the owner has ceased to be a legal entity (eg it has been liquidated) or is not engaging in business activities, or the trade mark gives a false or misleading indication of the product or its manufacturer.

- Where a trade mark has come into general use as a designation of goods of a particular kind.

- On renunciation by the trade mark owner.

### Rights of the trade mark owner

The owner of a trade mark has the exclusive right to use and dispose of the trade mark, and the right to prevent other parties from using it.

#### Use of the trade mark

The Trade Mark Law provides that a trade mark is 'used' if it is used by the owner, his assignee or licensee on the product for which it is registered or on the packaging. If such is not the case the trade mark is only 'used' if it appears in advertisements, printed documents, signboards or during demonstrations at a fair or exhibition in Russia, and there are good reasons for it not being used on the product or its packaging.

#### Assignment of the trade mark

The owner of a trade mark is free to assign it to another firm or individual, by concluding an agreement with that party regarding some or all of the products for which it was registered. The Trade Mark Law does, however, prohibit such assignment if its effect would be to mislead consumers in respect of the product or its manufacturer. The assignment will only be recognised if it is registered with Rospatent.

*Licensing*

Alternatively, the trade mark owner can grant to another person the right to use the trade mark under a licence agreement. The law requires that such an agreement contain a clause to the effect that the quality of the licensee's goods will not be inferior to those of the licensor (ie the trade mark owner), and that the licensor will exercise control over the licensee for this purpose. Once again, the agreement is invalid unless registered.

*Enforcement of rights*

Unauthorised manufacturing, importation, offering for sale or other business use of the trade mark – or of a denomination likely to be confused with it – constitutes an infringement of the trade mark. Disputes concerning this or relating to an assignment or licence agreement are heard by ordinary Russian courts, *arbitrazh* or an arbitration court.

The remedies available for unlawful use of a trade mark are:

■   cessation of the infringement;

■   damages;

■   publication of the court's ruling so as to restore the injured party's reputation; or

■   destruction or removal from the product concerned or its packaging of the unlawfully used trade mark.

### Registration procedure

The Trade Mark Register is maintained by Rospatent, which will accept applications for registration at their Official Patent Examination Office in Moscow.

*Application*

Applications for registering a trade mark should be filed at Rospatent by the prospective trade mark owner. Foreign firms and non-registered individuals should use a Russian attorney registered with Rospatent for this purpose.

The application must include:

■   A request for registration of the designation as a trade mark.

- The name and place of residence or registration of the applicant.

- The designation itself and a detailed description of it.

- A list of goods and services for which registration of the trade mark is sought, classified in accordance with international practice. (Russia is a party to the Nice Agreement on the International Classification of Goods and Services.)

- A receipt confirming payment of the registration fee.

All the documents contained in the application must be in Russian, or must be accompanied by a Russian translation (this may be supplied up to two months later than the original application).

*Priority protection*

Assuming the application is technically in order and all the required documentation is supplied, the trade mark has priority from the date of filing. Also a trade mark owner can claim priority in Russia from the moment an original application is filed in any country party to the Paris Convention on the Protection of Industrial Property, provided an application is received by Rospatent within six months of that date.

*Registration*

After a detailed examination process Rospatent will grant registration of the trade mark if it fulfils the conditions for registration. This should be carried out within one month of receipt of the application. The entry on the Register contains:

- the trade mark;

- information on the trade mark owner;

- the priority date of the trade mark;

- the date of registration;

- a list of goods for which the trade mark has been registered; and

- other data relating to the registration of the trade mark, including any subsequent amendments.

Within three months of registration, Rospatent will issue the trade mark owner with the trade mark certificate. Russia is a party to the Madrid Agreement on the International Registration System of Marks

1891, as revised, and applications for international registration may be filed through Rospatent.

## COPYRIGHT

Copyright is the protection offered to the creator of original literary, scientific or artistic work. In Russia, where years of isolation have fostered a formidable appetite for Western films, books and music, there is currently widespread counterfeiting and piracy. Thus an important consideration for the prospective foreign investor is the guarantees provided by the country's copyright legislation.

At present, the operative law in this area is contained in the Fundamental Principles of Civil Legislation of the USSR and Republics. These were adopted in summer 1991, and were intended to form the basis for new Civil Codes of the Republics of the Soviet Union. A new Russian Civil Code is under preparation, as is a law specifically on copyright protection. In the meantime, however, the Fundamental Principles apply.

### Protection of copyright

Copyright protection under Russian Law is granted to a work which is:

- the product of the creative activity;

- expressed in a material form; and

- capable of being reproduced without the participation of the creator.

In such a case, copyright automatically arises without any need for formal registration.

The copyright owner is the person by whose creative effort the work was produced. Generally copyright in work produced in the course of employment belongs to the employee, though the employer may use the work in accordance with the employment contract under a non-exclusive licence. Protection lasts for 50 years after the death of the author.

### Extent of copyright protection

The copyright owner is entitled to be recognised as the author of the work, to preserve its integrity, to use it and to publish it. Third persons can generally only use the protected work under contract with the copyright owner and on payment of royalties. In contrast to the traditional USSR system, 'free use' is only permissible in a limited number of cases. These are in line with Western norms.

### Protection for foreigners

Copyright protection for works by foreigners first published outside Russia is afforded only according to international treaties concluded by the USSR. Russia has assumed the obligations of the USSR under international law, and is thus considered a party to the Universal Copyright Convention (which the Soviet Union joined in 1963). By virtue of this, work with UK copyright enjoys protection in Russia on a non-discriminatory basis – ie the same as is granted to Russian nationals.

Russia aims eventually to accede to the Berne Convention, and the Copyright Law soon to be passed should facilitate this by bringing copyright protection in Russia up to the required standard. This should have the effect of increasing confidence in the Russian copyright protection system and will mean that copyright originating in the countries party to the Berne Convention, but not to the Universal Copyright Convention, will be protected in Russia.

### Monitoring and enforcement

Perhaps the most important recent development in Russia relating to copyright protection was the establishment of a new, forward-looking Russian Intellectual Property Agency, known by its Russian initials RAIS. This organisation took over from the Soviet State Agency for Copyright and Related Rights in July 1992, and is charged with monitoring the use of copyrighted work and enforcing the law relating to payments of royalties, conclusion of contracts and so forth. It will be financed from central funds and, with a total staff of nearly 400 people, should prove capable of performing these functions effectively.

## PROTECTION OF OTHER INTELLECTUAL PROPERTY RIGHTS

Towards the end of 1992 new legislation was passed in Russia in two areas – the protection of computer programs and databases and the protection of integrated microcircuits.

### Computer programs and databases

The law on the legal protection of computer programs and databases, passed in September 1992, protects computer software as an object of copyright. Copyright is afforded to preparatory materials and functioning programs, whether or not they have been published in a material form, but basic ideas and principles are not protected.

The copyright owner is the person by whose creative work the program was developed, or his assignee. Copyrights subsist for the author's lifetime, and can be notified by the inclusion somewhere in the program of an encircled letter 'c' beside the name of the copyright owner and the year of first publication of the software. In addition, the copyright owner may, if he wishes, register the computer program or database with the Russian Agency for the Legal Protection of Computer Programs and Databases.

The author of a computer program or database can transfer copyright ownership in full or in part to any other firm or individual. Copyright to programs developed in the course of employment automatically belongs to the employer unless the employment contract provides to the contrary. Otherwise, the ownership of copyright can only be assigned by a written agreement containing:

- the extent and means of use of the software;

- the amount of, and procedure for, payment of royalties; and

- the term and validity of the agreement.

Copyright is not infringed if a person lawfully possessing a copy of the program takes a 'back-up' of it for their own purposes, adapts it for their own uses or corrects any clear mistakes contained in it.

### Integrated microcircuits

The topology of an integrated microcircuit is protected under Russian law in a similar fashion to computer software. It is protected if it is *original* (ie it is developed as the result of the creative activity of the author – which is assumed unless the contrary is shown). As with computer software, protection is afforded automatically if this condition is satisfied but, if he wishes, the author may have the topology registered. Protection lasts for ten years.

# 28

# Forming a Company
*Frere Cholmeley Bischoff*

This chapter outlines the procedures required under Russian law for setting up and running a company.

## DIFFERENT VEHICLES

Foreigners can set up a business in any form permitted generally by Russian law. There are basically five different types, though Western investors are most likely to be concerned only with the first two – ie the joint stock company (also known as an 'open stock association') and the limited liability company (or 'closed stock association'). The uncomplicated structure of a limited liability company means it would be a convenient arrangement for a wholly-owned subsidiary, whereas a joint stock company would be more suitable for larger ventures with several backers. None the less alternative vehicles may be appropriate in different circumstances and should anyway be understood before trading or other links are forged.

### Joint stock company

The Russian joint stock company (JSC) is roughly equivalent to the British PLC. It has its own legal personality distinct from those of its shareholders, who are individually liable for the JSC's debts and obligations only to the extent of their contributions to its capital. These shares can be bought and sold freely, and the JSC must maintain a minimum equity of R100,000.

### Limited liability company

Russian limited liability companies (LLCs) can be compared to British private companies. Like JSCs the owners are protected by a 'veil of incorporation'. However, shares in a LLC can generally only be transferred with the agreement of a majority of the other shareholders, and the minimum capital is R10,000.

### Mixed company

The mixed company (or 'limited partnership') is a hybrid of the incorporated and unincorporated company forms. Although it has full legal personality, its capital is provided by both partners (termed 'full members') who are jointly liable without limit for the firm's obligations, and shareholders ('investing members') whose liability is limited.

### Partnership

Russian partnerships (labelled 'general companies') are similar to their British equivalent. They have no legal personality and all the partners have unlimited joint liability for the partnership's debts. The partners themselves may be individuals or firms, but the partnership must have its own name indicating its legal and organisational status and the name of at least one of the partners.

### Family business

Russian law distinguishes from other forms of enterprise the private firm owned by one individual or the members of his family only. Under this arrangement the extent of the owner's liability for the obligations of his business is defined in the firm's articles, and the firm must have its own name. There is a good chance that a number of family businesses will emerge following the privatisation of shops and other small concerns.

## FOUNDATION

The procedure for founding a company with foreign investment is set out briefly in the Foreign Investment Law, with more detailed instructions contained in the Regulations on Stock Companies enacted in December 1990 ('the Company Law').

### Preliminary examination

Foreign companies engaging in large-scale construction or rebuilding projects face the initial hurdle of a 'preliminary examination'. This will primarily be a question of convincing state-appointed experts that the proposed scheme is viable and that certain conditions will be fulfilled. Needless to say, it is impossible to give further guidance on this matter, as it will sometimes prove to be a mere formality and at other times may involve protracted wrangling. However, those intending to put money into such projects should be prepared on this issue, as on all others, to be persistent.

### Financing the company

The company's share capital must consist of an agreed number of ordinary shares, divisible by ten, with an identical nominal value. Contributions can be made either in cash (roubles or hard currency accrued or exchanged) or in kind, the import of the latter by foreigners being exempt from customs duties. The value of such contributions must, however, be expressed in roubles and is determined on the basis of world prices or, if no such prices exist, by mutual agreement of the founders.

If 50 per cent of the share capital stated in the founding documents has not been put up within a year of registration, the authorities have power to deregister and liquidate companies with foreign investment. Accordingly, it is prudent to fix a realistic figure for the new firm's capital in the founding documents. This can later be increased, if necessary, by a resolution of the shareholders.

### Company statutes

Founding documents similar to a British company's memorandum and articles should be prepared, stating:

- the name of the company;
- its place of business;
- the objects of its activities;
- the names and other details of the founders;
- the amount of the company's share capital and the procedure for forming it;
- the size of the founders' shareholdings;
- the structure, composition and competence of the administrative bodies of the company;
- the procedure for making decisions;

- the issues which require unanimity or a specified majority for valid determination; and

- the procedure for liquidating the company.

### Founders' meeting

Finally, all of the founding shareholders should hold a meeting to adopt the company's statutes, and appoint the firm's management by a three-quarters vote. This will also be a convenient time for all the founders to sign a written application for registration.

The Company Law states that it will not be necessary to hold a ritual first meeting if the company is being set up by only one investor. However, since both LLCs and JSCs must have a minimum number of directors, all of whom must also own shares, the process of transferring the shares from the sole founder to the other directors immediately upon incorporation would in such a case have to be embarked upon instead.

## REGISTRATION

Within 30 days of the initial meeting the founders should apply for the company to be entered in the State Register. Generally this application is filed with the local authority or city council, though firms with foreign capital of more than R100 million have to go through the Russian Finance Ministry. In fact, the Foreign Investment Law provides that such a high degree of foreign participation requires the permission of the Council of Ministers, but this should not prove a problem as the overall mood at government level remains generally in favour of encouraging investment from abroad.

UK companies setting up a wholly-owned subsidiary in Russia should provide the following:

- a written application for registration of the new company signed by the founders;

- two copies of the new company's statutes attested by a Russian notary;

- a document confirming the foreign investor's solvency – eg a banker's letter;

- a certificate of good standing from the UK Companies Register;

- the results of the 'preliminary examination' if one was carried out; and

- the registration fee – currently around R2000.

These requirements vary depending on the investment and corporate structure of the new company. Firms wishing to open a branch will also have to supply attested copies of their own company's statutes and of their original decision to establish an office in Russia, as will Russian parties wishing to register a joint venture. A foreign joint investor should submit evidence of his legal status in his country of origin.

All the documents filed should be accurately translated into Russian and properly witnessed as such. However, the registration bodies do not have preconceptions as to what the documentation should contain and they may be inclined to accept what is provided without question.

According to the Foreign Investment Law, the application must be processed in 21 days. However, experience shows that the city agencies, such as the Moscow Registration Chamber, are more likely to take about a month while the Ministry of Finance can take two to three months. In general, the higher a company's capital is, the quicker the registration period.

If the application is approved, the company is entered in the Register and a registration certificate is issued. The date of the certificate is the date on which the company comes into existence and acquires the rights of a legal person.

Registration may be refused if the correct procedure has not been followed or if the documents filed are unsatisfactory. The registrar must inform the applicants of the reasons for the rejection, but is not obliged to return the registration fee. However, the decision to turn down the application may be challenged, if necessary, in court.

A further point which should be noted is the requirement that companies with foreign capital intending to offer insurance or banking services must obtain a licence from the Finance Ministry or the central bank respectively. The Foreign Investment Law also enables the government to determine other activities which may be controlled in such a way, as has occurred with projects in the oil industry.

## INTERNAL MANAGEMENT

The administrative set-up for JSCs and LLCs formed in Russia is regulated by the Company Law. This establishes a three-tier management structure comparable to those found in American corporations.

### General meeting

The supreme organ of a Russian company is the general meeting of its shareholders, convened annually (maximum 15 months' interval) and extraordinarily on 30 days' written notice by the directors, auditors or holders of 10 per cent of the shares. The owners of at least 50 per cent of the firm's capital must be present for a general meeting to be valid, and resolutions are usually passed by a simple majority of those present on a one share/one vote basis. However, alterations to the company's articles, reorganisations of its internal structure or termination of its activities require 75 per cent of those attending and voting to be in favour.

### Board of directors

Responsibility for decision making between general meetings is assigned to a board of directors, who must themselves also be shareholders. The board must comprise an odd number of directors (with a minimum of five in JSCs and three in LLCs) elected by the firm's shareholders for two-year terms or, pending a general meeting, by the board itself. Board meetings should be held at least once a month and are presided over by the chairman of the company. Decisions are valid if taken by a simple majority on a show of hands if at least two-thirds of the directors are present.

### General manager

The day-to-day running of the company is overseen by a general manager, who must also be a director, appointed by the shareholders in general meeting. The general manager will in turn appoint other executive officers, the scope of whose authority will be determined by the company's articles. However, the law empowers the general manager to act on behalf of the firm without any additional authority.

## DISSOLUTION

A JSC or LLC can be wound up by a voluntary or involuntary liquidation. A voluntary liquidation is commenced by a decision of the shareholders in general meeting, who will appoint a liquidation committee to take charge of the company's affairs and pay off its debts. Any assets remaining can then be distributed among the shareholders.

If a company is unable to meet its obligations to creditors, its shareholders are obliged to declare it insolvent. The courts may then decide that it should be compulsorily wound up, in which case a commission will be set up to distribute its assets. Other aspects of involuntary liquidation are to be dealt with in an Insolvency Law, which awaits enactment.

# 29

# Finance for Business

## *Moscow Narodny Bank*

### TRADE FINANCE

Under the former centralised foreign trade system, all foreign trade financing was handled by the Bank for Foreign Economic Affairs of the USSR (Vnesheconombank) within the context of the state plan. When imports were financed by supplier credits, then Vnesheconombank was normally willing to supply financing guarantees.

Since the dissolution of the USSR and the difficulties in servicing former Soviet debt, the role of Vnesheconombank has changed radically and it no longer performs normal trade finance operations. By the end of 1992, however, there were over 2000 banks registered in Russia. Of these, some 60 had general licences authorising the conduct of a full range of rouble and foreign currency transactions while a further 100 had licences authorising a rather more limited range of convertible currency operations. A number of these banks will now open letters of credit, though the conditions under which they do so would appear very conservative by Western standards. Full cash cover is frequently required, a bank will often only be willing to open letters of credit for shareholders and credit terms are invariably short.

Given the sparsity of orthodox accountancy procedures and the even greater lack of credit analysis skills, it is not surprising that the new Russian commercial banks are making slow progress as far as trade finance is concerned. A further problem for the Western exporter, of course, is the lack of track record of the Russian commercial banks. After all, only five years ago there were only six Soviet banks, and it is usually difficult to interpret the accounts of the new banks. Thus, in most cases, presented with a letter of credit by a Russian bank with little track record, a Western exporter would be wise to look for confirmation from a first-class Western bank. By the end of 1992 a number of banks in the West had become more familiar with the larger and more able of the new banks and were willing to offer confirmations and guarantees on a limited basis. Such confirmations and guarantees are expensive and an exporter may have to shop around to find a Western bank willing to underwrite the obligations of particular Russian banks. Equally, it is prudent to find out prior to the opening of a letter of credit which Russian banks are acceptable and persuade the Russian importer to make use of one of these.

It must be admitted, despite a progressive development of orthodox trade finance methods, that letter of credit business is not easy to effect and a number of Western exporters look for advance payments with the balance paid on delivery. In the past, forfaiting (the discount of Soviet trade paper) was a frequent method of financing trade, but bearing in mind the lack of creditworthiness of most Russian enterprises, this type of business has virtually ceased.

## Countertrade

Given the opportunity of financing trade by traditional means, it is hardly surprising that countertrade has assumed increasing importance. Traditionally, this form of business was virtually impossible to effect outside the framework of bilateral clearing agreements. Indeed, the hostile attitude to barter was sustained with a decree in January 1991 that formally banned barter, not least as it was believed, with reason, that many so-called barter transactions were, in practice, unilateral transactions. However, the decree was rescinded when it was realised that, if effected (and illegal exports were difficult to stop) it could only damage trade flows further.

Within the context of existing legislation (eg the necessity for entities to have export licences to export strategic goods), a wide range of countertrade operations is now possible, spreading from one-off exchanges to structured agreements with governmental support. An example of the latter is an agreement between the Sverdlovsk oblast (region) around Ekaterinburg and the UK Health-Care Consortium whereby the regional authority has identified products to be exported, the proceeds of which are kept in an account held at Moscow Narodny Bank in London, in exchange for which health-care products and services are supplied for an integrated programme in the region. To ensure that all legislative and procedural requirements are met, formal federal government support was given.

## TECHNICAL ASSISTANCE

A number of programmes for providing finance to assist Russia's economic transformation have been initiated over the last few years.

### *TACIS*

The principal source of technical assistance funding for Russia is the European Community's programme of 'Technical Assistance for Economic Reform in the Commonwealth of Independent States' (TACIS). This scheme, first launched at the end of 1990 and renewed in February 1992, consists of non-repayable grants advanced from an annually approved budget (ECU450 million in 1992). From the outset, finance has been available for projects in five areas:

1.  Energy – with the goal of supporting the European Energy Charter, emphasis is placed in particular on improving safety at nuclear power plants, increasing efficiency in energy use, updating conventional power stations and introducing new technology to oil and gas development in specific areas.

2.  Training – concentrating especially on developing managerial skills, statistics and information gathering and helping the formation of new customs procedures.

3.  Food distribution – encompassing production, transport, transformation, wholesale and retail trade, and with special attention paid to fruit, vegetables, dairy products and bakery goods.

4.  Transport – with priority given to road haulage and improved co-ordination and efficiency of existing systems.

5.  Financial services – above all in banking, accounts, financial markets and insurance.

Responsibility for the administration of the programme lies with the EC's CIS technical assistance unit, based in Brussels, in tandem with a co-ordinating body in Moscow and the EC delegation to Russia, also in Moscow. The addresses of these bodies can be found in Appendix 2.

### The Know-How Fund

As its name suggests, the British government's Know-How Fund exists to help British firms supply advice and expertise needed during the transition to a market economy in Russia. A £50 million budget allocated to the fund for the former Soviet Union was doubled when President Yeltsin visited London in November 1992. Russia has so far taken up the lion's share of funds committed.

The Know-How Fund's priority sectors for technical assistance are:

■ food distribution and production;

■ the establishment of small businesses;

■ effective exploitation of Russia's oil and gas reserves, and efficient use of energy; and

■ practical advice and assistance in banking, accountancy, insurance, privatisation and other financial services sectors.

Finance is normally allocated through a process of competitive tendering. Details on participation can be obtained from the Joint Assistance Unit at the Foreign and Commonwealth Office.

Some assistance may be available under other initiatives launched by the British government, particularly if a scheme involves the placement of a Russian employee with a British firm. Interested parties should contact the British Council or the Know-How Fund.

## FINANCING INVESTMENT

The size of Russia and its rich endowment of mineral resources, together with a well-educated but low-paid work force would seem to make the country an ideal target for foreign private investment. Indeed, the Law on Foreign Investments in the Russian Federation, which was passed in July 1991, established a liberal regime for such investment, even allowing 100 per cent foreign ownership. None the less, the condition of the Russian economy, the poor state of Russian infrastructure and the uncertain and shifting nature of Russian legislation has led to a slow flow of investment funds following the initial wave of enthusiasm after foreign investment was first allowed in January 1987.

Since banks had to start creating provisions for Russian exposure in 1991, the chances of banks involving themselves in equity investment in, or direct loans to, Russian enterprises without some form of insurance cover or outside guarantee have become virtually non-existent. Moreover, the willingness of British industry to invest its own funds in such an environment has diminished substantially. Despite this, it is estimated that over 2000 Russian joint ventures were operating by mid-June 1992 and, in August 1992, the First Deputy Prime Minister, Vladimir Shumeiko, stated that cumulative foreign investment totalled over US$1 billion. Of these joint ventures, more than half appeared to be producing consumer goods, and this emphasis seems likely to continue at least in the near future.

Of the joint ventures registered in Russia, around 10 per cent appear to have a UK involvement, although the effective lack of cover provided for UK investment by ECGD between late-1990 and late-1992 had a major impact in retarding projects which had reached the developmental stage. In January 1992 an agreement to provide £280 million cover by ECGD was announced, subject to creditworthiness assessment, but it was not until November of that year that a number of projects, such as the John Brown/Gazprom polyethylene complex at Novy Urengoy, were identified as specific candidates for cover. To be acceptable to ECGD, deals have to be on Russia's 'preferred list' (a list formally identifying priority sectors for British involvement prepared by the Russian authorities), to be self-financing in terms of foreign currency earnings, have continuing British management support and preferably have a value between £20 million and £100 million. In addition, there is a preference for projects where co-financing can be arranged with international financial institutions, such as the European Bank for Reconstruction and Development. By the end of 1992, no EBRD financing in Russia had a specifically UK major component, but general projects such as the rehabilitation of St Petersburg clearly give opportunities to British industrialists.

It was announced in January 1993 that the International Bank for Reconstruction and Development (the World Bank) was considering waiving its negative pledge clause which prevents member states (and their state enterprises) from providing equal or more favourable treatment to investors than they have to IBRD. This means that a state enterprise cannot pledge future income from the sale of its output to other banks where such a pledge has already been given to IBRD. At least in principle, this waiver should provide the grounds for increased investment activity.

In referring to IBRD it should also be mentioned that its affiliate, the International Finance Corporation, has been successful in initiating and implementing privatisation projects in Russia, beginning with Nizhny Novgorod. The significance of the privatisation programme for foreign companies is that, having been privatised, the more dynamic enterprises frequently look for foreign partners and it is often at this stage that a foreign partner can make maximum impact, recasting the enterprise to free market conditions, while enthusiasm for change remains high.

In conclusion, it is clear that financing investment in Russia is difficult, but not impossible. Although bank funding in the West is often impossible to obtain, other sources and techniques (including product pay-back) can sometimes be used and government-backed assistance is now increasing. In any case, a market with the size and potential of Russia cannot be ignored and those who can make investments, after properly evaluating the viability of the project, may well benefit from the profits which will accrue as the economy stabilises.

# 30

# Dispute Resolution
## *Frere Cholmeley Bischoff*

A vital consideration for any foreigner dealing with a Russian party is the means for enforcing rights and resolving any dispute which may arise. In Russia, disagreements occurring between foreign and Russian entities will be settled through one of the following systems: the courts; State Arbitrazh; or arbitration.

The appropriate process in a particular matter may depend on the agreement between the parties, the nature of the case and the identities of the parties involved. Thus for a complete picture this chapter considers the structure, jurisdiction and procedure of each system.

## THE COURTS

Russian courts have jurisdiction over civil disputes to which at least one of the parties is a private citizen. The involvement of foreign citizens or enterprises does not affect this.

### The court system

*Structure*

The highest court in the Russian Federation is the Supreme Court, which oversees the intermediate supreme courts of the autonomous republics and all the other courts of the regions, territories, autonomous regions and autonomous areas into which the Federation is divided.

The lowest court, and the one in which about 90 per cent of first instance hearings are held, is the district or city People's Court. Cases are usually considered in the People's Court nearest to the defendant's place of residence. Where the defendant is not resident in the Russian Federation, the appropriate People's Court is the one at the place where his or her property in the Russian Federation is situated.

*Judiciary*

The bench in the People's Court comprises a judge and two 'people's assessors'.

Any citizen aged 25 or over with the right to vote may be elected a judge or a people's assessor. Judges are elected by the people's deputies in the locality served by the court for a term of 10 years, and usually have some form of legal training. The role of people's assessors, by contrast, is to ensure a lay element in the proceedings. They are selected by colleagues at their places of work and each assessor is required to sit in court for not more than two weeks per year over a five-year term.

*Nature of proceedings*

Russian court proceedings follow the inquisitorial model of most European legal systems, rather than the adversarial system found in Anglo-American courts. Thus the case is heard on the basis of personal examination of witnesses and other evidence by the court itself. The court has the power, frequently exercised, to hear independent participants, such as state bodies or labour collectives, in order to ascertain their views on how the case should be decided.

A notable aspect of the Russian system is the capacity of the court to refuse to accept a withdrawal by the plaintiff, admission of the claim by the defendant or indeed a friendly settlement reached by the parties. This may occur where the court considers such an order necessary to protect the rights or interests of an individual or organisation.

## Procedure

*Commencement*

A civil action is commenced by filing a written statement of claim, plus a copy for each defendant, at the appropriate court. The statement of claim must contain:

- the title of the court in which it is filed;

- the name and place of residence of the plaintiff;

- the name and place of residence of the defendant;

- the facts on which the claim is based and supporting evidence;

- the plaintiff's demands in the action;

- the value of the claim (if a valuation is possible);

- a list of annexed documents; and

- the signature of the plaintiff.

In addition, a duty is levied on the amount claimed. This duty is currently 15 per cent of the amount claimed unless the figure is R1000 or less, in which case the rate is 5 per cent.

The defendant can file a counterclaim at any time before judgment. The counterclaim should be set off against the original claim, must wholly or partly exhaust that claim and must have a mutual connection with the original claim so that the disputes are more expeditiously tried together. The counterclaim is chargeable to state duty in the same way as the statement of claim.

*Preparation for trial*

The procedure between commencement and trial of an action reflects clearly the inquisitorial character of the Russian system. The judge will question the plaintiff and, if necessary, the defendant about various aspects of the case and will explain the possibilities of settling the dispute by other means. The judge then determines what witnesses, and what expert or other evidence should be called. Strict time limits are imposed within which specified actions must be performed, with possible termination of the case to the benefit of the other party for failure to comply. When the judge decides that the case is ready for trial he will fix a date for the hearing.

*Judgment*

The opinions of each member of the bench carry equal weight, with decisions made by majority vote. The judge commonly votes after the people's assessors so as not to influence their views. However, it is rare in practice for the judge to be outvoted.

The judgment is drawn up and signed by all three members of the bench. It contains details of the time and place of the trial, a summary of the claim and the defence, an indication of the evidence accepted and reasons why any evidence was rejected, and a statement of the court's decision.

*Appeals*

There are effectively two ways in which the decision of a court may be reconsidered:

1. On appeal (known as 'cassation'). Either party can appeal against a first instance decision to the immediately superior court within ten days of the judgment being pronounced. At the cassation hearing the bench consists of three permanent judges, who review the whole case and not merely the points contested by the appellant. The decision thereby reached has legal force immediately and is not subject to further appeal by the parties.

2. By judicial supervision – upon protest by the procurator or a higher judicial instance. The decision of the first or cassational instance may be contested by the procurator or a higher court irrespective of the will of the parties to the dispute. If this occurs, the protested judgment is usually reviewed by the Presidium of the court whose decision is protested. The supervision takes the form of an assessment, on the basis of a full revaluation of the merits of the case, as to whether the protested decision was in accordance with the law and well-founded.

### *Costs*

Russian courts generally award all costs against the losing side, even if the winning side's costs were paid by the state. Costs include all expenses incurred in conducting the case, including the duty paid on commencement and legal fees for representation by an advocate up to 5 per cent of the total amount recovered.

## STATE ARBITRAZH

Under Russian law jurisdiction over disputes of a commercial nature, to which all parties are enterprises or registered entrepreneurs, is exercised by agencies of 'State Arbitrazh'. These are unique organs created under the Soviet system to defend the rights and interests of enterprises as protected by law. Their genesis arose from the need to ensure the implementation of the plan, if necessary by resort to the law.

It remains to be seen whether the system is appropriate for the regulation of market relations. Until recently, State Arbitrazh was not empowered to resolve disputes involving foreigners. This has now changed, and the State Arbitrazh system is accordingly the appropriate process through which to seek the enforcement of rights under a contract with a Russian enterprise.

### The Arbitrazh system

It is perhaps unfortunate that the system for settling disputes in the economic sphere is labelled 'Arbitrazh'. Although separate from the judicial system, the agencies of State Arbitrazh are possessed of certain characteristics of a court and are wholly distinct from arbitration tribunals.

Arbitrazh sessions are usually conducted between the adjudicator and representatives of the two sides to the dispute only. The process is designed to encourage the parties to reach an agreement, but if this does not prove possible the matter will be resolved by the adjudicator personally. Such a decision will be reached solely on the basis of law.

### Procedure

*Attempt to settle*

A particular aspect of the Arbitrazh procedure is the requirement that, before resorting to State Arbitrazh itself, the claimants seek a settlement of the matter by informal means (known as pryetyenziya – the 'pretension procedure'). Thus the claimant is obliged to send a letter (the 'pretension letter' – comparable to the 'letter before action' used by English lawyers) to the other party, listing his demands and requesting that they be satisfied without the need for recourse to the law. On receipt of a reply from the other party rejecting his demands the claimant is ready to bring the case to State Arbitrazh.

*Commencement*

Proceedings are commenced by presenting to the adjudicator a written statement of claim and the fee for State Arbitrazh.

The statement of claim is similar to that used to bring an action in the civil courts. However, it should also contain information relating to the attempts made to settle under the pretension procedure and there must be attached to it the pretension letter, the reply and, if appropriate, a copy of the contract forming the subject matter of the dispute.

The fee for State Arbitrazh is generally 10 per cent of the value of the claim. If the claim is, for example, for breach of a contract nominated in hard currency, the fee will be 10 per cent of the rouble equivalent of the contract value calculated according to the prevailing exchange rate, or, if the adjudicator so decides, the fee may itself be payable in hard currency.

The written statement of claim can only be rejected by the adjudicator on the following grounds:

- the dispute is not within the jurisdiction of State Arbitrazh;

- the contract between the parties stipulates that any dispute is to be resolved by arbitration; or

- proceedings relating to the matter have already been commenced in another forum.

If the claim is accepted the adjudicator will within five days issue a 'definition' (opryedyelyeniye). This will immediately be posted to both parties. The defendant should, within three days of receiving the definition, complete and return an 'answer' (otvyet) to the definition, stating the legal basis for his refusal to satisfy the claim.

## The hearing

In theory, an initial hearing should be held within one month, and a final hearing and decision made within two months, of the receipt by the adjudicator of the defendant's answer to the definition. However, owing to the volume of cases and a shortage of adjudicators, this period may in practice be extended considerably. The Russian authorities hope to resolve this problem soon by the appointment of more adjudicators. In the meantime, sizeable delays can be anticipated.

The decision of the adjudicator will be in written form delivered to all the parties in the case. It takes a similar form to the judgment in a civil court, summarising the claims of the parties, the decision reached and the evidence accepted to form the basis of that decision.

## Appeal

There are two levels to the Arbitrazh system: local agents of State Arbitrazh; and the Supreme Arbitrazh of the Russian Federation.

Appeal by way of cassation lies directly from the decision at the local level to the Supreme organ. In addition, as in the civil courts, the decision may be protested by the procurator.

To bring an appeal, the aggrieved party must file a 'cassational complaint' within one month at the agency which passed the decision. A fee is payable of five per cent of the value of the claim or, upon the direction of the adjudicator, half of the fee paid by the claimant on commencement of the case. The complaint will be considered by the 'Checking Commission' of the agency in question and a copy sent to all parties, who are obliged to submit answers. The matter will then be sent to the Supreme Arbitrazh, which must deliver its decision on the appeal within one month.

# ARBITRATION

The Russian Code of Civil Procedure permits the parties to a civil transaction to submit any disagreement between them to arbitration. Thus the necessity of bringing proceedings in the courts or through the State Arbitrazh system can be avoided by parties stipulating in their contract that disputes are to be resolved by arbitration.

An option favoured in the past by many foreign organisations was to take a dispute to arbitration in Stockholm. However there are two established courts of arbitration in Russia, both based in Moscow and having considerable experience in international trade disputes. The Arbitration Court (set up in June 1932 as the Foreign Trade Arbitration Commission) deals with all aspects of foreign trade and commercial relations. The Maritime Arbitration Commission (MAC), founded in 1930, deals with all types of maritime disputes. Both tribunals are attached to the Chamber of Commerce and Industry and have good reputations for fairness and impartiality.

## The Russian arbitration system

*Jurisdiction*

There are effectively two ways in which a dispute may be brought for consideration by the Arbitration Court or MAC: by written agreement of the parties; or by one party referring the matter to the tribunal and the other voluntarily accepting its jurisdiction.

The parties will normally agree in the contract that any dispute arising between them should be determined by the tribunal in question. If this is not the case, such agreement may be reached later, even after the dispute has arisen.

If a party simply commences an action in either tribunal, the tribunal will, if the matter is appropriate for its consideration, enquire of the respondent whether it will submit to its jurisdiction. If the respondent agrees, jurisdiction is established.

In the Arbitration Court, a contention by either party that the matter is not within the jurisdiction of the Court will not of itself mean that the matter is withdrawn from its consideration. Instead the arbitrators appointed in the case will examine the question of jurisdiction and may, if they conclude that the objection is ill-founded, proceed with hearing the dispute on its merits.

*Choice of arbitrator*

Both the Arbitration Court and the MAC maintain a list of approved arbitrators from which both the claimant and the respondent should choose their respective arbitrators. The lists contain the names of experts in the types of dispute which each tribunal entertains. There are currently no foreigners on the lists but there is no reason, in principle, why non-Russians should not be chosen in the future.

Under the Arbitration Court procedure, the arbitrators selected themselves choose a third individual from the list to act as chairman. If they fail to agree on this, the decision is taken by the president of the tribunal.

In the MAC only two arbitrators are chosen. However a third will be appointed to act as chairman if the two arbitrators are unable to agree on how to resolve the dispute. The parties may also agree for their case to be decided by a single arbitrator appointed from the list, either by their joint election or chosen by the tribunal president.

All arbitrators are required to be independent and impartial, though the rules of neither the Arbitration Court nor the MAC contain any procedure obliging an arbitrator to disclose any interest that he may have in the outcome of the case. None the less, either party can challenge an arbitrator if there is doubt about his neutrality.

*Applicable law*

Both tribunals will resolve a dispute on the basis of the applicable law relevant to the dispute, which will be either agreed between the parties or determined by Russian conflict of laws rules.

The parties will commonly define in the contract itself or by later agreement the law which is to govern disputes between them. Where Russian law is chosen, it is vital to ensure that the contract is validly executed in accordance with Russian law. Otherwise the agreement could be rendered invalid.

Under Russian conflict of laws rules, if the parties have not specified the law to be applied, their rights and obligations will be governed by the law of the place where the transaction was concluded.

## Procedure

*Commencement*

The arbitration proceedings are commenced by filing with the appropriate tribunal an arbitration fee and a statement of claim, in broadly similar form to that used to bring an action in the civil court.

The statement of claim must also contain the following information:

- the basis for the jurisdiction of the tribunal;

- the name and surname of the arbitrator chosen by the claimant; and

- proof of payment of the arbitration fee.

The arbitration fee is required to cover the general expenses of the tribunal. Its amount is assessed against the value of the claim on a scale laid down by the statute on arbitration fees.

Copies of the statement of claim and attached documents are sent to the respondent, who should within 30 days lodge a written defence, supported by relevant evidence, and inform the tribunal of his chosen arbitrator. The time limit can be extended on the claimant's request.

### The hearing

Arbitrations are less formal than fully fledged civil proceedings. The Arbitration Court conducts its hearings in private, with the presence of other persons permitted only with the consent of both parties and the tribunal itself. Hearings before the MAC, by contrast, take place in public unless one of the parties objects. It is, of course, common for interpreters to be present as the examination is usually conducted in Russian.

As regards evidence which may be adduced, the rules of neither tribunal provide for the discovery of documents, nor is there any comprehensive list of admissible evidence. In practice, written evidence is used widely and the tribunal will hear the opinions of experts and statements of witnesses. An assessment of the evidence is carried out by the arbitrators according to their personal judgements.

In either tribunal the parties are entitled to agree that their dispute be settled on the basis of written materials only, without an oral hearing being necessary. However, the tribunal can order that such a hearing be held if materials presented prove insufficient.

### The award

The rules of both tribunals urge that proceedings be completed, if possible, within six months of the election of the arbitrators. The decision is usually announced orally at the end of the hearing, with a written award sent to the parties within 30 days thereafter. The written judgment is signed by the arbitrators and contains the tribunal's reasoning.

The file of the proceedings is transferred to a People's Court for safekeeping. Awards are published only with the consent of the parties and the president of the tribunal, usually with confidential information edited out.

## *Appeals*

The possibility of appeal constitutes one of the few significant differences between the procedures of the Arbitration Court and the MAC. Whereas awards of the Arbitration Court are final and not subject to appeal, MAC decisions can be appealed within one month by either party, or protested by a higher judicial instance, to the Supreme Court of the Russian Federation.

Though not strictly an appeal, it is worth noting that a further hearing can be held before either tribunal if it transpires that the award made does not resolve all matters in dispute between the parties. Application in such a case should be made within 30 days (in the Arbitration Court) or 10 days (in the MAC) of the original award. Following the second hearing a supplementary award can be made.

## Costs

The rules of the Arbitration Court do not provide for compensation to be awarded to the successful party for legal fees and other expenses incurred in bringing the proceedings. Under the MAC rules, the losing party pays the arbitration fee and may also be ordered to pay other expenses up to a limit of five per cent of the claim. The parties themselves, however, can come to another arrangement regarding costs.

*Part IV*

# Case Studies

## Case Study 1

# British Gas

*Report of an interview with Tim Jones of the British Gas Global Gas unit.*

It was the astonishing events of 1989, culminating in the dismantling of the Berlin Wall, which attracted British Gas to Eastern Europe and Russia. In September of that tumultuous year the firm made its first contacts with what is now the former Soviet Union. The idea at the time was simply 'to go and have a look'. It soon became clear that Russia's potential for a multinational gas company was immense: Russia occupies one-sixth of the world's land mass and owns around 40 per cent of its total gas reserves. In addition, its population of 250 million is an enormous market of people who own fridges and TVs but little else.

## RISKS VS REWARDS

The risks of doing business in Russia are commensurate with the potential rewards. During 1990 and 1991 the political situation in the Soviet Union changed so fast and so frequently that British Gas felt unable to engage in any serious commercial negotiations. But at the start of 1992 the company entered into detailed discussions with Gazprom, its Russian counterpart. The first tangible steps towards co-operation were reciprocal study visits by senior managers, lasting three weeks at a time.

This exchange programme led to a proposal for British Gas to help establish a training facility for Russian energy managers in St Petersburg. This proposal is now near to fruition in the form of the Energy Management Training Centre (EMTC). It is possible that Ashridge Management Centre may participate in the scheme, and that it may even develop into a Russian MBA programme.

British Gas' activities in Russia are split into two parts by the great divide of the oil and gas industry: the upstream–downstream line. Upstream means exploration and production (drilling), while downstream is everything that happens once the gas is recovered from the ground: compression, transportation, sales and distribution. These two parts of the business have quite different approaches to the evaluation of project risk.

In the long term, British Gas is confident that Russia's reform process is now unstoppable. But it believes that the political and commercial environment is unlikely to stabilise for two or three years. Upstream people are accustomed to operating in the world's most inhospitable places – both geographically and commercially. It is a fact of life that most exploration wells do not produce product in commercial quantities, so huge investments must be made on a speculative basis.

British Gas already has two major upstream investment projects underway in the former Soviet Union, and it has two expatriates permanently based in an office in Moscow. In conjunction with Gulf Canada it is producing gas in the Arctic Komi region, while in Kazakhstan it is involved in an exploration joint venture with the Italian firm Agip. The upstream side of the company would like one more major project.

## DOWNSTREAM BUSINESS

Downstream investments in the oil and gas industry progress more slowly. It is more like a normal business, and no major investments are sanctioned without the reasonable expectation of a commercial return. For now, BG's Global Gas unit, which is responsible for downstream projects in the former Soviet Union, is investigating small and medium-scale development projects rather than major investments. The unit consists of four people, two covering the Russian Federation, and two covering the other republics.

The projects under development by this unit include pipeline rehabilitation, upgrading compressor stations, analysing the energy efficiency of power stations, and designing and installing computer control systems for gas distribution. Various multilateral development agencies have funds available for this sort of infrastructural work, and British Gas is keen to tap into these sources.

The biggest project it is chasing at present is an ECU1.7 million study sponsored by the EC's TACIS programme to investigate the status of the main Siberia–Moscow gas transmission pipeline. This pipeline crosses five major rivers, and submarines will be needed to carry out the work. Two other projects, each worth ECU0.75 million, involve installing a computerised transmission system and establishing an overall training structure for Gazprom.

Naturally, British Gas faces serious competition for these projects. The major gas utilities of Germany, France and Italy started buying Soviet gas several years ago; geography and commercial history have combined to give them closer ties with the Russians. When Tim Jones makes a solo visit to a facility in Siberia these days he is not surprised to be followed by a delegation of fifteen officials from Ruhrgas or Italgas. These continental companies have a significant lead over British Gas in the development of the relationships needed to conduct business with Russia.

## A COMPETITIVE EDGE

But while he cannot hope to match Gaz de France, Italgas and others for depth of experience in Russia, or in terms of resources available to investigate the market, he is confident that British Gas has some key competitive advantages. For a start the British firm's gas technology is equal to or better than any of its competitors, particularly in pipe-laying. The company undertook its first engineering job in Russia recently, laying 400 metres of polyethylene pipe in St Petersburg. By a happy coincidence, this demonstration of the firm's technology followed hard on the heels of an abortive attempt by Gaz de France to do the same thing.

A second advantage British Gas enjoys is its recent experience of privatisation. The Russian government wants to convert Gazprom to a joint stock company as a prelude to privatisation and sale to domestic and foreign investors. Gazprom managers are resisting this move, and the outcome cannot yet be predicted. Along with its continental competitors, British Gas is likely to seek a shareholding in Gazprom if the sale does go ahead, and it is in the unique position of being able to share with Gazprom officials the recent experience of being privatised. Privatisation is a worrying prospect for managers of a state monopoly, and Tim Jones is frequently asked to give presentations about what the process involves and how to react.

Asked for advice for other British companies thinking of approaching the Russian market, Tim Jones makes a number of points:

■ Russia's potential is enormous, but be realistic. Many people argue that companies need to be doing deals in Russia now in order to be ready for the time when the economy stabilises and the market really opens up. Failing to do so, it is claimed, will put you at a disadvantage to your German, Italian and French competitors who may already be active there. Tim Jones responds that this argument may apply to the largest firms (especially those in the energy industry) but that medium-sized British companies should beware of spending huge sums just to position themselves for the day when the market becomes viable. You cannot erase the closer ties enjoyed by continental companies; projects in Russia should stack up commercially, just like anywhere else.

■ If you do get involved in Russia, be sure you can afford a protracted period of business development. Exploring and negotiating deals in Russia takes a long time – often at least a year. And it is expensive. Hotel accommodation is dearer in Moscow than in London, and the cost of business flights reflects the booming captive market.

■ Be patient. Most Russians have absolutely no commercial experience, and it takes most Westerners several months to learn how to explain what they are trying to achieve in a way that Russians will understand.

■ An essential first step in doing business with a Russian is to win his or her friendship. This will not make business easy, but it may make it possible. Making friends invariably involves vodka. It would be hard for a teetotaller to do business in Russia!

*Case Study 2*

# The Littlewoods Organisation

*Report of interviews with Francis Ball, director, new business development, and Malcolm Landau, managing director, international retail and wholesale.*

Littlewoods is the first British retailer to make a significant commitment to Eastern Europe. Since 1991 it has been developing a range of opportunities in partnership with the largest department store in St Petersburg – Gostiniy Dvor.

Russia was chosen as the best investment prospect after a review of markets from Spain to Central Europe. Unlike mature, over-shopped markets in the West, it was felt that Russia offered scope to pursue a diverse range of retailing projects. There was also the opportunity to serve huge catchment areas with little or no competition. Against that, Russia is an unpredictable and risky commercial environment, where living standards are falling.

The first full year's trading of the joint venture in 1992 proved profitable and expansion in 1993 is being funded by retained earnings and limited rouble borrowings. No further injections of capital from the UK are required at present. Despite the risks of operating in such a volatile market, Littlewoods express no regrets about getting involved.

## THE STRATEGY

A dual track approach is being pursued. Hard currency shops stocked with imported western luxury goods service a wealthy new breed of consumers, while rouble stores stocked with local supplies cater for ordinary Russians. At the moment the two parts of the business are roughly equal, but over time the rouble element will predominate. In the long term, Littlewoods is aiming to develop a substantial retailing and mail order presence in St Petersburg and a significant position in the rest of Russia.

By the end of 1992, the company had set up two shops and three kiosks, one of which is for mail order, in Gostiniy Dvor at a total investment of £1 million. During 1993 it is planning to open three more shops and four more kiosks on new sites in St Petersburg and Moscow.

Russia is characterised by dormitory suburbs with few local services. At the beginning of 1993 Littlewoods opened its first food and clothing store in the suburbs of St Petersburg. It was the result of hearing about a store that had just been privatised, but did not have the funding to keep going. The joint venture took a majority stake and will have freehold title to the site. Within six weeks a refurbished clothes store had been opened with a food department to follow shortly.

Littlewoods is also looking at the potential for opening small specialist clothing shops in the city centre – forming reliable sources of particular lines such as knitwear. In the course of time it is hoped that these will expand into chain stores.

Mail order may be developed through kiosks in department stores. Some 50 lines are already available from stock and 1500 by order. The consumer orders these by placing a 25 per cent deposit and paying the balance on collecting the goods four weeks later. For the time being the customer has to do the walking because the telephone and post networks do not work adequately. In the future, mail order is seen as an effective way of selling to the major industrial conurbations in Siberia, where there is no flow of consumer goods, but which are generating hard currency and rouble income.

## BUILDING 'SUPPLIER CHAINS'

During 1993 Littlewoods is planning to start a programme of taking small stakes in local suppliers (critical in an economy unused to producing for a consumer services sector), as a way of acting as a catalyst for operations where the main limitation is working capital. These producers will be expected to produce a return through hard currency exports, as well as establishing Littlewoods as the privileged local customer.

Littlewoods' involvement with Russia had its genesis in a much wider review of potential for development in Europe. This sprang from the perception that the company was too dependent on mature markets within the UK, which were subject to cyclical conditions. The search for ways of achieving a geographical diversification of its existing strengths took Francis Ball to Italy and Spain and then on to Eastern Europe. 'The further East I went, the more mouth-watering the opportunities became', he commented. His view was that Eastern Europe represented large, untapped consumer markets suffering from an acute shortage of supply.

Francis Ball's first visit to Russia was in December 1989 in response to comments by President Gorbachev about the shortage of consumer goods. Despite visiting officials without appointments and wearing an autumn suit in temperatures of –25C, the retailing opportunities were apparent. Littlewoods' eventual joint venture partner, the department store Gostiniy Dvor, has a potential 1 million square feet of selling space at its disposal and attracts 300,000 customers a day. What was also apparent was the quality of the local production of textiles, notwithstanding poor styling and cloth.

There were three grounds for focusing on St Petersburg: it was removed from the bureaucratic infighting in Moscow; it was a natural gateway; and there was a so far unfulfilled promise from Mayor Sobchak of the creation of a free economic zone.

In the meantime, Littlewoods was continuing to investigate the potential for business development in Central Europe, but a number of good relationships meant that St Petersburg came on more rapidly – early contacts were with the commercial office of the British Embassy and with the British Soviet Chamber of Commerce. The first Russian point of contact was the Union of Soviet Friendship Societies, which may perhaps not have appeared very promising given that it was a state organisation. However, it was the one organisation that had ensured ongoing links with the West under communism. In Francis Ball's words: 'In the absence of any other institution, it was a hotbed of networking.'

The initial conclusions Francis Ball put before the Littlewoods' board were deemed sufficiently interesting to warrant a full feasibility study. A team of 12 people were selected to carry this out, but before starting they spent a week at a hotel getting rid of their prejudices about Russia. The conclusion was to go ahead with a joint venture in which Gostiniy Dvor and a local supplier held minority stakes.

## CONSUMER MARKET COMPARISONS

While living standards were certainly low, direct comparisons could not be drawn with Western incomes, as there is an entirely different price structure. People do not have to pay for rent or transport and pay next to nothing for the telephone. Disposable income is therefore higher than it might appear.

Littlewoods would also be servicing a catchment area of 7 million without any serious Western competition. In a consumer market as unformed as Russia, it is possible to pursue a wide range of objectives, in contrast to the West, where there is the need for detailed marketing analysis and a tight focus for all business activities.

The negotiations to set up the joint venture proved difficult, although using a local legal academic who knew the corridors of powers and who had already worked on some 20 international joint deals helped ease the process. In dealing with the bureaucracy, there were no shortcuts. It is necessary to visit everybody who might have any influence on the deal, then to distance yourself from those who cannot deliver. Only through experience is it possible to identify who are the real 'shakers and movers'; very often this proves to be the number two, not the number one.

The capital commitment was not large because the proposed joint venture would primarily hold merchandise and equipment in shops. As well as contributing cash, Gostiniy Dvor met the financial costs of occupying space and the local supplier provided merchandise. What these partners really bought, in the estimation of Francis Ball, was local knowledge. As projects develop, Western entrants may be tempted to squeeze out local partners, but 'it is important to recognise just how much you have to go on learning'.

It is not possible to establish the bona fides of potential partners by talking to credit reference agencies or even the banks, which are still at an early stage of development. It remains a question of judgement and rapport.

Working through interpretation is a technique that requires application. It is important to double check everything, otherwise the parties may agree on the basis of quite different understandings. Francis Ball once found himself looking at warehouses rather than potential retail outlets as a result of the literal translation of 'store'. On another occasion a discussion was complicated by the use of the phrase 'piece of cake', which a nervous interpreter translated to reflect how difficult it is to find any cake in Russia! The moral is to use someone whose English may not be excellent, but who has a grasp of the business fundamentals of a project.

It is similarly important to check that concepts are comprehended:

Russians always think of cash as notes and coins, rather than liquid assets on the balance sheet. Bringing Western standards of presentation and customer service is equally challenging. Littlewoods has recently increased its quota of expatriate managers in St Petersburg from two to five to underpin the implementation of the joint venture's developing range of initiatives.

## Case Study 3

# Amersham International

*Report of an interview with Bruce Beharrell, regional director, former Soviet Union.*

Amersham International, the British health science group, has been involved with the former Soviet Union for 30 years, but the scope of its activities have developed significantly since 1990 with the establishment of two joint ventures in Russia. The first of these is an integrated manufacturing arrangement to produce diagnostic reagents for the Russian market. The second is a marketing venture to purchase isotopes from Mayak, once the Soviet Union's largest nuclear weapons factory, now converted to non-military purposes.

Amersham is also one of the founder members of the British Healthcare consortium, along with Glaxo, Wellcome, Zeneca, Vickers Medical and Smiths Industries. The consortium has been set up to provide advice on the healthcare needs of regions within Russia and the first agreement has been reached with Sverdlovsk in the Urals.

## EARLY STRATEGY

As Soviet markets opened up in the mid-1980s, Amersham first opened an office, taking space from Lloyd's, and then as *perestroika* developed, started to look at joint ventures.

The first product area Amersham concentrated on was diagnostic reagents. As a means of measuring variations in hormone levels, these are used in detecting early signs of cancers and for testing for diseases such as hepatitis. In a country like Russia there is an almost unlimited need for products which allow early, preventive treatment. Although there were local equivalents, their shelf life is about six weeks compared to Amersham's six months – a distinct advantage in a country where distribution causes difficulties.

To develop this market, Amersham established a joint venture with a cardiology research centre it already knew well. The British-Soviet healthcare working group set up under the governments of Mrs Thatcher and Mr Gorbachev provided a supportive framework for carrying through the deal. Negotiations none the less took 12 months, mainly because Amersham's partners looked upon the process as a business course.

The joint venture, Amercard, was made up of equal contributions of £0.25 million. Amersham brought in new machinery and undertook to carry out a progressive transfer of technology. The cardiology centre contributed up-to-date plant which had been supplied by Western contractors. Once the agreement had been signed in late-1990, operations were up and running within five months. Attaining a standard compatible with good manufacturing practice was relatively straightforward, as Amercard was using modern equipment and the Russian staff had been trained in a protocol-driven production system. The venture is run by Russian managers with support from the UK as required.

The Russian healthcare market has undergone significant changes, as central purchasing structures are being replaced by regional ones. These authorities are being deluged with all sorts of offers of healthcare packages by international companies. However, managers have neither the time nor the expertise to assess what is required. In such circumstances making a sensible purchasing decision becomes quite frightening.

## CONSORTIUM OPERATIONS

The British Healthcare consortium was formed with the blessing of President Yeltsin to help with such problems and to upgrade regional health services. Given the scale of the task, a joint approach is more effective than individual companies or authorities working alone.

The consortium draws on expertise in the UK to provide consultancy advice, particularly through the Department of Health. It also ensures that opportunities from aid programmes are developed and used in the most effective way. To generate hard currency the consortium has put in place a financing arrangement with the Moscow Narodny Bank in London, which advises regional governments on products with greatest sales potential in the West.

Medical supplies are provided by the core members of the consortium and a separate procurement programme has been established to provide needs outside the capabilities of these companies. When construction of new facilities is required, Condor Projects co-ordinate the design and the management of the work for the consortium.

The agreement with the Sverdlovsk regional government covers assessment of healthcare needs, health service management training, the treatment of cancer and improving facilities for maternity and child care. Further programmes are expected to develop out of this work. The consortium is looking to extend such initiatives to other areas of Russia.

By early-1993 the Amercard venture was employing 55 people with a turnover of £2–3 million and had installed 50 testing centres in Russian hospitals. The next step is to look at the introduction of further products.

## ISOTOPES FROM MAYAK

Amersham's second joint venture was to consolidate its purchase of radio isotopes from Russia. These elements are used in healthcare, life science research and industrial quality and safety assurance. Amersham had been purchasing radio isotopes from Russia for some time and this source became increasingly important when the company's British supplies from the reactors at Harwell disappeared.

Under Soviet central sourcing, the identity of Amersham's supplier was not clear. As markets opened it was found that 80 per cent of the isotopes had been coming from Mayak, Russia's largest nuclear processing plant, situated in Chelyabinsk 65, a secret city in the Urals. The production of nuclear weapons had stopped, but uranium reprocessing was still carried out.

Amersham was able to start negotiations at the beginning of 1991 to set up a marketing joint venture. This would allow the company to service its own needs for isotopes, as well as trading them world-wide. Initially this is expected to bring Mayak $15 million a year in hard currency, with the prospect of revenue rising to $100 million.

Of the joint venture, known as Reviss Services, 60 per cent is held by Mayak and 40 per cent by Amersham, which is providing advice on the development, handling and distribution of radioactive products. The progress of the negotiations was eased by the importance attached to the deal by the Russian Federation.

Amersham found a high standard of engineering with good control systems at Mayak, although there have been health and safety problems in the past. Quality controls are well established as a result of military protocols. What Mayak lacks is any appreciation of the commercial process, as until two years ago it had no contact with the outside world and had no idea of who its customers were. On the world market Mayak's isotopes are certainly cost competitive, as well being of a high quality relative to international standards.

Bruce Beharrell is responsible for overseeing all of Amersham's operations in Russia. He visits the market every five to six weeks and is backed by an office staffed by three employees in Moscow. There are no expatriates posted in Russia, as Amersham's intention is to build up local staff bringing in expertise from the UK as it is needed. There are regular exchanges of personnel to effect transfer of technology.

Communications have proved remarkably good with satellite links both to the Moscow office and to Mayak. The most significant obstacle to working in Russia is that a common commercial frame of reference is often absent. In particular, it is necessary to convince people of the importance of sales and marketing and that once a product has been sold it has to be supported.

In nine years of experience in Russia Bruce Beharrell has learnt other lessons:

- There are no short-term results, so make sure you have the full backing of your board before entering the market.

- Do not go in on your own. Either find an umbrella, such as the British Healthcare consortium, which allows you to work with others, or work in the slipstream of other investments.

- Finding good Russian partners and staff is the key to making projects work. It is important to understand the milieu in which they are operating and to recognise the political and economic constraints they are facing.

- Winning political support for projects still makes an enormous difference in getting things done.

*Case Study 4*

# KBC Process Technology

*Report of an interview with Alan Perkin, business development manager, and Andrew Graves, senior consultant*

Russia has significant oil refining capacity, which to a large degree has been developed independently from the West. A typical refinery is 3 times as large as its Western counterpart producing 12 to 15 million tonnes a year. While domestic demand and the level of oil reserves will ensure that most refineries have a future, there is a widely perceived need among Russian managers to improve performance.

## REFINERY PRIORITIES

The opening of the market has led to refineries being overwhelmed with Western contractors and licensors offering new plant. This is giving Russian managers cause for complaint. New plant is neither what they need nor can afford at the moment. The priority is getting the best out of existing plant, as the refineries are at the stage of finding ways to hang on and survive. For a firm of process consultants such as KBC this represents a good opportunity, as its emphasis is on improving profitability and operations, not on selling capital goods.

KBC has served over 200 clients in the hydrocarbon processing industries throughout the world, providing advice on high-value, low-cost solutions using simulated computer models. It has been developing the Russian market since the late-1980s and has to date won some ten contracts, directly or through third parties, of various values. It is devoting 10–15 per cent of its marketing efforts to Russia, although it is careful not to attach a high viability to projects until they are up and running.

The purchasing process in Russia has undergone a fundamental transformation. The control of the refineries has now moved away from the ministries to the end users themselves, who often have substantial budgets at their disposal, although this may not be immediately apparent KBC's view of the starting point for any contract is to look at the most straightforward steps a refinery can take to improve yields and efficiency with minimum investment.

Marketing is carried out via two routes. Desk research in the UK yields a lot of good initial information: the DTI, the British Soviet Chamber of Commerce and others have proved to be a particularly valuable source. KBC also has an association agreement with Babcock contractors, whose production capabilities are complementary. The best results come from face-to-face meetings with the refineries themselves.

Alan Perkin has previous complementary Russian experience and was taken on by KBC to further develop the Russian market, as well as those markets like India, which employ Soviet-style technology. KBC is fortunate as well in employing an Eastern European consultant who speaks Russian. There are at least four other consultants among a staff of 50 in the UK who are now regularly working on Russian projects.

## PRACTICAL PROBLEMS

Dealing with the refineries has been straightforward. There is a tremendous willingness to change and Russian managers have proved good and fair negotiators. The main problem in putting contracts together is the lack of commercial processes. The chain of events that follow a transaction in the UK does not happen. Similarly, where one step in negotiations here might involve a phone call or a day trip, it can take weeks in Russia. Even fixing meetings can be difficult: Russian counterparts may find it hard to get to Moscow or may not even believe you are serious about coming on specific dates.

Getting in and out of the country is greatly simplified by multi-entry visas (if you can obtain one). It is important to remember too that the Russians are serious about customs declaration forms. Alan Perkin was lucky not to lose his wedding ring once. He had forgotten to declare it on entry and a customs officer accused him of taking out part of Russia's national treasure!

Outside Moscow travelling is arduous. Three star hotels are not what they might seem: make sure you take emergency supplies of high energy, convenience foods and cans of bug spray! Preparation for sales trips is all important.

Negotiations have proved straightforward. Managers are open and ready to listen, although it is important to take account of their pride. There is no mileage in stressing the superiority of the West's products.

The management in companies can change rapidly and to develop lasting relationships KBC tries to spot high flyers coming through the ranks. This fluidity of personnel has not caused any problems in either upholding or enforcing contracts.

One thing that it is worth clarifying is whether the Russian or the English version of the contract is the governing one, as there may be different shades of meaning.

## FINANCIAL ASPECTS

KBC receives stage payments in hard currency and ensures that it stays cash positive throughout the course of a project. It has found Russian banks to be more unpredictable than inefficient.

KBC has not benefited from any aid programmes to date, although it has made sure it is registered with the EC's technical assistance programme for the CIS (TACIS) and keeps the co-ordination unit in Moscow abreast of its activities.

Once a contract has been agreed, a project team from KBC will spend two to three weeks at the refinery assembling all the necessary data. A preliminary set of recommendations is made at the end of this survey visit and a more detailed report is then drawn up in the UK using KBC's simulation system. In total each project takes about six months to complete.

In carrying out profitability analyses, KBC's approach is to apply a set of free market criteria, although Russia is not operating fully on a free market basis. On one recent optimisation contract it was possible to recommend $15 million a year in savings on the spot and $55 million after processing. Once the modelling software has been introduced it is available under licence to the Russian managers.

While there are certainly difficulties in working with Russian systems and standards developed independently of the West, refining units do tend to be uniform across the country. Instrumentation and information systems are often lacking, although engineers have an excellent understanding of how the unit works. If you want a detailed drawing of a unit, for instance, it will often be made up there and then.

KBC has found the quality of Russian managers to be high and has experienced no resistance to the implementation of its proposals. The main limitation on its business is political stability. There are still many unpredictable elements but, if reform continues, business can only develop.

# Appendices

## Appendix 1

# A Survey by Sector

## *ALM Consulting and ExcelInform Ltd*

Any survey of the Russian economy should acknowledge the fact that chronic underinvestment and the breakdown of existing structures over the last few years, without replacement by new practices, has led to a crisis in many fields. This chapter aims to present a realistic view of the state of many key sectors, while highlighting the potential and opportunities for foreign investment in each area.

The review is by no means comprehensive and what follows is indicative of the state of most of the Russian economy. Telecommunications is covered in Chapter 23 given its relevance to all sectors.

## ENERGY

### *Electro-energy*

The development of Russia's electro-energy complex has been constrained by insufficient investment in its capital base. More than half of the equipment installed is between 10 and 20 years old. The estimated reserve level of energy potential does not exceed 5 per cent (whereas in Western European countries it is between 35 and 50 per cent) and possibilities for growth through increased production of electro and thermal energy have been exhausted. Furthermore, there have been serious delays in commissioning new facilities, as a consequence of which the burden placed on atomic stations has grown. These problems are being focused on by the EC through an energy centre based in Moscow which is linking technical assistance and the transfer of high technology for EC companies to access Russian oil and gas resources.

Independent Russian experts predict that electro-energy production will fall to 1022 kilowatt hours in 1992 – 25 billion less than 1992.

Since increased raw material prices and the inability of consumers to pay their bills is likely to leave the industry financially straitened, the formulation of a rational long-term energy policy is being addressed as a matter of priority by the Russian government. This is likely to centre around a controlled state energy market, with prices for oil, oil products and coal increased in phases to reach world levels during 1993, but the price of gas remaining fixed.

## Oil

Russia's oil industry plays a decisive role in the national economy. As the country's main export, oil has been a reliable source of revenue for many years. However of late, production has been declining sharply, and extraction levels for 1992 were less than 400 million tonnes – 150 million tonnes less than 1989. This fall can be explained mainly by the technical backwardness of the sector. Most fields are operating with old equipment capable of extracting only about 45 per cent of the available oil. In consequence, many unexhausted wells are now idle. Rosneftegas, the oil producers representative body, estimates that the industry can only function properly if new technology worth billions of roubles in hard currency is imported.

The position as regards refining is hardly better. While the USA, Canada and Germany obtain a 90 per cent yield from every tonne of oil, Russia can only manage 65 per cent. In fact this would probably be the most fruitful area for immediate capital inflow. An increase in refining quality to 75 per cent could produce a saving of 40 billion tonnes of oil each year. In 1992 the reduced oil output is expected to lead to a drop in diesel production of 3 million tonnes (5 per cent) and in other fields of 5 million tonnes (also 5 per cent).

The government's programme for the regeneration of the oil industry centres on privatisation. Many enterprises involved in extracting, processing, transporting and selling oil are being transformed into joint stock companies, and 40 per cent of their shares are to be sold during 1993 and 1994 (half of this tranche can be bought with vouchers, and foreigners can buy up to 15 per cent of the total stock of a single enterprise). The state will retain a minority shareholding (between 38 and 49 per cent) for the time being, though in the long term even this may be sold off.

## Coal

Russia's coal industry is also facing drops in output, though not as severe as those in the oil sector. In 1992 coal production was about

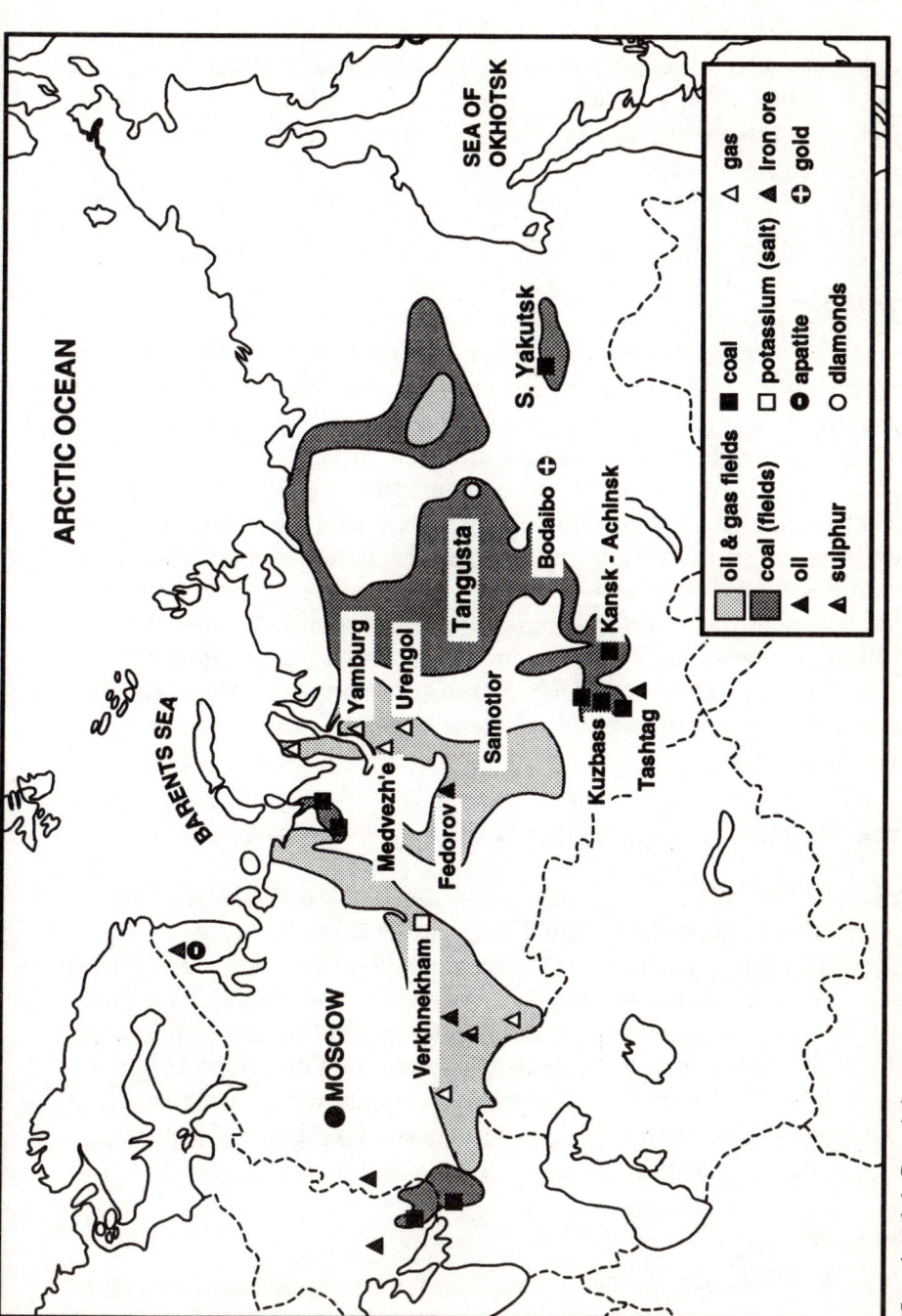

**Map App1.1** *Russia's resources*

Source:  Based on Aganbegyan, A (1988) *The Challenge: Economics or Perestroika*, Hutchinson, London, pp xi–xii.

350 million tonnes – slightly less than 1991, and a continuing lack of preparatory work, owing to a shortage of shaft support materials, is certain to reduce productivity still further.

Indeed the coal industry is particularly vulnerable to problems at either end of the mining process. Compared with 5 years ago, about 20 per cent fewer cleaning and drilling machines are now being produced. Meanwhile the construction of railway lines and wagons for bringing coal to the surface, and for taking it away from the coal face, is being hindered by insufficient supplies of materials and resources.

### Natural gas

By contrast with the other major sectors of the fuel energy complex, gas production has been increasing annually by 40 billion cubic metres for some years now. But here too, performance is expected to suffer from insufficient funding. A reduction in capital investment of about a third in 1991 is likely to mean that 1992 figures show no increase over the previous year. Unless the drop in investment is in fact avoided, output may actually contract over the coming year. Worn-down pumping units will increase the technological requirements of gas lines and decrease the volume of gas which can be utilised. On top of this, delays in the installation of gas gathering equipment on oil rigs, together with insufficient capacity in refining plants will mean that over 22 per cent of gas resources will continue to be burned.

## NEWS MEDIA AND THE NEWSPAPER INDUSTRY

The last few years have seen some great upheavals in the Russian media. Firstly *glasnost* lifted many restrictions on what could be reported, then the downfall of communism removed the structures on which the media industries were based. These changes, combined with the general economic malaise, have meant that the newspapers and broadcasting organisations have simply swapped dependence on the Communist Party for dependence on sponsors, advertisers and distributors. As yet, the requirements of end-users are still a secondary consideration.

### Newspapers

The printed media has been developing very rapidly in Russia over the last few years. Stimulated by *perestroika* the press changed its face radically – some long-established papers disappeared, others remodelled themselves completely and various new publications started. The number of different papers on the news-stands increased ten-fold between 1985 and 1992 and, as a result, competition is now intense.

Among the older publications retaining strong positions are *Izvestiya* (universal daily), *Argumenty i Fakty* (universal weekly), *Komsomolskaya Pravda* (daily for the younger generation) and *Ekonomika i Zhizn* (business-oriented weekly). Only a few of the newspapers founded recently have achieved nationwide circulation. Notable among these are *Nezavisimaya Gazeta* and *Rossiiskaya Gazeta* (both universal dailies). Also, in 1992 two new classes of newspaper were born: translations of prominent foreign newspapers and free advertising papers.

The biggest problem for newspapers now is distribution. The only way to get to their readers is through the state-owned distribution monopoly Soyuzpechat-Rospechat or through a local post office. Soyuzpechat's distribution costs now amount to about 60 per cent of the subscription price, and local post offices have introduced variable distribution prices such that subscription prices are undermined.

## Television

Traditionally all Russian TV stations were state owned. Although this is no longer entirely the case, airtime is still allocated centrally and under government control. In 1992 the former Soviet-wide stations were split into *Ostankino* – which covers the whole of the CIS – and the Russian channel.

Opinion polls show a general disenchantment with the output of the TV stations. During *perestroika* the television was less active than the printed press and now there is a saturation of advertising at prime viewing times. The enthusiasm of the TV managers for advertising revenue has led to a situation where there are more advertisements than programmes. Few people watch these, so major advertisers are now turning their attention towards sponsorship of established programmes.

## Radio

Radio is likely to be the most important section of the media over the coming years. As newspapers become more expensive, and their readership falls, the radio is likely to become more attractive to advertisers and readers alike. Already several music stations have been established and are attracting large audiences.

## REAL ESTATE IN MOSCOW

Prices for real estate in Moscow are now nearly all in hard currency, with amounts depending greatly on the dollar exchange rate. Some flats are sold for roubles, but the prices of these are usually 20–30 per cent higher than the dollar equivalent. This situation has been brought about by the number of foreigners now looking for apartments or office space, and most ordinary Russians have been priced out of the market. Every week dollar prices for property increase by 5–7 per cent, and in the last three months of 1992 rouble prices nearly doubled. At the end of 1992, flats were selling in Moscow for between $500 and $700 per square metre, or could be rented for between $600 and $800 per month, depending on location. The most prestigious areas are around the Leninskiy Prospekt and the Sadovoye Kol'tzo. Properties in Moscow are mostly sold at municipal auctions or through commercial estate agents.

An interesting result of this situation is the migration of many who formerly lived in the city centre to the country. A house can now be built outside Moscow for the same price as a flat can be purchased in the middle of town. Thus many Muscovites are selling their flats and building houses in the suburbs.

## ADVERTISING

The Russian advertising industry is very young, and consequently very naive. Skilled creative teams are a rarity, and many consider advertising simply an easy way of earning money. As a result there is an abundance of agencies and a dearth of skill.

### Agencies

Very few agencies specialise in a particular area – most are ready to undertake any kind of PR or advertising job. In the past 'advertising' meant simply attracting clients and distributing artwork and copy among all the available newspapers. This is now changing as clients are demanding more results, and some of the successful agencies have formed the Russian Advertisers' Association. The most competent organisations now offer recognisable campaign planning, corporate image-making, public relations and presentation services. Further development will depend on Russian firms learning to recognise the importance of advertising and image-making, which will take place only as the market itself becomes more sophisticated.

### Mailshots

Mailshot campaigns to a selected database, as occur in the West, are unknown in Russia. Apart from the problems of obtaining equipment for desktop publishing, the Russian postal system is far too slow and unreliable for any such strategy to work. However some 'enterprising' (and unprofessional) organisations have begun to send faxes to the 25,000-odd foreigners now living or working in Moscow. This is neither organised nor systematic – the parties responsible simply lift the fax number from one of the business directories and send messages offering everything from caviar to call-girls.

### Television

Advertising on television is more developed. Every channel has an advertising department, or at least a commercial directorate, and independent firms offer film and materials at widely differing rates. Some comparatively professional advertisements are now being shown (particularly for lotteries and banks), though most rely simply on pictures and simple, informative messages.

### Prospects

Advertising remains a growth area in Russia. Currently even the most amateur operations are managing to make money, though a dozen or so big agencies are emerging and seem set to drive some of the 'backroom' outfits out of the market. Both Russian enterprises (particularly converting defence factories) and foreign investors are anxious to publicise their products. Currently this is being done by agencies whose expertise lies at best only in their knowledge of the peculiarities of the Russian market. A partnership between such organisations and foreign firms well-versed in the professionalism and techniques of Western advertising may find that substantial rewards are available.

# FOOD

Most of the facilities and equipment currently used in the Russian food processing industry is between 15 and 20 years old. Over the last five or ten years producers have been actively searching additional capital while receiving little or no new investment. This fact alone explains the current problems of food shortages and the existing import structure.

Perhaps in consequence, the food industry is likely to be one of the most productive sectors for Western investment. While demand is stable, there is a lack of quality Russian-made food products, and Western imports tend to be highly priced. Also the government is very eager to attract investors who will help to produce food in Russia, so incentives and assistance are likely to be available.

The price of most food products is still controlled by the state. Under rules introduced at the beginning of 1993, the profits of producers are restricted to between 10 and 25 per cent of sales value.

### Bread

Bread has long been treated as sacred by Russians. Production has always been considered vital to ensure social stability, and was accordingly heavily subsidised by the communist regime. Even now, few private bakeries exist and most bread is made at huge factories before being distributed to retailers.

### Milk and meat

Russia's milk industry is in a healthier state than most. Factories are highly industrialised and the military-industrial complex has long helped in producing pasteurising equipment. Also about half of the machinery used in filtering milk is imported. All milk sold in state-owned shops is standard – pasteurised with 3.5 per cent fat and packaged in Tetra-Pak containers.

Similar standardisation is unattainable in meat production and distribution, and quality meat can often only be found in the private *rynoks* (markets) in cities. Right up to the early years under Gorbachev meat was still sent first to ordnance depots, in case of war, before it went to the shops, and even now the distribution system regularly fails to make deliveries to the shops before the meat ceases to be edible. This is true even of some of the meat provided by the EC.

### Drinks

The Russians are famous for their drinking, and vodka and other alcoholic beverages remain a profitable line for most retailers.

However domestic vodka producers have very high overheads and found themselves unable to compete with imported brands during 1992. In response, a 100 per cent import tariff was fixed on ethyl spirits at the end of 1992.

A similar position exists in the soft drinks industries. Western giants, such as Pepsi and Coca-Cola, have had interests in the Russian market for a long time and are now predominant in the major cities. Good prospects probably exist for other firms prepared to use imported technology and qualified Russian labour in producing soft drinks.

### Confectionery

Although the manufacturing of some confectionery has suffered of late, having been reliant on cheap supplies of raw materials from friendly communist states, Russian chocolate continues to be highly regarded both domestically and abroad. Bizarrely enough, Russian shops are now filled with imported chocolate, as the Russian manufacturers are exporting almost all their produce in order to fund new investment.

### Import structure

Currently, Russian commercial trade ventures and the state foreign trade organisations are actively importing a variety of foodstuffs from the West. Commercial traders concentrate mostly on vodka, confectionery and soft drinks, while the foreign trade organisations are importing fruit and selling it on to private retailers. As a result, Russians are beginning to become accustomed to purchasing quality foodstuffs.

## MACHINE BUILDING

Most Russian machine-building enterprises are equipped with old technology delivering a high ratio of energy and raw material consumption to output. Experts estimate that Russian machine-building plants use 50 per cent more material resources than their counterparts in the West. Thus the amount of metal used in producing railway cars is 50 per cent greater in Russia than abroad, in agricultural machines 30 per cent, in tractors 19 per cent, in the automobile industry 17 per cent and in the construction of road-making machines up to 230 per cent. So, for example, Russian excavators are more than 1.5 times heavier than German, Japanese or Dutch models.

It is forecast that 1992 production in the machine-building complex will be 15 per cent down on 1991. This is mainly due to the disruption of economic ties and interruptions in the supply of electrical energy. The sectors most likely to suffer as a result are those supporting the machine-building industry itself – ie suppliers of: metal-cutting, forging and stamping equipment, rotor and rotor-conveyor lines for machine building and processing, and computers.

## CHEMICAL INDUSTRY

Production of mineral fertilisers, which began to fall in 1990 owing to shortages of raw materials, has continued to contract. The situation is further worsened by insufficient supplies of packing materials. Other chemicals where output has been decreasing are sulphur acid, synthetic ammonia, caustic soda and micro-fodder for cattle.

Enterprises manufacturing chemical fibres and thread were reorganised in the late-1980s to form the state concern 'Chemvolokno'. This move failed in its goal of reversing declines in production which had been occurring for several years, and the future functioning of the enterprises is now in serious doubt. Faltering supplies of imported raw materials, as well as domestically produced synthetic dyes mean that the situation is unlikely to improve in the foreseeable future.

Environmental considerations have also caused the closure of a number of plants in the chemical-industrial complex. As a result, production of caustic soda, oil byproducts and semi-manufactured goods for synthetic dyes has been particularly hit. Most Russian chemical factories have an extremely poor ecological record and, as increasing importance is placed on such matters, existing production techniques will have to be reassessed.

## TIMBER AND TIMBER PROCESSING

Over 20 per cent of Russia is under forest. Among others, the Arch-Angel, Kirov, Perm, Sverdlovsk, Krasnoyarsk and Irkutsk areas are major centres for felling and sending raw timber by rail or river to processing plants situated predominantly on the Volga. However, Russia's timber industry is perhaps a showpiece for poor organisation, inefficient production, ineffective management, short-term planning and underinvestment. Though probably a consequence of the country's lavish endowment of timber resources, these factors have led to stagnation in the industry since 1980 and a dramatic slump in production since the beginning of 1992. Export orders have dwindled to reflect the Russians' inability to sort and categorise different varieties of timber for shipping, and output of cutting timber, glued veneer and chip board has also been reduced.

On top of this, vast quantities of timber byproducts, softwood and cedar are being wasted, and past strategies aimed at maximising production at the expense of developing a sustainable forest mean that new resources in Siberia and the far east of Russia are now having to be developed. None the less, the development of the Russian timber industry is likely to focus in the short term on expanding and upgrading existing capacity. Since most plants are situated in the western half of Russia, this should provide considerable opportunities for European-based firms – indeed many, mostly Austrian or Finnish, are already established on the market.

## METALS

The deteriorating situation in the metallurgical complex is a result mainly of the technological backwardness of its constituent enterprises. More progressive technical processes are being introduced only very gradually to steel smelting and sheet rolling operations, and over half of Russia's steel is still produced from open-hearth furnaces – a method long since superseded in more developed countries. Only 45 per cent of rolled steel can be transferred to pressure treatment, compared to over 65 per cent in the US and Japan.

The industry is also being crippled by a serious shortage of raw materials. The amount of iron ore mined has decreased, as has supplies of scrap metals, and insufficient inputs of coking coal have forced plants to cut production of coke. In response the Russian government has introduced emergency measures to divert coking coal originally destined for export or manufacturing enterprises.

## Appendix 2

# Bibliography and Sources of Further Information

## BIBLIOGRAPHY

### Books

*Business Opportunities in Central and Eastern Europe: EC Funded Projects and How to Secure Them*, European Systems Consultants and London Chamber of Commerce, Brussels, 1991.

*CIS Market Atlas*, Economist Intelligence Unit, London, 1992.

*Economic Aid to Eastern Europe: A Practical Approach to the Commercial Opportunities*, Insight International, London, 1992.

*Economic Review, Russian Federation*, IMF, Washington DC, 1992.

*Foreign Investment Opportunities in the 1992 Russian Privatisation Programme, A Guide for Potential Investors*, State Committee of the Russian Federation for the Management of State Property, Moscow, 1992.

*Mining in the USSR*, Economist Intelligence Unit, London, 1990.

*Privatisation in East Europe and the Former Soviet Union*, Financial Times Management Reports, London, 1992.

*Russia Country Profile*, DTI, London, 1992.

*Russia's Foreign Economic Activity*, Business Tass, Moscow, 1992.

*Sector Report, Oil and Petrochemical Industries, Russia*, DTI, London, 1992.

*Siberia at a Time of Change: New Vistas for Western Investors*, M. Bradshaw, Economist Intelligence Unit, London, 1992.

### Directories

*Directory of Oil Refining and Petrochemical Industries in the Post Soviet Republics*, AFI Ltd, 1992.

*Directory of Soviet Buyers of Medical Equipment and Pharmaceutical Products*, Flegon Press, London, 1991.
*Directory of Soviet Engineering*, Flegon Press, London, 1990.
*Directory of Soviet Hospitals*, Flegon Press, London, 1991.
*Trade Directory of the Russian Far East*, BSCC, London, 1992.

### Periodicals in English

*Arguments and Facts International*, monthly, AFI Ltd, Avenal, New Jersey.
*Business Contact*, monthly, Russian Federation Chamber of Commerce and Industry, Moscow.
*Business Eastern Europe*, bi-weekly, Economist Publications, London.
*Business Update Russia*, twice weekly fax service, Reynolds Associates, Innovation Centre, University of Reading.
*Central European*, monthly, Euromoney Publications, London.
*Commersant*, weekly, Commersant JSC, Moscow.
*Daily Review of the CIS Press and Bulletin*, daily, Novosti, London.
*Delovie Lyudi, Business in the ex-USSR*, monthly, Socpresse, Paris.
*Delovoi Mir-Business World*, weekly, Business World Consortium, Moscow.
*Digest of Science and Technology News*, Royal Society, London.
*East European Energy Report*, monthly, Financial Times Publications, London.
*East European Markets* and *Finance East Europe*, bi-weeklies, FT Publications, London.
*Ecotass*, weekly, ITAR-TASS, Moscow.
*Express Executive Briefing*, bi-weekly, *Russia Express Contracts*, monthly, and *Russia*.
*Express Geopolitical Update*, bi-monthly, International Industrial Information Ltd, Monmouth, Gwent.
*Image*, quarterly, KPMG International Headquarters, Amsterdam.
*Moscow Computer News*, monthly, Computer Weekly Publications, London.
*Oil and Gas Russia and the Post Soviet Republics*, quarterly, Oil and Gas Russia Ltd, Hastings.
*Plan Econ East Europe*, fortnightly, London.
*Russia Business International*, bi-monthly, BSCC, London.
*Statistical Report, Food and Agriculture Report, Business Report* and *Financial Report*, Interfax, Moscow.
*Summary of World Broadcasts*, daily or weekly, BBC, Reading.
*The Moscow Letter*, weekly, Interforum, London.

### *Periodicals in Russian*

*Ekonomicheskaya Gazeta*, economics daily.
*Finansovaya Gazeta*, financial daily.
*Finansy*, financial daily.
*Merkury, Sbornik Delovoi Informatsii*, Business News Digest, Russian Federation Chamber of Commerce and Industry.
*Pravitelstvenny Vestnik*, quarterly.
*Vestnik Statistiki*, monthly.

### *Information services*

ITAR TASS and RIA-Novosti provide online information services for businesses.

## SOURCES OF FURTHER INFORMATION

Alastair Tulloch
Frere Cholmeley Bischoff
4 John Carpenter Street
London EC4Y 0HN
Tel: 071-615 8000
Fax: 071-615 8080
(or Andrew Rosemarine Frere
    Cholmeley Bischoff Moscow,
    address and telephone number as
    per ALM Consulting)

Alexander Mamut
ALM Consulting
Malaya Semenovskaya 1
105023 Moscow
Russia
Tel: 7 (095) 962 1497
Fax: 7 (095) 963 6190

Michael Gibbins
KPMG Peat Marwick
1 Puddle Dock
London EC4V 3PD
Tel: 071-236 8000
Fax: 071-583 1938

Ken Crawford
KPMG Moscow
PO box 11
Delegatskaya Ulitsa 25
103473 Moscow
Tel:  7 (501) 882 3195 (satellite link)
      7 (095) 7 281 7584 (land line)
Fax: 7 (501) 882 3196
      (satellite link)
      7 (095) 281 8481 (land line)

Margaret Wood
Moscow Narodny Bank Ltd
81 King William Street
London EC4P 4JS
Tel: 071-623 2066
Fax: 071-283 4840

Nicholas Louis
Consultant
Westhumble Place
Dorking
Surrey RH5 6BT
Tel: (0306) 883460

Walt Jackson
Director
Brown & Root
150 The Broadway
London SW19 1RX
Tel: 081-544 6800
Fax: 081-544 6732

Jackie Carpenter
Consultant, Defence Conversion
6 Pembroke Close
Hillhead
Fareham
Hampshire PO14 3PP
Tel: 0329 668796

Dr Michael Bradshaw
School of Geography
University of Birmingham
Birmingham B15 2TT
Tel: 021-414 5543

CIT Research Limited
23 Dering Street
Hanover Square
London W1R 9AA
Tel: 071-493 9247
Fax: 071-629 9256

Dmitri Bogdanovich
Marketing Consultant
ExcelInform Ltd
PO Box 105
117296 Moscow
Russia
Tel/Fax: 7 (095) 137 8127

Tim Jones
Global Gas Operations
British Gas Plc
59 Bryanston Street
London WC1 2AZ
Tel: 071-611 2311
Fax: 071-611 1069

Bruce Beharrell
Amersham International plc
Lincoln Place Green End
Aylesbury
Bucks HP20 2TP
Tel: 0296 395222
Fax: 0296 85910

Alan Perkin/Andrew Graves
KBC Process Technology Ltd
KBC House
Churchfield Road
Weybridge
Surrey KT13 8DB
Tel: 0932 856622
Fax: 0932 854551

Malcolm Landau
The Littlewoods Organisation PLC
100 Old Hall Street
Liverpool L70 1AB
Tel: 051-235 2475
Fax: 051-236 2085

Francis Ball
The Littlewoods Organisation PLC
JM Centre
Old Hall Street
Liverpool L70 1AB
Tel: 051-235 3458
Fax: 051-235 3498

Konstantine Trofimov
Deputy Trade Representative
Russian Federation
Westfield
33 Highgate West Hill
London N6 6NL
Tel: 081-340 1907

CBI
Centre Point
103 New Oxford Street
London WC1A 1DU
Tel: 071-379 7400
Fax: 071-240 1578

East European Trade Council
Suite 10
Westminster Palace Gardens
Artillery Row
London SW1P 1RL
Tel: 071-222 7622

London Chamber of Commerce
East European Section
69 Cannon Street
London EC4N 5AB
Tel: 071-248 4444
Fax: 071-489 6391

BSCC
42 Southwark Street
London SE1 1UN
Tel: 071-403 1706
Fax: 071-403 1245

CIS Technical Assistance Unit
Directorate-General for External
  Relations
DG1/E/2
Rue de la Loi 86
B-1049 Brussel
Belgium
Tel: 32 (2) 236 2331

EC Delegation to Russia
Stolovy Pereulok 7a
121069 Moscow
Russia
Tel: 7 (095) 202 0136
Fax: 7 (502) 220 3245

TACIS Coordinating Unit
Radisson Slavyanskaya Hotel and
  Business Centre
Berzhkovskaya Nab 2
121059 Moscow
Tel: 7 (095) 502 224 1185
Fax: 7 (095) 502 224 1169

Michael McCulloch
Head of Unit
Joint Assistance Unit (JAU)
Foreign and Commonwealth Office
Old Admiralty Building
Whitehall
London SW1A 2AF
Tel: 071-210 1433
Fax: 071-270 3012

ECGD
2 Exchange Tower
Harbour Exchange Square
London E14 9GS
Tel: 071-512 7000
Fax: 071-512 7649

EBRD
1 Exchange Square
London EC2A 2EH
Tel: 071-338 6000
     071-496 6000
Fax: 071-338 6115

Department of Trade and Industry
Former Soviet Union Desk
World Aid Section
DTI
Room 402
Ashdown House
123 Victoria Street
London SW1E 6RB
Tel: 071-215 6157/6089

The Russian Federation Embassy
15 Kensington Palace Gardens
London W8 4QX
Tel: 071-229 3628
Fax: 071-727 8625

Russian Consulate (visa
  information)
5 Kensington Palace Gardens
London W8 4QS
Tel: 071-229 8027

The British Embassy
Nab. Morisa Toreza 14
Moscow
Russia
Tel: 7 (095) 231 8511
Fax: 7 (095) 233 3563

British Embassy – Commercial
  Section
Kotuzovsky Prospect 7/4
Moscow
Russia
Tel: 7 (095) 248 2001
Fax: 7 (095) 249 4636

The KHF Liaison Team
British Embassy
Kutuzovsky Prospekt 7/4
Moscow
Russia
Tel: 7 (095) 249 4936
Fax: 7 (095) 249 4636

British Consulate General
Room 252 Grand Hotel Europe
Saint Petersburg
Russia
Tel: 8 (71) 144 5136 (satellite link)

Ministry of External Economic
  Relations
Smolenskaya-Sennaya Pl 32/34
121200 Moscow
Russia
Tel: 7 (095) 244 1258

Ministry of Finance
Ulitsa Ulinka 9
103097 Moscow
Russia
Tel: 7 (095) 298 48 64

Ministry of Foreign Affairs
Smolenskaya-Sennaya Pl 32/34
121200 Moscow
Russia
Tel: 7 (095) 244 3448

Ministry of Agriculture
Gorlikokov Pereulok 3
107802 Moscow
Russia
Tel: 7 (095) 204 4828
Fax: 7 (095) 288 3580

Ministry of Industry
Petrovka Ulitsa 14
103 655 Moscow
Russia
Tel: 7 (095) 209 8282
Fax: 7 (095) 200 4534

Central Bank of Russia
Ulitsa Nieglinnaya 12
117049 Moscow
Russia
Tel: 7 (095) 237 5145
Fax: 7 (095) 237 5055

State Committee for the
  Management of State Property
  (GKI)
Foreign Investment Administration
Proezd Vladimirova 9
103685 Moscow
Russia
Tel: 7 (095) 206 69 15 (satellite)
     7 (502) 220 48 25

Russian Federation Chamber of
  Commerce and Industry
Ulitsa Ulinka 6
103684 Moscow
Russia
Tel: 7 (095) 298 32 31 (Foreign
  Relations Office)

Foreign Investment Committee
Ministry of Finance
Ul Okhotny Ryad 1
103009 Moscow
Russia
Tel: 7 (095) 292 7800

Russian State AntiMonopoly
  Committee
Prosp Vernadskovo 41
117947 Moscow
Russia
Tel: 7 (095) 434 2747

Russian State Customs Committee
Komsomolskaya Pl la
107842 Moscow
Russia
Tel: 7 (095) 975 3289

Russian State Property Committee
Prosp Vladimirovo 9
103685 Moscow
Russia
Tel: 7 (095) 206 1525
Fax: 7 (095) 230 24 55

Foreign Trade Arbitration
  Commission
Moscow
Russia
Tel: 7 (095) 205 28 53

Russian Commodity and Raw
  Material Exchange
Novaya Ploshchad 3–4
Moscow
Tel: 7 (095) 262 8080
Fax: 7 (095) 262 5757

# *Appendix 3*

# Trade Fairs

## SOME EVENTS IN 1992

Some of the exhibitions held in 1992 give an indication of the level of participation and subjects covered.

The international exhibition, 'Invecom-92' (Informatics and Computer Technology) opened in St Petersburg on 25 November. A total of 150 enterprises and design organisations from the CIS exhibited achievements in computer engineering, technology, communications and software. Exhibitors also included business partners of Russian firms from the USA and Europe. The programme incorporated seminars on information technology, electronics and telecommunications.

Similarly, the international fairs 'Our Home' and 'Office-92' took place in 1992. These were held on 25 November in Novosibirsk, Siberia. Some 400 factories, small enterprises and co-operatives as well as firms from Italy, Austria, the USA and other countries displayed their wares. Articles varied from door keys to individual homes to be built on a turn-key basis.

A representative from the Siberian Fair Commercial Centre, which organised the show, announced a work programme for 1993 at a news conference. It is planned to stage 100 Siberian international fairs. They will be held in Novosibirsk, Vladivostok, Barnaul and other Russian cities.

More than fifty Russian industrial and commercial enterprises and a number of foreign companies, which offer goods and services needed by farmers and enterprises in the agro-industrial complex, took part in the exhibition/seminar, 'Science, Business and Industry for Agriculture'. This was held in Moscow from 16 to 26 November. The event was organised by the Chamber of Industry and Commerce of the Russian Federation and the Sovincentr joint stock company.

The exhibition prioritised the latest products of defence

enterprises converted to peaceful needs, including new kinds of mini-equipment for farming, implements and advanced technology for dairy farming, high-yield crops, fruit processing equipment, and equipment for manufacturing meat and other food products. The most attractive exhibit was a business class aircraft designed to carry passengers and freight over long distances, adapted for agricultural purposes and not requiring a landing strip.

A number of enterprises from Moscow, Izhevsk and Tyumen exhibited universal means of transportation and a variety of engine units. Other exhibits included vegetation protection items, insecticides, milk processing equipment and bread ovens.

## THE 1993 SCHEDULE

The calendar of events planned for 1993 represents an informative selection of fairs, including the following:

| | | |
|---|---|---|
| Mar | 18–25 | Tourindustria '93. This is an exhibition on the tourism industry. Venue: Moscow. |
| | 19–23 | Bautech '93. This is an exhibition on building, engineering and city redevelopment. Venue: Moscow. |
| | 19–26 | Composit '93. An exhibition on the technology for production and use of new materials and composites. Venue: Moscow. |
| Apr | 14–21 | Igrushka '93. An exhibition on the equipment for the production of toys. Venue: Expocentr, Moscow. |
| | 19–23 | Obuv '93. An exhibition on machines and equipment for the shoe and leather industry. Venue: St Petersburg. |
| May | 3–7 | Euroexposhop-93. This covers shop fitting and equipment. Venue: Moscow. |
| | 10–14 | Myasoagroprom '93. An exhibition on machinery and equipment for the food industry and agriculture. Venue: St Petersburg. |
| | 12–19 | Obuv '93. Machinery and equipment for the production of footwear. Venue: Moscow. |
| | 17–21 | Meditech-93. This concerns medical engineering, plant and equipment for clinics and laboratories and specialised fields. Venue: Perm. |

| | | |
|---|---|---|
| | 17–21 | Euroexpomoda I-93. This exhibition covers ladies clothing, shoes and accessories. Venue: Moscow. |
| | 24–29 | Airport International-93. A specialised exhibition on the aircraft industry. Venue: Moscow. |
| | 24–29 | Autosalon '93. An international trade fair for the automobile industry. Venue: Moscow. |
| Jun | 1–5 | Euroexpomoda III-93. Children's clothing, shoes and toys. Venue: Moscow. |
| | 14–18 | Energy-93. An ever popular event covering extraction of raw materials, energy supply, materials and environmental technology. Venue: Moscow. |
| | 21–25 | Intersport-93. Venue: St Petersburg. |
| | 9–16 | Interbytmash. Fifth public services and household equipment exhibition. Venue: Moscow. |
| | 15–22 | First technical machinery fair. Venue: Moscow. |
| | 21–25 | Boat-93. Venue: St Petersburg. |
| | 28–2/7 | Polygraphbummash-93. An exhibition of printing machines, paper processing and converting, and packaging. Venue: Moscow. |
| | 28–2/7 | Technology-93. Advanced technologies in mechanical engineering, industrial projects, licences and know-how. Venue: Perm. |
| | 28–2/7 | Conversion—93. Machines and plant for restructuring of former defence industry companies. Venue: Perm. |
| Jul | 13–21 | Elektronmash. Sixth electrotechnical wares production and control equipment. Venue: Moscow. |
| | 15–22 | Spetsavtotransport. Third special purpose exhibition for automobile rolling stock. Venue: Moscow. |
| Aug | 16–21 | Aerotechnika-93. Aircraft equipment, security and communication systems. Venue: Moscow. |
| Sep | 6–10 | Techprodmash-93. Machines and equipment for the food processing industries. Venue: Perm. |
| | 13–17 | Interorgtechnika-93. Facilities and systems in banking, finance and administration, as well as office equipment and computers. Venue: Moscow. |
| | 13–17 | Euroexpo Stank-Components-93. Machine-tool components. Venue: Moscow. |

| | | |
|---|---|---|
| | 20–24 | Meat and Milk-93. Venue: St Petersburg. |
| | 23–30 | Zdravookhraneniye. Fifth health care, medical equipment and pharmaceuticals exhibition. Venue: Moscow. |
| | 27–10/10 | Metallurgictech-93. Industrial furnaces and pyrometric production processes, metallurgical engineering and foundry practice. Venue: Perm. |
| Oct | 4–8 | Flexible Automation-93. Universal manufacturing, assembly and transportation systems. Venue: Moscow. |
| | 11–15 | Euroexpomobel-93. Furniture. Venue: Moscow. |
| | 11–15 | Household and Hardware-93. Venue: St Petersburg. |
| Nov | 1–5 | Podyomtranstech-93. Lifting and handling, automatic and mechanised storing and storage technology. Venue: Moscow. |
| | 1–5 | Bakery-93. Venue: St Petersburg. |
| | 22–26 | Interplastech-93. Plastics and rubber industries. Venue: St Petersburg. |
| | 22–26 | Chemitech-93. Chemical and plant engineering, industrial processing and materials engineering, process control, logistics and recycling. Venue: Moscow. |
| | 22–26 | Woodworking-93. Venue: Moscow. |
| | 23–1/12 | Nauka. Fifth scientific research equipment and instruments exhibition. Venue: Moscow. |
| | 24–1/12 | Bioreaktor. Third fair on the automation of biotechnological processes in medicine and agriculture. Venue: Moscow. |
| | 25–1/12 | Mebelindustria. Fourth exhibition of equipment for the furniture industry. Venue: Moscow. |

Further information on these exhibitions and trade fairs is obtainable from the Barry Martin Group of Companies, 27, Kingly Court, Kingly Street, London, W1R 5LE, from Glahe International, Woodcroft, Bures Hamlet, Suffolk, CO8 5DU, or from Expocentr, 1a Sokolnichesky val, 107113 Moscow.

Western exhibitors are advised to provide plenty of advertising material in the form of brochures and other handouts, and where possible, with Russian translations. All preparations for participation in trade fairs and seminars should be made well in advance and usually takes at least three to six months.

It can also prove very useful to belong to such organisations as the British-Soviet Chamber of Commerce, which provides details of events in Russia and the republics as well as arranging twice yearly luncheons where it is possible to meet people from the UK and Russia to discuss business opportunities.

# Index